THE HEART OF PSYCHOLOGY

Unraveling the Mysteries of the Mind

HOWARD PAUL, PhD, ABPP, FAClinP
EDUARDO CHAPUNOFF, MD, FACP, FACC

FOREWORD BY ARNOLD A LAZARUS, PhD, ABPP
Distinguished Professor Emeritus of Psychology, Rutgers University

authorHOUSE®

AuthorHouse™
1663 Liberty Drive
Bloomington, IN 47403
www.authorhouse.com
Phone: 1-800-839-8640

Names and identifying characteristics of persons found in this book have been altered to protect their identity and to maintain confidentiality.

Published by AuthorHouse 3/6/2012

ISBN: 978-1-4685-3842-7 (e)
ISBN: 978-1-4685-3843-4 (hc)
ISBN: 978-1-4685-3844-1 (sc)

Library of Congress Control Number: 2012900155

Any people depicted in stock imagery provided by Thinkstock are models, and such images are being used for illustrative purposes only.
Certain stock imagery © Thinkstock.

This book is printed on acid-free paper.

Cover photo courtesy of Michael Davenport

FOREWORD

There is much we will learn by reading this informative book of conversations between Dr. Eduardo Chapunoff, an accomplished cardiologist whose inquiring mind goes far beyond medicine, and Dr. Howard Paul, a seasoned and learned clinical psychologist, who sheds light on questions and issues in an understandable format. Dr. Chapunoff poses questions about people that many of us may well wonder about, and raises issues that many of us may not have thought about. Various discussions between Dr. Chapunoff and Dr. Paul provide additional information, as well as food for thought.

If you review the chapter titles in the Table of Contents, you will have an idea of the interesting and important territory these two doctors cover. A few examples of what they discuss include what lies behind human cruelty, obsessive-compulsive disorders, uncontrollable anger, jealousy, sorrow, guilt, anxiety, greed, self-esteem, stubbornness, bullying, and codependency.

The book is also sprinkled with humor, which adds to the joy of reading it. It is noteworthy that Dr. Chapunoff self-discloses the factors that gave rise to many of his questions, and Dr. Paul draws a distinction between data-based findings and speculative assumptions. Suffice it to say, perusing their manuscript was an enjoyable and often enlightening experience for me.

Arnold A Lazarus, PhD, ABPP

Distinguished Professor Emeritus of Psychology,

Rutgers University

President, the Lazarus Institute, Skillman, New Jersey

CONTENTS

ABOUT THE AUTHORS

Howard Paul, PhD is professor of psychiatry at the University of Medicine and Dentistry of New Jersey-Robert Wood Johnson Medical School, New Brunswick, New Jersey and a field supervisor at the Graduate School of Applied and Professional Psychology, Rutgers University, New Brunswick, New Jersey. He graduated from Rutgers University with a degree in clinical psychology and completed his internship at the American Institute for Mental Studies. Dr. Paul is board certified in clinical psychology through the American Board of Professional Psychology and a fellow of the Academy of Clinical Psychology.

Dr. Paul is currently the book review editor for the journal, *Child & Family Behavior Therapy*.

Dr. Paul is a master therapist, trained in clinical and school psychology, as well as neuropsychology and behavioral medicine. He lectures on integrative, empirically informed treatments and provides clinical supervision to both psychology interns and psychiatry residents. He maintains an active psychotherapy practice, and for the last 45 years, he has written over 100 articles, including studies, book reviews, and book chapters.

Dr. Paul's web site is www.howardpaulphd.com

Eduardo Chapunoff, MD is the chief of cardiology at Doctors Medical Center and its six facilities in Miami, Florida. He received his medical degree from the University of Buenos Aires Medical School and completed his postgraduate training at the University of Miami School of Medicine. He is a diplomat of the American Board of Internal Medicine and the American Board of Cardiovascular Disease, a fellow of the American College of Physicians, and a fellow of the American College of Cardiology. He was a clinical associate professor of medicine at the University of Miami from 1985 to 1997.

Dr. Chapunoff is the author of several books: *Sex and the Cardiac Patient, Answering Your Questions about Heart Disease & Sex, Morbid Obesity: Will You Allow it to Kill You?, and How Not to Drop Dead! - A Guide for Prevention of 201 Causes of Sudden or Rapid Death.* All of his books have been translated into Spanish.

He has been included in the biographical records of Marquis Who's Who Publication Board, Personalities of America, Community Leaders of America (American Biographical Institute), and the International Who's Who of Intellectuals, (International Biographical Centre, Cambridge, England). He was named International Man of the Year 1991-1992 by the International Biographical Centre, Cambridge, England. The Customers' Research Council of America 2009 selected Dr. Chapunoff as one of America's top cardiologists.

Dr. Chapunoff's web site is www.dreduardochapunoff.com

INTRODUCTION
Mysteries Encountered-Questions Followed

In the mid 80s, Frank, a patient of mine, was in the hospital's intensive care unit because of a massive heart attack. He died. A couple of minutes after he was pronounced dead, his second wife and his 50-something-year-old son from his first wife, went into Frank's room and began to scream at each other. But that was not all. They each grabbed Frank's hand and tried to remove a gold and diamond ring from his fourth digit. During the struggle, Frank's hand and arm moved all over the place. In fact, they moved his limb so much, one had the impression Frank was alive and had joined the fight with them. A nurse supervisor stopped the confrontation. I never knew what happened to the ring, and it doesn't matter. What was important to me was the behavior of Frank's widow and his son. How could they act like that, showing no respect for their husband and father? What was more intriguing to me was to ask what kind of psychological backgrounds these two people had that led them to behave the way they did?

Not everyone reacts negatively to tragic events. I once treated an octogenarian, British woman who had been in London during WWII when the Nazis dropped tons of bombs on her city. She was educated and bright. She told me she *"had had a beautiful experience during the blitz."* I asked her, *"I don't get it, how did you find something beautiful while people were being killed or maimed by the bombs?"* She answered, *"Yes, it was beautiful, indeed, to see how people who didn't know each other helped those who were wounded, risking their own lives in the process. I never saw anything more beautiful than that!"* You can appreciate how different the emotional-psychological response of different individuals may be. This extraordinary woman gave me the impression that she had actually enjoyed, not the devastating destruction and carnage, but the fact that she was able to assist people with very serious physical and emotional damage, and share heroic performances with other courageous individuals.

Skin scars last forever, unless a plastic surgeon removes them with a scalpel. Emotional scars seem to have the same fate, unless a psychologist frees one from burdensome and damaging effects. Scars of the mind may range from minor to terrible. They may be tolerable and not significantly disruptive, or they may evoke bitterness, sadness, disappointment, pain, frustration, hatred, and other unpleasant reactions.

For many years in my cardiology practice, I observed people's gestures, arguments, and actions. These observations left me with a preoccupying collection of question marks. I also dealt with an assortment of clients: intellectuals, corporate executives, policemen, antiterrorist experts who defused bombs every week, artists, physicians, politicians, psychologists, engineers, attorneys, CIA operatives, plumbers, construction workers, taxi drivers, window-cleaners of New York highest skyscrapers, members of mafia families, drug dealers, men and women with abject poverty, and others who had so much money they didn't know what to do with it. I do not remember even one of these individuals who presented without some sort of emotional disorder or behavioral dysfunction.

Over the years, I interacted with numerous US veterans of World War II, the Korean War, the Vietnam War, and more recently, the Gulf War. It would take volumes for me to relate their experiences to you. A few of their struggles included the Normandy invasion or D-Day, life (and death) in concentration camps, airplane dog-fights, the fear of being in a submarine that was the target of depth charges exploding nearby, hand-to-hand fighting with the enemy in the jungles of Southeast Asia using machetes and bayonets, and the survival of marines lost in places where they had to eat what they could, such as insects and the fluid of a snake's body. It was not easy; first, the marine killed the snake, then with a knife, he opened up the middle part of the snake's body and suctioned the *juice* of the reptile with his lips. Most of these veterans suffered from Posttraumatic stress disorder (PTSD), and in some of them, the condition reached disabling proportions.

We sometimes live in a difficult world - I do not hesitate to call it a crazy world. It may often appear full of violence and polluted with angry and destructive minds, including an abundance of greed and corruption in governments and corporations. Many individuals have erroneous thinking, disturbed emotions, and behavioral dysfunctions; some are worse than others are, but a certain degree of emotional or mental dysfunction may be universal.

Those who appear and sound *normal* may have mental issues they have to reckon with. We sometimes watch as drugs, rapes, and wars destroy people's lives. Some married couples do not know how to reach harmony and happiness, let alone peace of mind. Many have to deal with marital or extramarital relationships, personal lives, parents and in-laws, children, sibling rivalry, jealousy, financial hardships, unemployment, loss of their homes because of an inability to afford mortgage payments, serious illnesses, disabling accidents, legal battles, conflicts with coworkers (bosses and subordinates), and let me not forget, their sex lives.

As you read the questions I posed to Dr. Paul in this book, it will become obvious to you that I am not particularly interested in the *facts and realities* about each story of the participants. We all know, a liar is a liar, a bank robber is a bank robber, and a rapist is a rapist. What we often may not know, and what I want to know is, why and how do these dysfunctional behaviors occur? What caused the minds of these subjects to became so twisted, so crooked, and so abnormal? Did family, cultural, educational, or social problems affect them, or were they born with dislocated genes?

We often see suffering and dysfunctional behavior of noble people, whose parents provided them with a less than effective upbringing. The parents were probably good people, but had no idea what was required in their children's development. They may have lacked knowledge, time, motivation, or the ability to raise children; they made mistakes. Good people sometimes have an array of personal, interpersonal, intimate, and family conflicts that generate expressed or repressed unhealthy emotions. My basis for having these conversations, to honor the truth, is to find answers to my questions that are a reflection of my ignorance, not my knowledge.

Over the years, I have amassed many unanswered questions on human behavior. They have piled up and now resemble the shape and size of an Egyptian pyramid. I am equating the top of the pyramid with my desire to understand human behavior. I often saw myself climbing the pyramid, but never able to reach the top. It reminds me of the mythological story of Sisyphus, where he was condemned by the gods to roll a boulder uphill, only to watch it roll back down again. He was sentenced to do this for all eternity. The story of Sisyphus is mythological, mine is not.

Recently, I decided to engage a prominent, senior psychologist and master therapist in a dialogue that would help me get answers to my questions and maybe put the pieces together in the puzzle that is human behavior. The learned psychologist I enlisted was Dr. Howard Paul, a very experienced clinical psychologist, medical school professor, and supervisor of other psychologists and psychiatrists. Dr. Paul is renowned internationally and enjoys prominence for his academic achievements, multiple scientific publications, and book reviews. After 45 of years of experience in private practice, he continues to exert remarkable influence on his patients, colleagues, students, and society. Throughout his career, Dr. Paul has provided support to thousands of concerned patients and dealt with situations and complications, almost all manageable, even if difficult to treat.

During my conversations with Dr. Paul, he explains why and how negative emotions occur. He tells us what may be the best way to prevent them and offers guidance on ways to positively deal with them.

I invite you to read our conversations, and give some thought to his comments. Take your time. Do not read his words too quickly. He has many cryptic metaphorical phrases that teach us valuable lessons. His friends and those he counsels call them, *Howardisms*. Most are his, although some are borrowed. Here are but a few that he has shared with me:

- It isn't a good idea to keep putting your finger into an electric pencil sharpener

- If you really want to mess up your day, start off with a wish you know won't come true

- People who argue with freight trains are called casualties. Sometimes it is best to simply get off the tracks

- The biggest tiger that people face is the fear that their inadequacy will be discovered and eat them up

- There are big deals, medium deals, and small deals. Most of what people think are big deals are just highly aggravating little deals

- If you do not know where you are going, you are sure to get there!

- We are creatures of habit, not of knowledge

- If people really did what they knew was best, psychologists would all be unemployed

- Never speak unless you have a pair of ears ready to listen

- The mind is a dangerous place. Don't go in there alone

In this book, Dr. Paul shares a lifetime of experience, knowledge, and the wisdom that results from them.

Let us get immersed together in this exploratory journey as we learn more about the origin of feelings, thoughts, and behaviors and try to unravel the mysteries of the mind.

Eduardo Chapunoff, MD, FACP, FACC

THE CONVERSATIONS

1

THE CONTROVERSIAL NATURE OF SORROW
Emotional reactions can be difficult to explain

Dr. Chapunoff: It was 10:00 PM, I was lying in my bedroom, and my wife, Cristina, was in the living room. My beloved 10-year-old Yorkie, Duke, was nearby. Duke had not been feeling well for several days and was under veterinary care. At one point, I noticed that Duke was motionless, and I thought he was sleeping. Then I saw his beautiful eyes, open but expressionless, and I realized he was dead. With the speed of light, I began cardiopulmonary resuscitation, and the only response was a brief agonizing sound. His eyes kept on looking at me as if he was saying, *"Dad, I'm no longer here, I'm gone. You will have to accept it. I love you and I always will."*

After Duke's death, my suffering and grief reached excruciating proportions. I found them nearly intolerable. I thought if someone applied a hot iron to one of my eyes, I would not experience as much pain as I was dealing with Duke's death. The point I want to make is, when my parents died, I did indeed cry, but I cried less than following the demise of my pet. I adored my parents, and I felt perplexed by the way I acted and somewhat guilty about it.

Can you tell me what happens in the depths of our souls (or at least, my soul), that can explain why the expression of grief for my beloved dog was far more intense than the emotional pain I felt when my parents died?

Dr. Paul: Ed, please accept my heartfelt condolences for your loss. You are correct that the bond between a person and a cherished pet can be very deep, and the loss very real. The degree to which humans are able to form attachments varies from person to person. Our early life and the type of bond established by our parents often influence the quality and intensity of our attachments. A great deal of psychopathology is thought to emanate from early attachments gone wrong. Much of the ability to form and

1

sustain long-lasting, positive attachments emanates from positive and supportive parenting that, most fortunately, works to our advantage.

For those who may be interested, Edward Mostyn "John" Bowlby (1907-1990), a British psychiatrist, is credited with much of the work on attachment theory. He believed that an infant needed to develop a relationship with at least one primary caregiver for strong social and emotional development to occur normally. He also believed that further relationships would build on the strengths of this early attachment. While attachment theory was meant to address the quality of bonds between people, I believe it applies to the relationship between anyone and a loved object, especially a pet.

Strong attachments become a base of strength from which our early exploration of the world take place and ultimately influences our emotions, thoughts, and expectations of future relationships. Interestingly, if we have been fortunate enough to have positive attachments as an infant, followed by quality relationships as an adult, the sense of loss and upset when a loved one is no longer there, can normally be quite intense. With strong attachments, we always wish to be near the attached object, and then we deeply miss it when it no longer exists. While loss can be painful, it is in fact adaptive. It is also a time of high vulnerability, and as a result, the probability of the emergence of less adaptive behaviors increases.

Early experiences with our caregivers have a significant impact on our thoughts, memories, beliefs, expectations, behaviors, and emotions, as they pertain to us and to others. The experience of our early attachments creates, what is sometimes viewed as the internal working model of future social relationships. Time and experience modifies this. The quality of early experience establishes the core.

Dr. Chapunoff: From what you're saying, Howard, one must logically conclude that defective, early life attachments with our parents or caregivers represent a prelude to, or anticipation of, future psychological dysfunctions.

Dr. Paul: That's right, Ed. Mary Dinsmore Salter Ainsworth (1913-1999), a Canadian developmental psychologist, expanded on Bowlby's work and identified what can go wrong with attachment styles. She noted that attachments could be secure, which is what one hopes for, but they can also be insecure. When attachments are insecure, children and the adults they grow into can develop behaviors of avoidance, ambivalence, and resistance, or have attachments that are disorganized. For example, when parents discourage crying and overly encourage independence, and at the same time, show little or no response to genuine distress, avoidant attachment patterns can arise. As a practicing behavior therapist, I often work with parents who overly respond to distress, and inadvertently expand and reinforce such behaviors, which is not a good thing. Both not reacting to genuine distress and overreacting to lesser degrees of distress can create problems.

Children with less responsive parents tend to have difficulty sharing and expressing warmth with others and often have poor self-esteem. Sometimes, parents respond appropriately to distress but are inconsistent and occasionally neglectful of distress. These parents tend to respond only after a youngster has amplified his or her distress responses. The parents are not perceived as providing a secure base, resulting in increased distress on separation, sometimes associated with feelings of ambivalence and anger, and subsequent reluctance to warm up to caregivers. Such children seek contact but then respond angrily when they achieve it. Others cannot easily calm them, and they typically always feel anxious, as they are never sure of the positive availability of their significant caregiver.

Caregivers are often frightened in disorganized attachment patterns by the distress of their child and can behave with withdrawal, negativity, and role confusion. Abusive exchanges are often associated with this particular pattern. The affected children often display contradictory and disoriented behaviors, such as combining approach and avoidance at the same time; showing high levels of fear when either leaving or returning to an attachment figure.

Dr. Chapunoff: From all the patterns of insecurity a child may have, which is the most detrimental?

Dr. Paul: Disorganized attachment is the most damaging of all the insecure patterns. Fortunately, two thirds of individuals have secure attachments. This, however, leaves one third of all individuals with high vulnerability to one or another form of emotional distress and mental illness.

3

Ed, returning to your question as to why you felt so much distress over the death of your dog, I would say that because of your positive attachment with your parents, you were able to deeply experience the loss of your beloved pet. There is little doubt that in the process of your own individuation, you established independence from your parents. This individuation of yours in no way diminished your caring for them. It did establish a positive and adaptive emotional distance between you and your parents. With a pet, this individuation cannot be because we remain constant companions and caretakers to them. The bonds between pet lovers and their animals are apt to become very intense.

For the rest of my comments, I need to put on my cognitive psychotherapist hat. When we are children, if we sustain an accident, like falling off a bike and scraping an elbow, and we approach our mother and say something like, *"Mom, I fell off my bike, and I'm having a little discomfort in my elbow."* She will probably not pay much attention to the complaint. We soon learn that if we come in and say, especially with distress in our voice, *"Mom, I fell off my bike and my elbow is killing me,"* there is a much higher likelihood that we will get the desired attention, without that elevated distress, she might not get off the phone!

An inexorable force works to teach all of us to use amplificatory language when we talk about distress. Ed, you are obviously a man who uses language positively and with some style; you addressed your grief as *excruciating and intolerable.* The language we use determines, at some level, the intensity of our emotional reaction. Often, the internal scripts we use to create these amplifications of distress are never heard. We can sense these amplifications are there by the way people describe their pain.

Dr. Chapunoff: Could you explain to me what the mechanism was that caused my guilty feeling?

Dr. Paul: Ed, you felt guilty that the intensity of your reaction to your pet's death exceeded your reaction to the death of your parents. It would seem to me that on a subconscious level you were stating that you should not have more intense feelings toward your pet than you do toward your parents. Because of that internal demand, you became angry with yourself; that anger was expressed by guilt.

4

Dr. Chapunoff: Knowing psychology, obviously makes a huge difference! Guilt and, I presume, other emotional dysfunctions become aggravated when you do not know why and how they happen.

Dr. Paul: Correct! You were irrationally and unknowingly demanding of yourself that you had to love your parents with intensity greater than you loved anything else. Your inability to confront this with adult reasoning became compromised, as you did not know what you needed to argue against.

Parents, no matter how beloved they may be, if they do their job correctly, must at some point, say no. Pets almost never say no to us, and very rarely disappoint us. On the other hand, parents must teach us to cope with disappointment in order to socialize us. Even if we understand unconditional love, as it pertains to parents, it is more complicated than that of pet ownership. We seldom have conflicts with our pets. They usually do not tell us what to do or, if they do, we are clear that it's a request, not a demand.

Ed, I would like to end this discussion by noting that there is a continuum of feelings that begins with joy and ends with sorrow. Sorrow is different from depression. Sorrow, while it is unpleasant, is normal, necessary, and not diminishable. Beyond this joy-to-sorrow continuum, we may experience feelings contaminated by distorted beliefs. It's almost impossible, in this day and age, to escape these distortions. This is the reason why, when feeling pain, we need to be diligent to not amplify distress beyond its true level. **No level of undistorted thinking can make a bad thing good, but it doesn't take much to make a bad thing worse.**

There are also societal issues to contend with, especially as they relate to grief, sorrow, and pain. Sorrow is painful, and no one likes pain. Many people have come to believe that feeling pain must be avoided at all costs. Unfortunately, one easy way to reduce pain is to become angry at others, or, at ourselves. When you stated that the pain felt unbearable, you were, at some unconscious level, telling yourself that the pain was beyond your ability to tolerate.

One of the actions that enable people to finally mourn and move on, is to reframe the loss as something they can and will manage. Your pain was very real. Even though you may not have been aware of what you were doing, it was unreasonable of you to make a contest of the extent of your loss between your pet and your parents. I am also suggesting that your selection of words amplified your distress. I do not offer this as a criticism, but mention it as an example of how we can come to make a truly painful event even more distressing.

Dr. Chapunoff: Howard, this was the first question I presented to you, and I already learned plenty. In my opinion, most people never consult a psychologist, and many individuals probably have unresolved psychological problems - the *guilt feeling* I had when I cried for my lost doggy more than I cried when my parents died is undisputable proof that I am one of them. From the lucid explanations you just provided, I learned the following:

A) The mechanism and importance of early life attachments to parents or caregivers, and what goes right or wrong with good or defective attachments

B) Suffering is inevitable with attachment bonds of superior goodness and quality. The more of them one has, the more one suffers when a loved one is lost. That is *not diminishable*, as you suggested. Those who fail to understand this concept seem to be destined to unmitigated grief

C) The *individuation* that one develops, leads to a certain independence of feelings that does not exist with a pet. With parents, we have frequent companionship, but with pets we have constant companionship. Whether we'd like it to be that way or not, it doesn't matter, since that's the way it is

You helped me a lot, Howard, and although the sadness over the loss of my beloved pet is *undiminished*, I no longer have guilt for expressing my feelings more intensely for my pet than for my beloved parents. Suffering is a normal, inevitable reality in our lives. On the other hand, guilt is an intrusive element that imposes a heavy burden on us.

The way I see it, suffering makes us feel sad, but guilt makes us feel miserable. Suffering is inevitable, guilt is not.

2

UNCONTROLLABLE ANGER
A fired bullet with an unpredictable destination

Dr. Chapunoff: Henry, a man in his early 50s, was referred to me by an internist because of uncontrolled hypertension even though he was properly medicated. There are several reasons that explain unresponsiveness to adequate medical management of high blood pressure; one of them is anger, and Henry had an abundance of it. His severe emotional stress was evident by the expression of his eyes, the tightening of his lips, the shirt wet from excessive perspiration, an accelerated pulse, and his very high blood pressure. Henry divorced his first wife and lost two million dollars in the process. He married again, and this time had a very happy relationship. He was successful in his business and again made a couple of million dollars in about six years; not bad. The trouble was his hatred for his first wife was so intense that it did not allow him to enjoy his new life. The fact that his ex-wife destroyed his old business and ran away with one of his closest friends tormented him. His newly found marital happiness and the substantial capital he remade did not mitigate his *emotional misery*. I told him that if he was to control his blood pressure and find a way to get rid of his anger, it was essential that he seek the assistance of a psychotherapist. Unquestionably, he was a candidate for a stroke, a heart attack, or other dreadful complications. He moved to another state, and I never saw him again.

Howard, I'd like to know what kind of psychotherapy, drugs, or both you'd provide to a person like Henry, who exhibited chronic, unresolved anger.

Do people respond to management and change their thoughts, feelings, and attitudes, or is anger of this kind incurable? Is it possible to eradicate anger? Are angry people capable of overcoming the bitterness of the past and developing the ability to be at peace with themselves and the rest of the world?

7

Dr. Paul: Ed, this is a great question. Almost all human emotions are understood best if they can be broken down into their simplest form. Anger is a perfect example.

For the first year of life, whenever we are hungry, we cry. More often than not, a consistent and loving caretaker comes to us and feeds us. If you remember my discussion about sorrow, when caretakers are neither caring nor consistent, derangements in attachments occur. For most lucky babies, a warm and dependable caretaker is there to respond to our crying. There is usually a very reliable relationship between babies crying and someone tending to their needs.

At about one year of age, most of us begin to develop language and form our early, basic, and crude understandings of how the world works. We begin by believing the world is a great place! We get whatever we want, and when we do not, we make a fuss, and someone comes and gives us what we need. We like this! This nirvana doesn't last forever, and when we begin to be somewhat mobile or ask for something in excess, we hear this strange, new, two-letter word that we don't like. The word, *no*, becomes an affront to our sensibilities, as it represents a conflict with our nascent model of the world in which we get whatever we want; a world where fussing almost always works. The desire to return the earth to truth and beauty begins to grow, culminating in the *terrible twos* - when children go to war with their parents.

Dr. Chapunoff: Howard, please remember that people of many different cultures will read this book, and not all of them will be familiar with the term *terrible twos*. Would you please explain a little further?

Dr. Paul: Ed, *terrible twos* is a term used to describe the developmental phase many children go through at about two years of age. At this time in their lives, many children try to return their environment to that golden time when they got whatever they wanted and fussing almost always brought the desired response. During the *terrible twos*, parents have the daunting task of teaching children the three basic ideas that will provide comfort for the balance of their lives:

1) You cannot always have what you wish

2) It isn't terrible

3) You can live without getting what you want. In other words, you can cope with it

We then spend the rest of our lives trying to outgrow the *terrible twos*. Whenever anyone is angry, from a developmental standpoint, he or she has returned to *terrible twos*! Most adults do not like this notion, but, when you think about it, the truth becomes very clear. When we are angry, we are making one of two cognitive errors: we are saying, what is cannot be, or we're saying, what is not, must be.

Neither of these statements are logical in that what is, can be. It's foolhardy to say that something cannot be when it does exist. Likewise, if we say that what is not, must be, we are again clearly incorrect in that, if it does not exist, it does not have to.

Dr. Chapunoff: In observing the faces and attitudes of people, anger appears to be a disturbingly common and often socially accepted phenomenon. In fact, politicians, artists, executives, athletes, and people in different professions and endeavors frequently use angry expressions that are celebrated by many. Anger is also used as a weapon. Dictators typically do that.

Dr. Paul: You hit the nail on the head. We live in a unique society where anger is praised and sorrow is feared. Unfortunately, this idea transcends cultures and is true in far too many parts of the world. Anger is seen as a source of strength and power, rather than as a destructive force that creates rigidity, narrow focus, poor perspective, and stereotyped ways of responding.

Let me relay a small story. When I was in high school I joined the fencing team; my weapon being the saber. I was fortunate enough to be undefeated my junior and senior years while on the varsity team. Even then, I tended to be an observer of others' behavior. At one meet, early on in my junior year, I noticed one young man, from Olney High School in Philadelphia, do something quite unusual at the beginning of each of his bouts. When the referee started the match with the word "Alez," this young man would run up, in the guise of a Flash Attack, and purposefully step on the toes of his competitor. Not surprisingly, many of the competitors became angry, and then this young man would beat them.

He was not a very accomplished fencer, and I easily beat him in every match. But, those that he made angry would lose some composure, become overfocused on *getting back at him*, and as a result, become rigid in their approach and lose their form, allowing him victory.

Dr. Chapunoff: Could it be that an angry person feels that he or she will better impose a point of view because of a display of anger?

Dr. Paul: Yes, humans, uniquely, will repeat what they know does not work, somehow believing that if they simply do it longer or louder (or both), it will finally lead to success.

Many cultures prize machismo, and unfortunately, the backbone for this is often anger with its associated set of demands.

Dr. Chapunoff: What is the real origin of anger? I'd like to know about the initial mental process that evolves into anger.

Dr. Paul: Anger is generated by distorted beliefs that we *must* always have our way. It really is a very simple concept. Whenever someone is angry, they are reverting to two-year-old thinking, and incorrectly saying to themselves that they must have their way or things must work out only the way they wish. There is a huge difference between *what I would like, what I think might be best,* and *what has to be.* It is when we make the transformation from *what I would like* to believing that *it must be,* that anger forms. Dealing with anger involves the reverse process of teaching people to finally transcend the *terrible twos* and have as their guiding internal concept the reality that things do not have to be the way they wish.

Dr. Chapunoff: You seem to suggest that an angry individual, at times, verbalizes anger in an imperative mood.

Dr. Paul: Exactly, Ed! There are a series of words termed categorical imperatives, which include *must, should, have to, ought to, got to,* or any other phrase which implies demand. These are all anger-creating words. If you think about it, none of these words are logical. The only thing we *must* do is die. All other *musts* are corruptions of *what I might like,* or *what I think is best.* Unfortunately, demand words are inescapable. Our culture, including our vocabulary, is insidiously jammed full of such faulty demand notions.

10

Dr. Chapunoff: Almost every time a demand is issued, it seems to carry at least a drop of poison called anger, doesn't it?

Dr. Paul: Yes, Ed, to understand the impact of demand words - words that take on the characteristics of *commandments* - the following example may be helpful. I do not use this analogy to bring religion into this discussion. Instead, I refer to it as an easy example for one to relate to:

If you ask some people, *"How does God feel when someone breaks one of his commandments?"* they will typically respond that breaking a commandment brings on the wrath and anger of God. If you then ask, *"What do we call people who break commandments?"* individuals will universally respond, *"We call them sinners (bad and worthless people)."* If we then ask, *"What happens to people who are sinners and break commandments?"* the universal response, *"They will be punished and burn in hell,"* will typically follow. There is no difference in the meaning between, *Thou shalt* and *You must!*

I often quip that if God can make commandments, humans would best make suggestions!

As you suggested, imperatives, or any abridged demand statements, leads to anger on the part of the person issuing the commandment. This is also associated with the firm belief that the person who breaks our commandment is either inadequate or in some way not a good person. Not only do we believe, truly believe, that the person is not acceptable, but anger also imbues us with the sense that we are rightfully entitled to punish the offending person.

Dr. Chapunoff: It then appears that individuals who are angry and demanding, generate an atmosphere of discontent and create a bad disposition in others, making them less likely to comply with their demands.

Dr. Paul: Correct, Ed, that is one of the problems associated with the use of demand words. If I say to you, *"You must do something,"* typically, the little voice in your head will say, *"No I don't!"* Far too often, demand leads to opposition and resistance. This applies to physicians who give directives to their patients, and then don't understand why patients don't comply. There is a range in the severity of resistance people may

11

generate. Many are able to overcome their resistance, listening instead to their own common sense and choosing to be compliant. But, the more things are demanded, the more frequently people will rebel, simply because it was delivered as a commandment, leading them to ignore the content of the request, even if it's reasonable or prudent to listen.

Dr. Chapunoff: How do demanding people deal with the *responsibility factor*? Does demand imply a release of responsibility or its transfer to someone else?

Dr. Paul: Ed, you have identified one other complication of demand. If I tell you that you must do something, in my head, I am placing responsibility on you. I developed a very important rule that says, *whoever owns the desire, owns the responsibility.* If I want you to do something and I tell you that you must do it, in reality, I own the responsibility, as I am the one who wants it. Because I say you must do it, I am actually placing the responsibility on you and ignoring the fact that it is truly mine. Responsibility is an interesting commodity; it can only be taken and almost never be given.

Dr. Chapunoff: I presume that when you say, "Responsibility can almost never be given," you are referring to the military. In the military, an order is a delegation of responsibility. The individual who receives the order is generally not allowed to resist it.

Dr. Paul: There are certain circumstances that make it seem responsibility can be given, such as the military, law enforcement, corporations, hospitals, educational institutions, and many others. In these organizations, orders are commonplace, and there is the perception that responsibility can be given. In fact, these are all circumstances where the person who gives orders and who makes demands has enough control over your life that you will most likely choose to comply. Wherever this is the case, there is inherent resistance that goes along with demand, and there tends to be a large amount of grumbling in the ranks.

To summarize, demand leads to opposition and resistance and results in the mistaken perception that responsibility can be given to the other person. We create anger when our demands are not followed, and we think poorly of others and wish to hurt them. The message of anger is that you are no good, and the agenda of anger is pain to be inflicted on the other person.

When people think of uncontrollable anger, they typically think of loud fussing, such as yelling, screaming, kicking, throwing things, and/or being cruel and aggressive. People can also be passively angry and internalize anger or be angry with themselves. Anger, whether uncontrollable or not, has very clear and understandable roots. I offer a few examples to further make my point.

One of the original science fiction TV shows was called *Flash Gordon*. Flash Gordon's nemesis was the personification of anger, Ming the Merciless. Ming had a large and devoted following, and many people loved to be near him. However, they knew they could never say "no" to him. As long as they were on his *right* side, he treated them admirably and more than equitably. He threw great parties and was a wonderful entertainer. He believed he was always right. He always had to get his own way and no one could say "no" to him. If he wanted something, it instantly needed to be delivered. Anyone who thwarted him or his way of thinking became an instant archenemy. He felt justified in being cruel and merciless toward his enemies and extracting pain and revenge from whoever got in the way of his wishes.

After hearing this tale, sometime in the future you may wish to speak to me about human cruelty. Our current discussion on anger will serve as one of the bases for that discussion. Not everyone can be reduced to a caricature like Ming the Merciless, so I will provide a few more real life examples of how anger can get out of hand and adversely affect others.

One of the ideas we mentioned earlier was that responsibility gets corrupted when people are angry. When people are angry, they displace responsibility and blame the other party for not providing them with what they want, which they elevate to *needs*. I often do marital therapy and would like to introduce you to a couple that is prototypical.

The Faults have been married for about eight years. The husband, Notmaya Fault, is a passive man who is very conflict-avoidant. When pressured, he tends to withdraw and become reclusive. His wife, Itzyoura Fault, is quite the contrast to Notmaya. She is demanding, very verbal, and unfortunately, always angry with her husband. The first time I met with them, Itzyoura produced a long list of dissatisfactions about Notmaya's behavior. When I asked her, "*What would make you happy?*" she reiterated her list of demands. When I asked her, "*Whose job is it to provide you with your happiness and to make all these changes?"* she clearly stated that the responsibility was totally her husband's because he was not giving her what she wanted and needed. I asked her, *"Who wants these things?"* She stated very clearly that she wants these things deeply. However, when I followed this question with the idea that since she wanted these things, it was her responsibility to try to achieve them, she was aghast and became angry with me! Itzyoura felt entirely justified in berating her husband, demeaning him, and yelling at him whenever he disappointed her. The notions that he did not *have to* provide her with what she wanted and that it was *her responsibility* to behave in ways that might increase the odds of her getting what she wanted, were foreign to her. Fortunately, as therapy unfolded, she came to realize that change was, in part, hers to make. In order to gain more of what Itzoura wished, she would have to take more personal responsibility and not always blame him. Itzyoura also learned that some of her demands were unreasonable and, fortunately for the couple, she became easier to live with. Notmaya was taught to be more assertive and better communication strategies were developed between the two of them. They lived more happily ever after!

In another example, I recently worked with an attractive, 20-something, young woman who had been involved in numerous motor vehicle accidents. She had what is commonly termed, *road rage.* While driving, if someone did something she didn't like, she would manage to get in front of the person, blow her horn, and shake her fist at them. After she was in front of them, she would then stomp on her brakes, often causing the person behind her to hit her in the rear. She knew that the person who hit her from behind would be charged with the responsibility of the accident, and she took great pleasure in the vindication she felt when they struck her car! She also took pleasure in the fact that the person who she believed offended her would have to pay for the accident, often receiving a police citation and points on their license. After her car was repaired and repainted a few times, her rage, rather than being reduced, escalated. One day she was out driving, and as she saw it, the driver of a nearby car came too close to her. She became so enraged that, rather than taking the time to get in front of the other car, she simply swerved into them pushing them off the road, causing damage to the vehicle, and sending one of the passengers to the hospital. The police looked unkindly upon her actions and *threw the book at her.* One of the outcomes of the court proceedings against her was that she was ordered to be in anger management. This brought her to me. In working with her, it was very clear she had a faulty ideational system. She believed that every car around her should know of her presence, show her infinite respect, and do nothing that would distress her, as it pertained to driving. Instead of understanding that not everyone is a good driver and she must drive defensively, she believed that everyone *had to be* a good driver and that it was her rightful duty to punish them if they transgressed and drove poorly. It has been a few years since she had a motor vehicle accident, and since correcting her faulty notions, she is in much better control when driving. This result also had a positive impact on her relationships, in general.

Before returning to Henry, the gentleman you brought up in your opening set of questions, I'd like to add a little information on autonomic reactivity. Ed, I am sure I don't have to tell you about the autonomic nervous system; however, it may be helpful for our readers to know that we all have one.

The autonomic nervous system has two major components: the sympathetic nervous system and the parasympathetic nervous system. The sympathetic nervous system activates us, producing both fear and anger. The parasympathetic nervous system is the nervous system of calm, comfort, and positive feelings. All emotions have two basic components: one is physiological, based on sympathetic nervous system activation, and the second is mediated by cognitive process, which determines the expression of our sympathetic activation. Everyone has an autonomic nervous system, but there are significant variations in the way our nervous system functions from person to person.

Some individuals are more reactive than others are. Henry appears to be an individual with a very reactive sympathetic activation process. This balance of sympathetic and parasympathetic reactivity is described often as temperament. Some people are hard to shift from being parasympathetic; they are hard to arouse, slow to anger, and typically have little inappropriate fear or anger. By contrast, there are individuals with highly reactive nervous systems who shift into sympathetic activation quite quickly.

The neurotransmitters in our sympathetic nervous system influence whether our reactivity will be biased toward responses of fear or biased toward responses of anger. Independent of the way our sympathetic nervous system responds, it is our beliefs that ultimately determine the expression of our activation.

For the most part, when I speak of anger, I speak of the cognitive portion of our reaction based upon our faulty demand-based beliefs. I will try to use the term, activation, to mean the changes that occur in our body due to sympathetic responses, and when I speak of feelings, I am referring to the combination of our activation and its modification by our beliefs.

Many people are familiar with the fight-or-flight reactions of our nervous system and understand that flight could be equated to fear, and fight would be equated to a higher propensity to anger.

People can be taught various relaxation skills to help temper their sympathetic activation and enable them to reacquire parasympathetic tone; strategies that are seldom sufficient alone. If a more robust treatment is desired, it's best to combine relaxation and other strategies with alteration of faulty cognitions and training to replace them with more mature, realistic ways of thinking.

Dr. Chapunoff: What about drug therapy to control anger; do you frequently use medications?

Dr. Paul: In most cases, pharmacology is not required in order to achieve better anger management. Occasionally, beta-blockers are prescribed for some individuals with highly reactive sympathetic activation. Antidepressants, atypical neuroleptics, and in some cases, certain seizure medications are used to reduce central (brain) irritability, which can assist in taming uncontrollable anger responses. These drugs may be necessary if there is a related mood disorder, especially a bipolar disorder. For the most part, good cognitively oriented psychotherapy does the job alone.

I noted earlier that anger leads to functional fixity, rigidity, and stereotyped behavior. *Anger is the glue that keeps us stuck to what we need to put behind us.*

In Henry's case, this is clearly true. Because of the potential risks associated with his uncontrollable hypertension, some pharmacological intervention might have been appropriate. In my opinion, as I outlined above, the most important thing in his case was to teach him the cognitively based basics. Henry never overcame his *terrible twos*. He never accepted or understood the fact that bad things can happen, and we do not always have to have a positive outcome. He never came to terms with the reality that while his first divorce was financially costly, it need not have been emotionally disastrous. He never understood that this was something he could have coped with. I'm sure that one contributor to the intensity of his rage was his ongoing sense of helplessness when things didn't turn out just the way he wanted. There's an old joke, "How many psychologists does it take to change a light bulb?" The tongue-in-cheek response is, "Only one, but the light bulb really has to want to be changed."

Dr. Chapunoff: Howard, once again, some people might not get what you are saying. Could you please explain a little further?

Dr. Paul: Sure, Ed, changing a light bulb is a simple task that almost anyone can do. Creating motivation is a different story. In order for psychologists to be effective, they work best with someone who is motivated to do the work. Without motivation, nothing, not even a light bulb, will be changed!

In answer to the question, "Is Henry helpable?" the answer is clearly, yes. However, Henry would need to be motivated to put in the work necessary to overcome his heightened emotional reactivity and to relearn a more realistic set of controlling ideas about how the world really is. The easy part of his treatment would be to have him understand why his belief system was unrealistic and produced his distress. The hard part would be to get him to do the rehearsal necessary to actually make a difference by creating a new and strong pattern of thinking.

The final concept I'd like to introduce in this discussion is that of habit. What I mention here may be reintroduced in a later conversation, but, it's so important that I may say it more than once. *We humans are creatures of habit, not of knowledge. We may know how to do something, but we fail to do it because we did not acquire the habit to do it!*

Getting Henry to understand this idea would be the first step in actually making a difference. The real work of therapy for Henry would be him putting in the time necessary to create and strengthen a new cognitive response pattern.

Dr. Chapunoff: Your explanation about uncontrolled anger was very didactic. You showed us how specific therapy can be applied psychologically, by cognitive therapy methods, and when applicable, the use of psychotropic medications, beta-blockers, seizure medications or antidepressant drugs, and some neuroleptic drugs.

In my opinion, these available therapeutic resources are not deployed with the frequency they should be used. Many who suffer from uncontrolled anger, never consult a psychotherapist. One of them, whom I knew, was a physician. He invited me and others for a dinner party. I arrived at his home, rang the bell, and a maid said, *"Come in, Sir."* I did. What did I find? He was kneeling on the ground hitting his pregnant wife in her face as she was lying on the floor crying and screaming. I intervened to avoid additional injuries to the unfortunate woman. He finally achieved some degree of control, particularly when he saw other guests arriving at the party. I was nauseous and dizzy. I needed fresh air. I saw a tree in the front yard. I embraced it and threw up. I was so upset! Years later, I learned that his violent outbursts had continued. To the best of his closest friends' knowledge, there was no indication that he had undergone any kind of treatment.

Another story: I saw on television an incident that occurred during a soccer game of Spain's league. A player hit another with his foot, not accidentally but on purpose, in a very aggressive, nasty way. He was suspended for several games and obliged to pay a fine of 10,000 euros. One year after that incident, I saw the same offender physically attacking another player during a game, in an obvious display of uncontrolled behavior. Did he ever receive any kind of therapy for his anger bouts? I doubt it!

This procrastination in avoiding or delaying the treatment of uncontrolled anger is a prescription for disaster. Persons who suffer from this condition do not often accept the fact that they need professional assistance.

Regrettably, the same phenomenon occurs with a host of other mental disorders, and I don't have to tell you how much suffering and even chaos result from that attitude.

There are also physical consequences from anger - controlled, repressed, or uncontrolled - such as strokes, myocardial infarctions, acute congestive heart failure, life-threatening cardiac arrhythmias, and sudden death. I urge people who suffer from chronic anger to consult both a psychotherapist and a cardiologist.

3

JEALOUSY
Anger-In, Gone Awry

Dr. Chapunoff: I've met a number of jealous people throughout the course of my life. Invariably, they presented with very serious and disruptive problems.

I observed jealousy in the context of marital, as well as fraternal relationships. There are many other situations in professions or politics where jealousy creates enemies as well.

Here is an interesting example of jealousy. John and Rose have been married for 20 years. He is successful professionally, mentally and emotionally well balanced, and enjoys, or tries to enjoy, his powerful sex drive. His wife does not have any of the same qualities. She is intellectually flat, and as he describes her, a cold fish during intimacy. When John's mother recently visited, John placed his arm around her shoulder, expressing affection for her. His wife had a near violent reaction when she said, *"What are you doing with your mother?"* Another incident occurred with John and Rose when they invited another couple for dinner at their home. One of the guests, Alice, is a violinist, as John is. When Alice attempted to remove her violin from its case to prepare to play a duet with John, Rose reacted rudely, nearly crushing the violin that never made it out of the case and said, *"There will be no violin playing here!"* The dinner that followed was tense and had a charged atmosphere. John reported that this aggravating incident demanded *gallons of Maalox®* to relieve his heartburn.

A second example of jealousy involved a 70-year-old psychiatrist, who confessed to his 65-year-old, prominent executive brother that he hated him for many years because he believed their father showed a preference for him during their childhood. The psychiatrist's training in adult and child psychiatry was useless to resolve this issue. He also said that he felt tremendous jealousy every time his younger sibling succeeded economically, socially, or professionally.

In the third example of jealousy, Mary and Richard were married for ten years and had two children. Richard was a devoted family man, charming, intelligent, and hard working. He never neglected his wife and kids, and he was home on time every evening. His in-laws described him as the best man their daughter could have married. But, there was a problem, a big problem! Mary was morbidly jealous. She checked his suits, looking for imaginary motel receipts and proof of extramarital affairs. She called him constantly at his office and was jealous of all his female coworkers. She was afraid that one of those women might steal her husband. Every day, and many times a day, she questioned him about the women he saw at his place of work, the gym, and other places. Richard, who was a friend of mine, once told me, *"Ed, if I continue to be married to this woman, I'm going to die of a heart attack from the stress she puts me through."* After 12 years of marriage, he couldn't take it any longer. The couple consulted a psychotherapist, who found it impossible to correct her morbid jealousy. She became severely depressed after they divorced; he did not.

Howard, can you please tell me how, when, and where jealousy starts and why? We are more aware of how it ends; often in a turbulent disruption of the relationship. When the victim of a jealous person or the jealous person consults you himself or herself, how do you approach therapy, and what are the usual results of your intervention?

Dr. Paul: Ed, jealousy is a topic that well follows our previous discussion of anger. In Richard's case, anger is not aimed outward, manifesting itself by chronic, unreasonable demands toward others. It has its roots in anger, aimed inward, affecting peoples' views of themselves and contaminating their self-images in chronic, destructive, and negative ways. To answer your question about jealousy, I think it will be helpful if I introduce, and then discuss, a number of different topics that may appear unrelated. It will be important for you to understand these concepts in order to tie things together, and then you will see how they interrelate.

Let me begin my answer to you by saying that jealousy is an anger process. It's easy to see that people who are jealous easily become angry with others. In reality, they are chronically angry with themselves and by doing so, unwittingly maintain their sense of ongoing inadequacy. I'd also like to introduce a developmental perspective, pointing out how our parents' backgrounds and their interactions with us can influence and even create our insecurity.

Negative parental interaction patterns get learned and internalized. Through habit, they are maintained and strengthened. It's helpful to understand that habit operates on an unconscious level. We are usually unaware of the internalized scripts that drive our emotional behavior.

In your second example of jealousy, you described a 70-year-old psychiatrist who maintained intense sibling rivalry throughout his life, his significant psychiatric training notwithstanding. It might be instructive to start with this example. As we can plainly see, jealousy has roots that go deep into childhood.

Just imagine, for the first few years of your life you had sole possession of your parents' attention and received all of their largesse and gifts. Then one day, you are told that a baby brother or sister would soon to be joining your family. The expectation is that you will be happy about it. Shifting gears, now imagine that your parents won the lottery and every week for the same few years, you received a sizable check, leaving you with very little to wish for. One day, you are told that next week you will begin to share this prize with a brother, leaving you with only half of the weekly check. Given this scenario, most people would be less than thrilled with this new proposition. If you think about it as a parallel circumstance, when a sibling is added to a family, it is not unreasonable to expect a similar, not so pleasant reaction.

Dr. Chapunoff: And, the source of pathological rivalry, it seems!

Dr. Paul: Rivalry is a euphemism for a jealousy-based phenomenon. What reduces sibling rivalry, or any jealousy for that matter, is our own sense of security and personal adequacy. If we were fortunate enough to have parents that fostered strong attachments, and even more importantly taught us that we have personal merit and value that is not diminishable by our errors or failures, and not enhanced by our successes, we will have a resilience factor to guard against jealousy.

Dr. Chapunoff: I've seen enough parents congratulating their children for their accomplishments and then getting upset, criticizing, or punishing them when they fail to pass exams or get good grades. Kids seem to be confused when that happens.

Dr. Paul: Unfortunately, far too many parents don't do a good job getting across the concept of unconditional value and self-worth. Far too many people see themselves as <u>only</u> being judged personally adequate by their positive performances. If, as children, we are taught to believe that we are only as good as our last success, and then, if someone else displays more talent, beauty, and intelligence than we do, we will probably believe they are better than we are. The flip side of the, *you are better than I am* coin is *I am less worthy than you.*

Many children come to believe they *must* be better than others *in order simply to be adequate*. If I *must* be better than you, then anything you do well can become a threat to me. Ed, I'm sure you can see how this relates to the psychiatrist you mentioned. He actually felt threatened any time his sibling demonstrated accomplishment or success. This was not about the successes of his brother; it was about circumstances that he believed meant that he was less worthy than his brother. This core fear of inadequacy is the basis of many different emotional problems.

If you read my previous sentences carefully, you detected an anger-producing, categorically imperative word, *must. Must, should,* and *have to,* as I previously explained, are language constructs that produce anger. You may recall my earlier explanation - anger stems from believing our wants and desires *must* be fulfilled. With jealousy, there is still a core of anger. However, in the case of jealousy, the *must* turns itself inward and becomes, *I must.* Behind jealousy, there is a damaged sense of self. People do not see themselves as good enough, and therefore, demand they *must* be perfect (or some variant of it). They believe that if they fail, or someone else outshines them, their inadequacy will be exposed, further eroding their sense of worth and creating fear and over-focused obsession.

Dr. Chapunoff: From what you're saying, Howard, one can conclude that a jealous person is angry on two fronts or different directions. I'd call it bidirectional anger - anger aimed at the self and anger aimed at another individual.

Dr. Paul: That's right, Ed. As I previously noted, if I'm angry with you, I will have negative and derogatory thoughts about you. By the same token, if I'm angry with myself, the same negative and derogatory thoughts will exist, only now they will be aimed at me!

Dr. Chapunoff: Evidently, not a nice prospect!

Dr. Paul: No, it is not a nice prospect! Behind jealousy, there is an ongoing, insidious, constant self-anger reproducing and strengthening negative thoughts about the self.

Let me take you through the various steps of self-aimed anger, and then we'll tie it together as it relates to your questions regarding jealousy. Just as *anger-out* starts with an externally focused demand, *anger-in* starts with internally focused demand - I must, rather than, you must. Similarly, if I make a demand of you, and you comply, there is every probability that there will be some internalized opposition and resistance.

Dr. Chapunoff: When people struggle with feelings of jealousy, are they aware of the jealousy status they are going through and the fact that it is causing damage to them and to others?

Dr. Paul: When people are angry with others, Ed, they know they are angry. When people are angry with themselves, they are often unaware that anger is behind their feelings. Furthermore, when people place demands outside of themselves, they externalize responsibility. When demand is aimed at the self, the individual retains responsibility, but the opposition and resistance created by the demand still exists, only now they create negative energy, leading to blockage and procrastination. People are seldom aware of this process.

Dr. Chapunoff: How does the mind handle the blockage and procrastination you're referring to, Howard?

Dr. Paul: In order to overcome internalized, negative reactivity and resistance, people marshal their energies and in the process, can become obsessive, narrow-focused, and may suffer a significant loss of perspective.

Dr. Chapunoff: I'm under the impression that in all of the cases of jealousy I presented to you, the jealous persons lost their sense of perspective.

Dr. Paul: Yes, Ed. It's clear, in each of the examples of jealousy you provided, these individuals lost their perspective and became overfocused, desiring to control their partner in order to reduce their own fear and anxiety. Just as with anger-out, self-demand once failed leads to anger-in. If my demand is aimed at you, I will be angry with you. By the same token, if my demand is aimed at me, I will be angry with me. If I am angry with you, I *will* know that I am angry. However, if I have a set of demands aimed at me, and I fear or believe that I have failed them, I *will not* know that I am angry with me. I will, instead, be enmeshed in my own sense of feeling worthless. I may try to mask that with jealousy.

Dr. Chapunoff: Howard, this feeling of worthlessness you speak of, must be one of the worst frontal attacks on a person's self. Is that true?

Dr. Paul: Yes, it is, Ed. Many people believe, if anyone else discovers their deep, dark secret that they are worthless, it will be catastrophic. This is especially true in the case of jealousy, where along with the sense of feeling inadequate, comes the belief that everyone else might be better than you; better than you, through and through. Any time someone else does something that we believe is better than what we might be able to do, we react as if it confirms our own sense of inadequacy.

Dr. Chapunoff: Is it reasonable to think that a person who suffers from jealousy also suffers from significant anxiety and/or other important emotional dysfunctions?

Dr. Paul: Yes, often there are associated emotional and behavioral dysfunctions. Some people develop significant anxiety with jealousy, while others cope with a dread of their own inadequacy by obsessively trying to control the world around them. This action, they hope, will ensure that the secret of their presumed inadequacy will never be revealed. Unfortunately, these people become blind to the reality that their behavior creates their insecurity, which is obvious to others.

Dr. Chapunoff: People with repressed anger might release it at the least expected moment. They remind me of a guy who has a machine gun that could be activated at any time.

Dr. Paul: You're so right, Ed. That is exactly what can happen. If I'm angry with you, I will want to attack you. I may do this overtly, covertly, or internally. If I am angry at myself, I will probably try to escape somehow, or I may attack. This attack can be directed at me or anyone who happens to be in front of me and within my range of attention. With jealousy, people attack the person who they fear will cause their inadequacies to be discovered. Unfortunately, this person is often a close family member, such as a sibling or a spouse. It's wise to think basically, if you are to understand people's emotions and behavior.

Dr. Chapunoff: How does one do that, Howard?

Dr. Paul: Our emotional control system is laid down as soon as we begin to develop language, and it is frequently consolidated and well formed by the time we start kindergarten. We may grow up, but all too frequently, our emotional control system does not.

A brief story: I frequently lecture at the Mental Health Center of the University of Medicine and Dentistry of New Jersey (previously known as Rutgers Medical School), where I am a professor in the Department of Psychiatry. I often poll the audience, comprised of psychiatrists, psychologists, and social workers, by asking, *"Who of you enjoys working with children?"* Typically, about 25 percent of the audience will raise their hands. I then ask, *"Who here only prefers to work with adults?"* I then offer my condolences to the 75 percent of therapists who responded that they prefer to work only with adults. I gently chide them by noting, "Irrespective of the age of our patients, we only work with children!" This is not at all meant to be demeaning, just accurate.

Dr. Chapunoff: At the beginning of this conversation you mentioned that negative parental interaction could produce defective emotions and behavior in their children. Would you please elaborate a bit on this negative parental role?

Dr. Paul: There has been a notion that psychologists have it in for parents, in that parents are typically blamed for any problems their children may have. I would like to make it clear that I do not blame parents, as they are simply doing what they have also been taught. I often say, there are no villains, only victims. This is not a hard and fast rule, but this is something I say to help people be charitable and understanding toward parents who made errors that disrupted the emotional development of their children.

Dr. Chapunoff: That is so true! I've also observed that poor emotional development of a parent is a prelude to poor emotional development of the child.

Dr. Paul: That's correct, Ed, but it doesn't always apply. There are times when parents are not implicated in the transmission of faulty messages learned by children. Sometimes, children incorrectly presume what the parental message is, leading to their own faulty learning. Often, but not necessarily all the time, parents teach us our early emotional control system by conveying the beliefs that they have been taught. Our early understanding of the world that becomes the base of our emotional control system results in a well-learned habit.

I'm taking time here to be sure you understand, as one of your questions to me was, "How do I go about trying to deal with jealousy?"

Ed, we are creatures of habit, not of knowledge. This was well borne out by your example of the psychiatrist; he clearly knew better, but was unable to do better. Getting people to behave differently and acquire more mature patterns of emotional responses requires the building of new patterns of habit. It is fascinating to me that when it comes to our emotions, people believe that talking about them will somehow change them. This is seldom the case. Habit is defined as something we have done so frequently, we are no longer aware of it. Habit operates on an automatic level. The internal messages that we send to ourselves are unconscious. Most people, especially those who have not entered into therapy dealing with internal scripts, such as cognitive behavior therapy, are typically unaware of the emotional control programs they unconsciously carry. If you ask most people, *"When you are walking, are you aware of the messages your head is sending to your feet?"* they will respond that they are not aware of such messages. People understand that walking is a habit, and they also understand that their feet will do only what their head tells them (their feet) to do. Just as with walking, people, as a rule, do not hear their own self-talk. We are aware of what happened to us, and we are aware of how we reacted. However, as far as emotions are concerned, we are not aware of the messages we send to ourselves that determine our emotional responses.

Let's now return to your three examples. You described Rose as having difficulty with intimacy and also being jealous and controlling. There is every probability that early on Rose saw herself as not good enough. She might very well have believed that everything she did was an *ego contest* that would reveal her inadequacy or finally prove her adequacy. Unfortunately, with this kind of system, the baseline is always one of inadequacy. Sex, rather than being an expression of love and intimacy, probably became something she felt she was not good enough at and tried to avoid it by suppressing her feelings.

Dr. Chapunoff: In other words, she feared she would prove to be inadequate during intimacy and that led her to act like the *cold fish* that her husband referred to, right?

Dr. Paul: It's certainly a possibility, Ed. There are many reasons why people fear intimacy and are unable to tolerate genuine and spontaneous emotional expression, especially during sex. I don't think this discussion on jealousy is the venue to explore all of the factors that may impinge upon her needing to maintain such physical control. I will bet, however, that negative self-judgment played a significant role in her having to suppress her feelings. Rose's example helps us to understand how she may have been threatened when her husband, John, put his arm around his mother. The very thought that John might be more attached to his mother than to her was devastating to Rose. Her internal demand that John *must* be more devoted to her than to anyone else was certainly activated in such a circumstance. This internal statement that I'm sure she was unaware of, led her to be angry and possibly attack in some way. I do believe that the same dynamic held true and explained her reaction to her guest, who wished to play a violin duet with her husband. It's sad that so many opportunities for joy became circumstances for her to feel threatened, leading her to be inappropriately controlling and hostile.

In the case of the 70-year-old psychiatrist, somewhere along the line as a child, he no doubt formed the belief that to simply be adequate he had to be better than his brother. He based his competence and sense of self, not on his own accomplishments, but as the inverse of his brother's success. Given his age, and the fact that cognitive psychotherapy was born at the time he went through his psychiatry training, it's no surprise to me that he was unable to understand the silent root of his problem. He may have been psychoanalytically trained and had some insight into his problem. As I said earlier, we are not creatures of knowledge, but of habit. Someone would have to have taken him through exercises to build a better emotional control system and help him understand that his brother's successes were in no way related to his adequacy and worth. If he came to believe that his own worth was noncontingent, he'd be able to overcome his pain, hatred, and jealousy.

In your third example of jealousy, it is very clear that Mary carried an internal view of herself that was less than charitable. She feared that since she was inadequate, no one would stay with her. All the love, care, and devotion of her husband, was not sufficient to overcome her core, internal belief of being inadequate. In fact, the more true to her and caring that he was, the more anxiety it probably created. Her hidden internal demand, that Richard be faithful to her, was coupled to her own sense of inadequacy. The dissonance between her demand that he be faithful, and the anxiety that she was not worthy of his faith, was the probable dynamic behind her unremitting jealousy. She was actually working to always disprove the fear that she was rejectable. She was on a quest for constant reassurance that, unfortunately, only led to worsening anxiety and an increased need for heightened control. When Richard finally left, she saw that as an affirmation of her inadequacy and worthlessness. It is no surprise that a morbid depression ensued.

Dr. Chapunoff: Howard, if you have a patient at your office with a jealousy problem, what kind of therapy do you offer?

Dr. Paul: Ed, I am often consulted by people who are jealous. If they are able to understand that jealousy is really about their own negative self-image, and they are willing to put in the effort to build a better emotional control system, the outcome is typically quite positive. However, I must say that a damaged and negative self-image is a challenge to overcome. Some individuals are very damaged, and it takes some time for them to heal their childhood wounds. It is possible to do, but it takes diligence and significant motivation.

Dr. Chapunoff: The cases of jealousy I witnessed in the course of my life were all so recalcitrant that the best psychologist in the world would have a most difficult time trying to correct them. You mentioned how you would manage a jealous patient. Can you please give us some idea about the psychological management of the jealous person's victim?

Dr. Paul: Yes, Ed, I certainly can. When I'm consulted by the victim of jealousy, the therapeutic course of action typically consists of increasing their acceptance while decreasing their own emotional reactivity, including anger, in response to the pressures of their spouse. What I do is dependent upon the goals of the person seeking my support. If they wish to maintain their relationship and are willing to learn ways to take the other person's problems less personally, then I am able to teach them strategies to do so. It is important to understand that I do not create the goals of therapy. Goals come from the person seeking my assistance. As long as their goals are licit and reasonably accomplishable, I will work with them to achieve the outcome they wish.

Dr. Chapunoff: The three cases of jealousy I presented ended badly. In the first case, Rose and John got a divorce. He was fed up and exhausted with Rose's interminable, irrational recriminations, and he could no longer take it. One morning, after having a light breakfast, he headed for a divorce attorney's office.

The psychiatrist's brother ended the sibling rivalry by disconnecting himself from his brother, the psychiatrist, who had been trained in mental disorders but was incapable of using his knowledge (if he really had that kind of knowledge) to correct his jealous fits.

In the case of Richard and Mary, circumstances became unbearable for Richard. Among other things, his wife searched his pockets looking for anything that she could find to blame him for infidelity. One day she found a condom. The couple had often used prophylactics during intimacy and Richard only intended to use it with her. But, as usual, she accused him of cheating. He was unable to convince her she was wrong. Richard was so relieved by his divorce that he described his mental reaction as, *"the freedom one may feel skydiving."* Fortunately for him, his parachute opened at the right time.

4

A METHOD TO YOUR MADNESS

Dr. Chapunoff: Howard, I must say that I've enjoyed our exchanges up to this point. You have a way of responding to my questions that is clear, concise, comprehensive, and very understandable. As I go through my questions about sorrow, anger, and jealousy, there appears to be an unfolding, conceptual system that you use to unify your thinking, enabling you to provide a cohesive backbone to your responses.

I understand you have been working with people for about 45 years. It appears to me that you have put in a great deal of effort to deepen your understanding of people and how you can help them enjoy a more comfortable life. This might be a good time for you to share what your system is and how it has grown and matured over the years.

Dr. Paul: Ed, you are correct and quite perceptive. Over the years, I have developed ideas that help me understand people and provide me with a comprehensive and consistent approach to deal with people's problems. This conversation will be a little bit more of me sharing information and may not allow for as much back and forth as other talks. Bear with me, as I think these ideas are very important. They will help lend clarity and understanding to much of what we may be speaking about later. Now, let me take you through how this approach has unfolded and grown over the years.

When I began working with people in 1966, I was trained as a behavior therapist. The technology of that time was to observe antecedent conditions, which simply means conditions that happen right before any behavior in question occurs, and consequent responses, or what happens right after the behavior occurs. This system worked very well in the management of children or people in psychiatric hospitals, where there was control over their environment and one was able to control what happened to them and how they responded.

Research psychologists carefully developed experiments that led to the discovery and understanding of the laws of learning that were clear enough to apply to human behavior, sometimes with startling success. These laws revolved around two different kinds of learning:

1) The Pavlovian learning pattern is when a normal automatic body reaction is paired with a novel sound or shape. In time, this learning pattern produces a physical reaction. When a tone is paired with the sight of food, it normally causes saliva to be formed. After a number of pairings of tone and food, the tone alone will also produce saliva. This learning pattern, discovered by Pavlov, is often referred to as Classical Conditioning.

2) The Skinnerian learning pattern is when behavior is followed by some incentive (reinforcement) or a punishment that leads to more or less behavior, depending on what follows. This type of learning, studied by Skinner, is referred to as Operant Conditioning.

1960s: Psychoanalytic vs Behavior Therapy

During the 60s, there were two competing schools of thought within psychology and psychiatry. The primary and most well-represented school was psychoanalytic, comprised of individuals who were the followers of Freud. At that time, Freudians had a great deal of disdain for the emerging field of behavior therapy. They saw it as limited, trite, and far too unsophisticated. Psychoanalytic therapists were not much for looking at either antecedents or consequences, believing that what went on within the black box (subconsciously) was where the meat of treatment existed, and where the focus of psychoanalysis needed to take place. The contrast is seen easily in this schematic:

School	Antecedents	Internal Process	Consequences
Psychoanalytic	Not important	All important	Not Important
Behavioral	Most important	Not important	Very important

Dr. Chapunoff: Howard, the differences between these two methods could not be more striking!

Dr. Paul: That's right, Ed. As you can see, both groups approached understanding human feelings and what determined people's behaviors from very different perspectives. Behavior therapists did not deal much with feelings, focusing instead on behavior, as their name implies. One other major difference was behavior therapy's strong foundation of demanding empirical support for concepts, coupled with a dedication to utilizing procedures that were developed and corroborated in the research laboratory.

The psychoanalytic tradition early on was primarily a tradition of discussion, insight, and theory with very little reliance on research to corroborate ideas.

It wasn't long before an active technology developed in behavior therapy that had great utility in dealing with changing many problematic behaviors. Along with effectiveness, came a good deal of success and the number of people who consulted behavior therapists grew exponentially. As the number of people who sought my assistance began to grow, an increasing number of them wanted to talk with me about their feelings. I was trained to examine antecedents and recommend an alteration of consequences, not to talk to people about how they felt! Initially speaking with them about feelings was seen by me as a distraction that kept me from doing a comprehensive behavioral analysis and following through with environmental alterations to help them achieve their goals. I was not alone in this dilemma, and in the early 70s the cognitive revolution occurred within behavior therapy.

1970s Cognitive Revolution

A classic story that may help to explain why behavior therapists had to grow their theoretical base:

Driver #1 is happily motoring along when suddenly a very poor driver abruptly cuts driver #1 off. He says, possibly subconsciously, *"You can't do that to me, I'm going to teach you a lesson."* He then becomes angry, fumes, and pounds the steering wheel; his blood pressure goes up, and he becomes red in the face. If we were to walk up to this driver and ask, *"What do you think you have just said in your mind to cause you to make yourself angry?"*, there is a very good chance that this individual wouldn't understand the question, be unable to answer it, and might take his anger out on us. If we were to simply ask this driver, *"Why are you mad?"* he or she would explain that they were angry because they were cut off.

When people are asked to explain their feelings, they become very behavioral and describe only antecedents and their emotional consequence; they deny or avoid looking at any internal process!

A little further down the road, driver #2 is cut off by this identical, poor driver in the identical manner. Unlike driver #1, driver #2 says subconsciously, *"Oh my God, this is awful and terrible and horrible. That person is going to cause an accident."* This driver will have a very different emotional experience from the first driver. Rather than anger, this person will probably have anxiety, worry, or other high levels of concern. If we ask this driver why they are anxious, we would get the same response that driver #1 gave us. The difference is that it would be delivered with a very dissimilar affect; not anger, but some level of fear.

To complete my story, let me introduce you to driver #3, who had been seeing me for an alternative problem. This same poor driver likewise cut off driver #3 in the identical fashion as driver #1 and driver #2. Driver #3 thought, *"Wow, what a good job I did avoiding an accident!"* As you can see, this individual had a very different emotional experience, even when the identical circumstance happened to them as happened to the other two drivers. The response of driver #3 is very different and mediated by a more positive and constructive internal thought process and script.

These examples caused problems for behavior therapists as the identical, antecedent condition happened to all three of the drivers, yet three very different consequent reactions emerged. It became clear that in order to predict emotional reactions accurately, it was necessary to understand internal thought processes. Once the internal thought process was clear, highly accurate predictions of emotion became possible. With this new awareness, came the cognitive-behavioral age. Cognitive behavior therapists, however, still cling to the tradition of research-supported, empirically informed procedures.

Dr. Chapunoff: Howard, thank you for explaining concepts related to the psychoanalytical and behavioral methods. Now, will you please explain to us what you mean by *empirically informed procedures*? Would you also tell us in a few words what cognitive therapy stands for?

Dr. Paul: Sure Ed. Empirically informed procedures are strategies used in treatment that have been investigated scientifically and proven to have merit. They work better than chance and are better than simply caring and showing interest in the person. Cognitive behavior therapists have a goal - to make a difference in how people function - to have them develop new skills, better emotional controls, and more functional behavior.

One additional, key difference between psychodynamic therapists and cognitive behavior therapists is that the psychodynamic therapist's goal is to understand the patient's problems, not necessarily make a change in their behavior. However, there has been some necessary change in that position, of late.

Habit-based Behavior

In our last discussion, I introduced the concept of behavior as habit-based, and I explained that the goal of therapy is to create new, more adaptive habits. If you recall, I said a few times that humans are creatures of habit, not of knowledge. If people actually did what they knew was best for them, I would probably be unemployed. There is little danger of that happening. Our beliefs become habit and operate silently in the background.

I believe I explained that most of our emotional-control habit system is formed at an early age. When we are young, we are taught the belief system of our caretakers, our community, and our society. We are not mature enough to critically assess whether what we are taught makes real sense. On examination as an adult, we see that some of what we learned is faulty. If we are lucky, some things work well. It is helpful when our belief patterns are functional; often our belief-based habits maintain their childish base, leading to dysfunction.

Dr. Chapunoff: You just said that humans are creatures of habit, not of knowledge. I believe this is an extraordinarily important concept. Habit would imply an automatic behavior, something that is repeated over and over again, automatically. I never think when I tie my shoelaces. I do this automatically, don't I?

Dr. Paul: Yes, Ed, you do! Habits are things we have rehearsed to the point of automaticity. Automatic thoughts are synonymous with the unconscious.

Dr. Chapunoff: I didn't know that! I never thought that tying my shoeslaces was part of my subconsciousness!

Dr. Paul: Yes, Ed, in a way, it is. Early learning forms the significant base of our beliefs, and most of these beliefs (habits) formed at a young age. As habits do, they operate on a level below awareness. By focusing on habit, cognitive behavior therapy borrowed a page from the psychoanalytic field and resurrected the unconscious, labeled it as habit, and recreated the notion that early experience and learning are important psychological developmental variables.

Dr. Chapunoff: Humans are plagued with dysfunctional thoughts and beliefs of all kinds. Can you tell us what basic dysfunctional beliefs create so much emotional and behavioral chaos?

Dr. Paul: To my way of thinking, there are three core dysfunctional beliefs that create almost all psychopathology. In our discussions on anger and jealousy, I noted that people make three basic cognitive errors:

1) We make demand statements (categorical imperatives) that create anger.

2) We denigrate whoever is the target of our anger and perceive the target as a less-than-worthy person, even if the target is ourselves. Demand and denigration are a one-two punch and always go together.

3) The third cognitive error is something that I call, awfulization - something we are all taught to do, to a greater or lesser extent.

In our previous discussion on sorrow, I explained that when we were children, if we had an accident like falling off a bike and scraping our knee, and we approached our mother saying something like, "Mom, I fell off my bike, and I'm having moderate discomfort in my elbow." There is reasonable doubt that she would ever get off the phone to help! We soon learn that if we approach her and say, with distress in our voice, "Mom, I fell off my bike, and my elbow is killing me." There is a much higher likelihood that we will get the desired attention. An inexorable force works to teach us to use amplificatory language when we talk about things that distress or upset us. The language we use determines, at some level, the intensity of our emotional reactions. Often, the internal scripts we use create these amplifications of distress, and we seldom hear them. We can understand that they are there by the way people react.

Now that we have covered the three, core, distress-producing, faulty beliefs behind most dysfunctional behaviors - demand, denigration, and awfulization - I would like to provide you with a model of how these dysfunctional scripts create our problems.

Problems, Problems, Problems

Dr. Chapunoff: People usually complain about problems and more problems. Besides specific solutions for different problems, do you have a general philosophy of operation to deal with them?

Dr. Paul: Yes, I do, Ed. Many people come into therapy to eliminate problems. I take great pain to impress upon people that problems are a normal part of living. The role and goal of therapy is not to eliminate problems, but to increase solution-focused behaviors. When problems confront us, there are only three possible paths to choose: attack, escape, or solution.

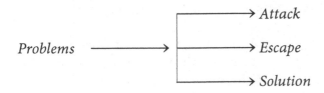

To begin, we must bring the external problem inside of us and internalize it. This involves transferring what we see, hear, feel, smell, and taste from the outside world into our internal representation of what is outside of us.

In the process of internalizing the real outside world, there are errors of transfer that can color our understanding of what is real. There are many impactors on the quality of this information transfer, including mood, sleep or lack of it, medications, cyclical variations of hormones, light, the type of nervous system we were born with, and the list goes on.

Part of good therapy is to examine the many factors that interfere with good transfer of information from the outside to our internalized model, and use this insight (among other tools) to select our therapeutic methods.

After we internalize the problem, we encounter the belief processes that are our internal scripts. They help us understand (or misunderstand) and interpret the world, modifying our reactions and giving form to our emotions and behaviors.

Anger
Let me briefly discuss anger as an example.

Unfortunately, many of us believe that words are more important than the message anger conveys. Parents, who are often angry with their children, rationalize and say, *"I never said you are no good."* Instead, they insist that they only said, albeit angrily, *"I don't like your behavior."* Unfortunately, the message the child hears is, "You are no good (inadequate, evil, bad, irresponsible, etc)." When anger is directed at the self, our own feelings of inadequacy are amplified. Remember, *the message of anger is inadequacy; the agenda of anger is pain!*

After we become angry with someone and attribute bad things to them, we set about attacking them. There are three methods of attack:

1) <u>Active aggression</u> is what most people think of when they think of attack; yelling, screaming, throwing things, hitting, kicking and tantrums. If I hit you over the head with a two-by-four piece of lumber, there will be blood and splinters. This will be messy! In the process of socialization, most of us are taught that having such loud displays of temper is unacceptable. I call these overt and loud attacks *loud fusses.* These attacks often cause scenes and our parents or

caretakers dissuade us from behaving so. Unfortunately, there are many elements in too many cultures that see such anger-based behaviors as a show of strength. These ideas reinforce these behaviors. Sadly, watching any news program will attest to the potency of the reinforcement of such behaviors.

2) <u>Passive aggression responses</u> are what I call, *soft fusses*. People will pout, moan, groan, plot revenge, burn the dinner, and in essence, do things that they know the other person will not like.

3) <u>I refer to internalized aggression</u> as *inside fusses*. People get sick, depressed, or anxious. Some people can do these all at once.

Dr. Chapunoff: As I understand it, when people are angry with themselves, they increase their own anxiety and sense of inadequacy. They try to escape from their self-inflicted pain. Howard, will you please make some comments on inadequacy, denial, and escape attempts?

Dr. Paul: I'll be glad to do that, Ed. Humans can be very creative in their varied schemas to protect themselves from the anxiety of facing their own fear of inadequacy. There are four basic strategies that people use to escape. The first and most universally popular, is the ever classic, *I can't stand it*. I doubt there is anyone who, at one time or another, has not used such a phrase.

Dr. Chapunoff: Howard, I hear that phrase so often, and as you point out, it is used universally, how can it be so bad? I hear so many variants, such as, *"I can't stand it!" "I can't handle it!" "I can't tolerate it."* They all appear to be linguistic twists that mean the same thing.

Dr. Paul: Ed, this is a perfect example of how words and phrases we use become so ingrained in our language that they have a subconscious negative impact on the way we feel. As an example, let's say you and I are walking down the street. We turn the corner and see a large group of angry looking people coming towards us swinging clubs and chains. What would be a good plan? I think we would both decide to go the other way, quickly! We would come to two similar conclusions:

1) The challenge exceeded our capacity (It's too big).

2) We did not have the resources to cope with the presenting problem (I'm inadequate).

With these two views activated, the only sensible thing to do is to escape. "I can't handle it", along with its many variants is code for these two beliefs:

It's too big and **I am too small**.

The second strategy is an adolescent strategy that begins with *I don't care*. The persons claiming a lack of caring typically do indeed care, and care so much that they must protect themselves from the pain of caring and the associated self-attribution of inadequacy, caused by failure to satisfy their own and other's demands in order to succeed.

When we cannot escape the pain of caring and believing that we are a failure, and our strategy of, *I don't care,* is not sufficient to shield us, we simply refuse to acknowledge the problem! That is what denial is all about. Escape strategies are usually adolescent but adults use them too.

The third strategy is a plan I call the, *some day my prince will come* fairy tale. This represents the externalization of responsibility and expectation of salvation. We feel entitled to succeed, and when we do not, with no sense of personal responsibility, we expect to be rescued.

The fourth strategy occurs when escape drives our actions. In this case, the easiest possible option is usually the winner. Escape options are 180 degrees opposite of my working definition of maturity: 1) the ability to choose and then do what is best or most valued over what is easiest or most fun, and 2) the ability to identify our demands, recognize that they are faulty, and correct them by returning them to a statement of desire or affirmation of what we believe is best.

Ed, you asked about escape. The challenge of escape is that when we are done, the problem still exists, and we are engaged in a large circularity with amplification, anger with self, self-attribution of inadequacy, and continued failed coping reverberating in an escalating cycle.

I've tried to detail what I believe explains how things go wrong, now I'd like to switch gears and talk about how we go about making things right.

Dr. Chapunoff: I love it!

Dr. Paul: Ed, perhaps you can see from our previous discussions that it is our internal belief systems that create the overt expression of our feelings. When people say, *you make me mad* or *it makes me frightened,* they are actually incorrect. It is their internal interpretation of external events that creates feelings. *We make our own feelings; what happens outside of us represents things we do not like.* We combine things we do not like with our internal beliefs, which modify our actions, producing our feelings and responses.

I previously emphasized that we are creatures of habit; knowledge alone does not alter our ongoing behavior patterns. To change behavior reliably, we must create alternative habits. Fortunately, we are able to create and then strengthen new scripts (beliefs) that, when brought to sufficient strength through practice, will influence our feelings and behavior.

Dr. Chapunoff: Howard, how do you handle the link that exists between feelings and behavior? Abnormal feelings translate into abnormal behaviors. What about the awareness factor; how aware are people about their inadequacies? These will inevitably lead to dysfunctional behavior. How do you put all of this together and choose the appropriate therapeutic response?

Dr. Paul: Ed, there's a logical progression I take people through to make a difference in their behavior and feelings. If people are of a mind to do so, step one begins with the person's ability to be sensitive to and understand our habit-based, belief system, and determine if there are errors in it. This is a bit of an initial challenge in that our beliefs often operate at a level below awareness. It is difficult to change something when we don't know it's there! Something called an antecedent, belief, consequence (ABC), or cognitive analysis, is helpful to enable people to hear their silent beliefs.

I ask people to take a piece of paper and draw three columns. In column A, I ask them to write down what happened to them. This may be either an event or a thought. I then asked them to go to column C and write down how they felt and what they did. Then, I assist them with exploring what ideation, faulty or correct, may have connected A to C and place that in column B.

There are three faulty, core beliefs that create the bulk of our distress:

1) Catastrophization: A distorted idea that magnifies a thought or a problem and creates a feeling of doom or impending catastrophe

2) Demand: A request that represents an imposition - I *must,* you *must,* or *he or she must do as I say*

3) Denigration: Worthlessness aimed toward the self or others

Dr. Chapunoff: After a person reaches a state of awareness of any of these faulty thoughts, what's the next step to attempt their solution?

Dr. Paul: Once individuals get a sense of their faulty ideations, they are in a place where they can begin to decide on alternatives that are more realistic they wish to strengthen. We then begin to develop reasonable beliefs, such as the development of strategies of de-awfulization, the capacity to turn demands into preference, or what we think is best, and a recognition that even if we are disappointed by someone's behavior, or even our own, it does not relegate us or them to the realm of the inadequate and unworthy. Since this is habit-based, we set up practice programs and environmental cues to signal the need for rehearsal. There's an old joke about a musician who hails a cab in New York City and asks to be taken to Carnegie Hall. He tells the cabbie, *"Take me to Carnegie Hall."* The cabbie answers with the question, *"How do you get to Carnegie Hall?"* The musician answers, *"Practice, practice, practice!"*

The simple fact is habits are only strengthened by practice. It's like going to the gym. If you go only three times, it would be imprudent to say, *"I tried it, but it didn't work."* If you go to the gym with any degree of regularity and apply yourself with any degree of diligence, it will work, period. The same is true for the creation of any habit. If you practice anything, even thoughts, the habit will strengthen and with persistence, will grow in power until it is able to compete with older, less adaptive habits.

Dr. Chapunoff: I presume that for a newly formed habit to work, it has to be fully developed. If a habit has the consistency of jelly, so will the resulting behavioral change, right?

Dr. Paul: That's not quite correct, Ed. People need to build up new habits. If things are calm, they can begin to express themselves early on. However, when push comes to shove, old, strong habits will prevail. The good news is that once a habit is at full strength, even an old habit that has been with us for many years, it cannot get any stronger. A well-practiced, new habit can compete with a strong habit of many years' duration. Habits are like fuel tanks. Once they are full, they can't get any fuller!

Dr. Chapunoff: I don't know what happens in the practice of psychology, but in my practice of cardiology, I explain to patients what they suffer from and the corrective methods. Some appear to understand the instructions, but often fail to implement my recommendations. Do you see a similar behavioral pattern with your patients?

Dr. Paul: Yes, Ed, I do. When working with people, the easy part is figuring out what might be wrong and then helping them know what to do. The hard part is getting people to actually do what will help them. Often, when I lecture to my psychiatry residents or other staff at the medical school, I say, in a somewhat tongue-in-cheek fashion, that therapy has three parts: the easy part, the hard part, and the harder part. The easy part is figuring out the problem and giving instruction on the solution. The hard part is getting people to do the work, and the most crucial and hardest part is getting people to keep doing their homework long enough to actually make a difference.

Diligence, creativity, and a research-informed, treatment plan will only work if people do the homework necessary to create, strengthen, and sustain new habits. This may sound reasonable and simple but it does mean real work.

Dr. Chapunoff: Is this why psychotherapy sometimes fails to solve the patient's problems?

Dr. Paul: Most people have a poor outcome in therapy because their therapist is stuck on insight and not on behavior change, or their therapist is not working to create motivation and diligence to create and strengthen better ways of doing business.

Dr. Chapunoff: Howard, we are now at the end of our fourth discussion and we still have a long way to go. I am enjoying these talks and I also find them extremely useful. You showed us some ways to avoid negative, emotional reactions and how to deal with them. It's clear that the understanding of psychological processes that cause anger, other dysfunctional feelings and behaviors, in addition to receiving specialized treatment when necessary, are crucial to achieving peace of mind and avoiding potentially dangerous confrontations with oneself and others. Now that I'm referring to the avoidance of *confrontations*, I remember a joke that shows how one can do that! Shall I tell you the story?

Dr. Paul: By all means, Ed, go ahead.

Dr. Chapunoff: Joe and Dick are two psychotics. Joe visits Dick and they have an exchange.

Joe: *"Dick, I came to visit you."*

Dick: *"That's impossible!"*

Joe: *"Why?"*

Dick: *"Because I'm not here!"*

Joe: *"Are you nuts or what? What do you mean you are not here? I'm talking to you right now!"*

Dick: *"I told you, and I insist I am not here!"*

Joe: *"Well, that's too bad, because I came to pay you the $500 I owe you!"*

Dick: *"Wait a minute! If that's the case, I'm here!"*

Joe: *"That's too bad, Dick, because I'm gone already!"*

There's always a way out, isn't there?

5

THE MENTAL HEALTH OF YOUR THERAPIST AND THE MENTAL HEALTH SYSTEM

Profound knowledge of mental disorders by learned psychotherapists does not guarantee preservation of their own mental health

Dr. Chapunoff: Fred was a 50-year-old patient of mine who consulted a psychiatrist because of his severe stress related to serious marital conflicts. I asked him, *"Fred, how was your first interview with the psychiatrist?"*

He replied, *"That was my first and also the last interview with him."*

"Why," I asked,"what happened?" "He spent one hour with me and dutifully charged me his professional fees. For 50 to 55 minutes, he talked about himself and his problems. I tried to suggest to him that I was the patient, not he. But, this was to no avail. He kept on describing his marital problems and all kinds of aggravating situations with his widowed mother and his own children. He even told me that his wife was frigid. When the session was over and I left his office, I had a sense of relief knowing that I wasn't going to see him again. My problem now is that I'm reluctant to consult another psychiatrist or any therapist. I'm afraid the same situation might happen again and frankly, I don't feel I can endure it."

Howard, I have known psychiatrists, psychologists, and medical professionals of other specialties, who suffered from personality disorders and various kinds of mental illnesses, sometimes more serious than those of the patients who consulted them. As a practicing cardiologist, I saw physicians who suffered from mental illnesses, some ending in suicide. During a two to three year period, one physician jumped from the seventh floor of a hotel and another put a bullet into his heart; both suffered from depression. A third one - a cardiologist with bipolar disorder, who was making hospital rounds screamed at the nurses for minor irregularities, calling everyone's attention to himself. Finally, he shot himself in the head. These situations were indeed sad, but there were no apparent mental illness consequences on the patients that were treated by these professionals. It may be quite a different matter for a mentally affected patient to consult a psychotherapist who suffers from neurosis, a personality disorder, or psychosis. During my long years of medical practice, I knew psychotherapists who gave me the impression they were walking repositories of psychopathology.

What I don't know is what exactly transpires during the interaction between a sick patient and a sick therapist. I'd also like to know what signs patients should look for when dealing with a mental health professional that might alert them that something is not quite right with their psychotherapist. When a patient becomes aware of a practitioner's dysfunction, at what point would it be best to decide that enough is enough and terminate therapy?

Dr. Paul: Ed, just like you, I do not know what might go on between a sick therapist and a sick patient. I am sure that it will not be good for the patient. However, I can shed some light on what one might look for. Simply put, if a therapist is too preoccupied to have you feel you are getting close to 100 percent of their attention, find someone else. As you point out, if they are too busy with their own stuff to hear you, find someone else. I do, on occasion, share personal stories and information, but only to increase rapport, help people feel more comfortable with me, or allow them to feel a sense that I understand their pain or dilemma. Storytelling, when it is a metaphor, can be a powerful tool to convey information and learning. However, just telling stories is altogether different. There are two kinds of patients: those that come to tell stories and those that come to get better. Just telling stories, by either therapist or patient is a bad plan.

Unfortunately, there are times where lonely or sexually frustrated therapists use their lonely patients to satisfy their own needs. This can be very destructive.

Dr. Chapunoff: The professional relationship with a doctor, particularly a psychotherapist, may evolve into something emotionally deeper than affection, namely, love. Falling in love affects a normal person's rational-emotive process. If a patient who is suffering from almost any psychological disorder falls in love with their therapist, it seems to me that the situation is heading for trouble. Howard, how should the client behave after discovering that he or she fell in love with their therapist? What about the opposite situation, when the therapist falls in love with the patient?

Dr. Paul: If you think that your therapist has romantic feelings toward you, find another therapist. If you, as a patient, have romantic feelings toward your therapist, this is a real danger sign, and you should attempt to discuss it with your therapist. It may be necessary for you to find a therapist, where feelings of love will not interfere with the therapeutic process. If you feel, you are falling in love with your therapist - not that hard to do when you finally have someone who gives you unconditional regard, caring, and undivided attention - it may not be safe or therapeutic to continue working with that person. From a therapist's standpoint, this is a very sensitive issue and care would best be taken to not cause hurt or trauma to the person who has developed caring feelings towards you. Sometimes, this can be worked through. Sometimes it cannot. If it cannot be dealt with therapeutically, then changing therapists becomes very important in order to not create an even bigger problem.

Love is a much romanticized and interesting process. It produces clear changes in the biology of our brain. While love may make the world go around, it can also spin our head around and make sound decision-making a real challenge. As you know by now, I jokingly say, "Love is the only sanctioned psychosis!"

Dr. Chapunoff: By sanctioned psychosis, Howard, I presume you mean a medically authorized psychosis, correct?

Dr. Paul: Well, Ed, that is not exactly what I mean. There is no official sanctioning body. This is just a tongue-in-cheek way of saying that love is supported by everyone, not just the medical community of psychologists and psychiatrists - even when we are in it, we are loco. When people are in love, they are truly out of their mind and do the silliest things! Love makes us put on rose-colored glasses and be blind to the difficulties that other people may have, especially someone who returns the *"I love you"* words with *"me too"* whether it be a prospective mate or a therapist. While I understand I might be criticized for such an unromantic view of love, when mixed with high need, pain, or even adolescences, it can put people into jeopardy because their decision-making is altered. While falling in love may be joyous, falling in love with your therapist can be dangerous.

Dr. Chapunoff: Falling in love with someone who is not your therapist can also be dangerous. Individuals with emotional disturbances are more vulnerable than those who are fortunate enough to have no emotional disturbances. Vulnerable persons - patients or therapists - may think about using their love object for reassurance and protection and behave in ways that are exploitive.

Dr. Paul: What you are saying is correct, Ed. Just as medical physicians must work to do no harm to their patients, so must therapists. In medicine there is an oath, "above all, do no harm." In psychology, there are ethical principles, but no oath. It is said that physicians have a license to kill; psychotherapists only have a license to maim.

Dr. Chapunoff: Vulnerability, I'm sure, makes a bad situation worse.

Dr. Paul: There are many vulnerable patients and therapists alike.

If you, as a patient, believe that your therapist is using you to help him or herself rather than you, go the other way quickly. The therapeutic relationship is reciprocal; however, the benefit from such a relationship needs always to be imbalanced and very much in favor of the patient. If you have the sense that your therapist sees you as a paycheck or an annuity, once again, go the other way quickly.

Dr. Chapunoff: Isn't it true, Howard, that a good therapist should always try to solve the patient's problems in the shortest possible time, and of course, with the most effective therapy?

Dr. Paul: Absolutely, Ed. I tell patients that my job is to get rid of me as soon as possible. It is important that I try to provide therapy that is sufficient, targeted, empirically supported, time-limited, and effective. If you get the sense that your therapist is not of a like mind, find one who is.

Ed, in answer to other parts of your question, as you act in your cardiology practice, providing treatments according to the abnormalities you see, therapists also provide counseling according to the type of challenge they observe in the patient and how much of the problem limits the patient's ability to function. Ed, the way you state your question implies that you believe there may be clearly defined boundaries between normal, neurotic, and psychotic conditions.

Dr. Chapunoff: Oi, oi, oi. I think that my lack of psychology knowledge is getting me into trouble!

Dr. Paul: It may well be. But don't worry too much about it, Ed. If we were discussing cardiology, I would be having similar lapses. To my way of thinking, there is no such thing as normal.

Dr. Chapunoff: This is shocking to me, Howard! If you and I are not normal, can you tell me why we are writing this book?

Dr. Paul: We are assuming, Ed, that you and I are more normal than many people are.

Dr. Chapunoff: Oh, I see! Well, that is reassuring!

Dr. Paul: Ed, everyone is, to some extent, neurotic. Neurotic means behaving in a way that is against one's best interest. At one time or another, we all do this. To me, a goal of therapy is not to make people normal, but to get them to a point of being comfortably neurotic!

Dr. Chapunoff: Up until one minute ago, I thought I was a normal person. Your explanation convinces me that I was wrong. I'm thrilled about my new title. From now on, I will consider myself a comfortable neurotic.

Dr. Paul: I am so glad you accept you new status, Ed. Good for you! Most of what we psychologists consult with people for is not mental illness, but faulty learning, and we help them with problems of living. When we speak of mental illness, there has been an alteration in the meaning of the term over the last few years. There are those who are psychotic with a disorder, such as schizophrenia. To use the vernacular, schizophrenia has been popularly termed, crazy. Psychotic implies that one is not in good contact with reality, hearing voices and seeing things that are not there. This term, crazy, has been popularized and greatly expanded to mean almost any strange or counterproductive behavior.

As we learn more, disorders such as major depression, bipolar disorder, attention deficit hyperactive disorder (ADHD), obsessive-compulsive disorder (OCD), as well as some other anxiety disorders, are seen as forms of mental illness, as they are biologically and genetically influenced. Even with biologically based disorders, problems exist on a spectrum with some being less severe and others more severe.

When I was in college, I had a chemistry professor who was obviously psychotic, a paranoid schizophrenic. He believed that aliens had implanted a transmitter in his gut, and when he reached the age of 45, the transmitter would broadcast all the information that he knew about chemistry to other scientists. With this self-imposed deadline, he worked night and day to achieve greatness before that fateful day came, and others would steal his work. While crazy, he was a very good teacher and reached some modicum of fame due to his positive contributions to science, even in the face of his mental illness.

Dr. Chapunoff: You reminded me of an elderly woman patient of mine, who was psychotic and believed she had a computer in her vagina. When the scans, ultrasound studies, and gynecologists proved that she did not have a computer in her vagina, she accused the technicians and the doctors of conspiring against her. She kept on saying, *"I'm sure my computer is right where I told you it was."*

Dr. Paul: Ed, one real danger to patients, rests not in a therapist's mental illness, but in a much more common and insidious problem - arrogance. I am currently dealing with an issue involving a complicated patient, who has chronic pain and a blood disorder. The patient was taken to the emergency room of a hospital, due to a medication-induced delirium. Because of her blood disorder, she is unable to take standard pain-relieving medications, due to the complication of bleeding and clotting. The only drugs left for physicians to prescribe are narcotics. With the right combination (or wrong combination as the case may be) of negative events, she becomes delirious and looks and acts psychotic. However, it is really a drug reaction and is medical, rather than psychiatric. The emergency room psychiatrist, who believed she had bipolar disorder as well as schizophrenia, significantly overdosed her with potent antipsychotic medication rendering her a drooling and dysarthric mess. She was unable to speak and unable to defend herself against this doctor. I spoke to the emergency room psychiatrist and acquainted him with 15 years of her history - the fact that this had occurred before and that it always cleared in two or three days with proper medication management. In the past, if she was transferred into a psychiatric hospital, she was discharged within a few days when it became clear to the next doctor that it was, in fact, a transient medical condition. The arrogant, emergency room physician was unwilling to accept information from me or other physicians familiar with her medical history, concluding instead that he was right and everyone else missed the diagnosis. He ignored the patient when she told him she was allergic to certain medications and proceeded to give them to her anyway, producing a significant rash, other complications, and risking a potential permanent dystonia. Finally, when the weekend came, an alternative psychiatrist was covering. The first doctor's overdosing was eliminated, and the patient cleared. However, by this time it was too late. The first doctor had already forced a court hearing and involuntary commitment.

Dr. Chapunoff: Your description of this doctor makes one think he has a personality disorder.

Dr. Paul: I suspect one could argue that this doctor has a very clear personality disorder, but arrogance is a problem shared by many in positions of power. Too many doctors, independent of their specialty, become angry if patients wish second opinions. Too many doctors become angry or simply give up when there are compliance issues. They do not see them as potential mental health issues.

Dr. Chapunoff: There are many wonderful doctors, but I've also known physicians who feel they are larger than life. Spiritually, in my opinion, they are smaller than bacteria.

Dr. Paul: You are so right, Ed. There are many, many, responsible, caring, and very good doctors. However, far too few doctors take the time to refer people to psychologists, psychiatrists, or other mental health specialists when there is a need.

Dr. Chapunoff: I totally agree with that, Howard. The personality and character flaws of some doctors at times create problems for patients, and on top of that, the health system in the United States has its own maladies. We are discussing psychotherapists' mental and behavioral dysfunctions, and they are part of a health care system that has its own share of dysfunctions. Would you mind adding your thoughts about that, Howard?

Dr. Paul: I would be happy to, Ed. In fact, I welcome that question. While everyone should be concerned about the mental health of their mental health provider, what really concerns me is not only the status of mental health delivery, but also the general health of our total health care system. We have a health system that has many, many strong points, but it only tends to work well if you are fortunate enough to be relatively healthy and have good insurance. Far too many people do not have good health or good insurance. If you are uninsured, or if you have Medicaid, or even Medicare without a secondary policy, and you get very sick, you may well be in jeopardy. As long as you are not too ill and you can take readily available generic medication, you will be okay. If you have drug sensitivities or need specific branded medications, you will probably suffer because these medications are not available or will not be approved and filled by your pharmacy unless you pay the full amount; often several hundred dollars. If you have a complex medical condition and need coordinated care, you will probably not receive it.

It is strange but true, if you have absolutely no money, you will get free care. If you have some money, just enough to put you at or slightly above the poverty limit, there will be countless doors shut in your face, due to the lack of affordable care.

When it comes to the delivery of mental health care, there is a significant shortage of sufficiently trained providers. All you need do is watch any news program to understand the need for enhanced mental health services, yet mental health workers are the least well-paid professionals, with psychiatry among the lowest paid specialists within the medical field.

Dr. Chapunoff: How do you view the managed care situation with mentally ill patients?

Dr. Paul: Managed care has almost taken over the provision of mental health services in the United States. In mental health centers and many child guidance programs, the workers are not primarily at a doctoral level. Far too many mental health workers have not been trained in the provision of empirically supported treatments. There is some relationship between the services you receive and what you pay for, but providing mental health services on the cheap is not the best way to go. A second problem is that because of limited graduate school space, there are far too many people who wish to become mental health providers and are unable to gain acceptance into programs offering appropriate training. When I applied to graduate school, there were eight positions and close to 1000 applications. The school whittled down the over 1000 applications to the best 400 applications. All 400 final applicants were qualified, but very few were accepted. Not only do we need more psychologists, but also I think you will agree we need more well-trained physicians.

One way to decrease costs is to increase supply. This holds true for any commodity. I noted in an earlier discussion that I have been involved in medical education for about the last 35 years. We are just not making enough doctors.

Dr. Chapunoff: How would you advise those in need of psychotherapy to inquire or search for a competent professional?

Dr. Paul: I would advise anyone seeking a therapist to ascertain the training and credentials of whoever is considered. Ask them if they are board certified; many psychologists are not. Ask them if they are professionally trained in cognitive behavioral therapy or other more modern, dynamically oriented, and empirically supported treatments. This is not a guarantee of good treatment, but it sure increases the odds that you will be dealing with someone who knows what they are doing.

Dr. Chapunoff: Howard, please tell me how a therapist might handle patients who are difficult to deal with or show a poor response to different modes of therapy? It's also a fact that an occasional patient will never respond to even the most exhaustive and knowledgeable modalities of treatment.

When does the therapist conclude that no hope of improvement with treatment can be offered, and how does the psychotherapist tell the patient that services will no longer be provided?

Dr. Paul: Ed, what a good question! You are correct that not everyone can help everybody. There are occasional patients where you do not see eye to eye on either the problem or the solution, and it better serves their interest to refer them elsewhere.

Of the thousands of people I have seen, there were probably only a handful, where either I missed something important or we just did not click; therapy was very brief with them seeking an alternative therapist. I believe this happens infrequently with me, in part, due to the way that I work. When someone comes to me, the first order of business is to try to determine what exactly we are going to work on. I jokingly say, "If you do not know where you are going, you are sure to get there!" When I am working with someone, I try to help them develop a clear, measurable, and focused set of goals, so we will both know what works and what does not work. After determining clear goals, I work to educate my patients about how I think conceptually and what our work of therapy will be. After we develop a unifying vocabulary, so there is less misunderstanding when we speak, I present the therapeutic plan, and we begin to work. I often give patients homework that we will review at each session. As I said earlier, there are two kinds of patients: those that tell stories and those that get better. Therapy is not simply for coming in and talking. Therapy is meant to make a difference by creating learning to help people reach their goals. At set times during the course of therapy, progress is measured. If progress is being made, we continue. If progress is being thwarted, we examine the obstacles that we encountered and develop problem-solving strategies to reduce or eliminate barriers to success. The therapy I usually plan with patients is short term and measured in months, not years. I do have a few patients that I have been seeing for an extended period, but this is the exception and not the rule.

Dr. Chapunoff: Howard, please tell me, what are some of the mental disorders that therapists usually find more pleasurable and gratifying to treat? In addition, which are the most refractory and professionally frustrating?

Dr. Paul: Ed, this is an interesting question. I don't think that disorders are what therapists find more or less pleasurable, but the people who are more or less pleasurable. I enjoy working with any challenge. Some therapists develop a particular expertise in one type of problem or another, and others prefer a wider range of people to work with. As the day goes on, I personally prefer the changing landscape of ages and types of problems. Some people come in and believe therapy is about rehashing negative emotional experiences and telling stories. These people tend to be refractory; it is difficult to get them actually to do the work, especially the homework. Few people like doing homework, but those who do it get better much faster than those who do not do it. There are personality issues that complicate therapy.

Dr. Chapunoff: Is there a separate diagnosis made for personality disorders as opposed to mental illness?

Dr. Paul: Ed, let me explain how a diagnosis is looked at. When a psychiatric diagnosis is made, it is divided into five different areas, each one called an Axis:

Axis I   Diagnoses that define and identify psychiatric disorders

Axis II   Diagnoses of personality disorders

Axis III   Identification of existing medical disorders

Axis IV   Identification of the life stressors people are confronting

Axis V   Global Assessment of Functioning Scale (GAF). GAF is measured on a 0 to 100 scale with good functioning being scores above 80. A score of 70 denotes mild symptoms, 60 denotes moderate symptoms, and 50 and below denotes increasing levels of severity

When people present with Axis II problems, they tend to have a lower prognosis and increased challenges to produce therapeutic change. Some examples of Axis II problems would be borderline personality disorders, narcissistic and dependent personality disorders, and others. These are the types of problems that are typically produced by severe and significant early trauma, attachment problems, or faulty learning transmitted by similarly affected parents.

Dr. Chapunoff: One would think that the extensive training and qualifications of highly qualified psychiatrists and psychologists would assist them in dealing with their own mental, affective, or emotional dysfunctions. However, this does not always appear to be the case. At the same time, professionals can continue with their practices and counsel patients, who have similar mental pathologies to what they may have.

Why is it that therapists may not effectively deal with their own pathology but can work effectively with similarly challenged patients?

Dr. Paul: Ed, once again, we need to consider the type and severity of problems being experienced by the therapist. Sometimes, a little bit of the same problem can make you more intuitive, increase your understanding of what the problem is, and help you relate better with the patient. It is easy to know what to do; sometimes it is just hard to do it. I may have mentioned earlier, *"If people really did what they knew was best, I would be unemployed."* Just because therapists know better, does not mean they will do better. This is part of the unique nature of the human condition. As a rule, the more well-put-together therapists are, the better the job they will probably do. Listen to your stomach. If it is doing flip-flops, and you are uneasy with the information your therapist is giving you, or you are uncomfortable in their presence, consider looking for someone else to work with.

6

THE STRUGGLE BETWEEN
SINCERITY AND DISCRETION
SEX, SEX, SIX!

Dr. Chapunoff: I was blessed with wonderful parents. My father died when I was 16. He was a great influence on me. He used to teach me certain things by throwing short sentences at me that contained important messages. The words that follow weren't his creation; he told me that. But, he still wanted me to keep them in mind, *"Before talking, think, and after thinking, keep your mouth shut!"*

The questions I'm going to raise, Howard, have to do with telling the truth or not telling the truth, under selective circumstances. Honesty is a wonderful thing. However, there are situations where telling the truth, and nothing but the truth, may be a poor choice leading to increased distress, rather than more trust.

Where do we draw the line between honesty and discretion? In intimate relationships, where are the dividing lines between sincerity, not telling the truth, and ethics? When is it wrong to choose *not* to divulge the past? When is it right to tell it like it is (or like it was)? Isn't it sometimes much better to bury the past like a hidden treasure, even if it was fools gold?

A dear friend of mine of 45 was madly in love with a 38-year-old, beautiful woman. He had the most serious intention to marry her. Their sexual chemistry was *better than perfect*. There was nothing he considered erotic that she wouldn't be happy to comply with. And she truly obliged with total joy and pleasure for both. One night, they practiced anal intercourse for the first time. Everything was as pleasurable and happy as usual. That is, until she said, *"John, would you believe it, I only had anal sex with six men? One was a Brazilian soccer player, another was a French journalist, and the third was a marathon runner from Belgium, yeah, I think he was from Belgium. There also was an Italian businessman. My previous husband was the first one and you are the last to do it."* My friend felt as if a ton of ice had dropped over his body. He ended the evening without saying anything to her about her comments. If my friend's girlfriend had not been so sincere and explicit, he probably would have married her. He was deeply in love with her, as well as extremely attracted to her. The exposure of her liberal sexual past disturbed and preoccupied him intensely. He developed a sense of insecurity about her and thought he could no longer trust her. One night, following this traumatic incident, he struggled with doubts of whether to continue the relationship with her or to end it. He developed intense tension headaches that disturbed his sleep. He heard screaming voices coming from his own tormented thoughts that kept on repeating, *"Sex, Sex, Six, Sex, Sex, Six, Sex, Sex, Six."*

The woman was gentle and educated, and he wished she had never brought up her past intimacies. But, she did. She crossed the line where trust turns into trauma. He was in shock and could not recover from it. Shortly thereafter, he ended the relationship. He told me, *"Ed, I was very disappointed. All of a sudden, my prospective wife turned out to be just a good lay."*

This brings the topics of sincerity and integrity in a relationship to the surface. It appears that being totally honest all the time may not be the best course to follow. I believe that there is a limit to what a man or woman should tell their sexual partner, even in the context of a sincere, honest, and loving relationship. I think the woman I just referred to made a huge mistake by telling her lover she had performed anal intercourse with several other men. Please, correct me if I'm wrong, Howard. I believe it's usually imprudent and counterproductive, for a person of either sex, to offer detailed accounts of sexual activities with past sexual partners. Keeping some secrets to yourself may not intend falsehood or dishonesty, but caution and discretion. Just as there are times we don't want to say too much, there are also times we don't want to hear too much.

Something similar happens with sexual fantasies. If one feels guilty about them, perhaps one should consult a psychotherapist, not a sexual partner.

In the forgoing case, the woman was not obliged to tell the truth. There was no previous commitment between them always to tell the truth. In my opinion, she acted like a guy who is found carrying an explosive device in a subway, and when asked what he intends to do with it, he answers, *"I don't know; I guess I wanted to have some fun!"* In my view, she acted childish like the guy in the subway!

There is a crucial distinction between this couple's conflict and the one I'll describe below. We'll be speaking about a formal commitment a couple made to always tell each other the truth and only the truth.

Howard, you may deploy reasoning concerning what the first couple should have said or thought. However, with respect to the next case, I would appreciate a yes or no answer.

A man and a woman are in love with each other and ready to marry. Both are educated, decent, honest, and straightforward. They made a commitment to each other to *always tell the truth and never lie.* Sexually, the man is a conservative fellow. On the other hand, the woman has been far more liberal in her intimate experiences with others. He doesn't know how many men she previously had sexual relations with or if she ever had any sexual relations with others. The man proposed they not have sex prior to their marriage because of his educational and family background, as well as tradition. A couple of months before the wedding he asked her to speak honestly and tell him with how many men, if any, she previously had sexual encounters. Remember, both had previously made a commitment to be *always* truthful with each other. What is she supposed to answer? The reality is that she had sex with five men. Should she tell her fiancée the truth or not? If she tells him the truth and he then asks if she ever experienced cunnilingus, fellatio, and other interesting variants, should she lie? Should she continue to answer truthfully? On the other hand, should she find ways to minimize or soften her past intimate interludes? Clearly, a decision to minimize or soften her past would be viewed as a failure on her part to honor her previous commitment to *always* be truthful.

Now, the other side of the coin, was it a smart decision by the man to ask her those questions? Obviously, he wanted the truth about the woman he loved. Did he really need to know the truth? It seems to me that he jumped into an abyss without a parachute and put his fiancée in a very difficult position. It appears to me there are times when a few words, delivered at the wrong time or to the wrong person, can have devastating consequences. Where do you draw the line between sincerity and retaining a sense of privacy in intimate relationships? In my opinion, smart management of a relationship can prevent it from becoming a conflict-laden, sticky mess. Do you agree, Howard?

Dr. Paul: Ed, for many of our discussions, we dealt with diagnosable problems, where I had the ability to rely on scientific-based knowledge to assist with my answers to your questions. With this question, we are entering the realm of belief and opinion, where values and judgments, rather than data-based findings must be considered. There is a huge difference between fact and opinion, and it is crucial to have the ability to tell which is which.

I often quip that people only fight over two things: issues that are fact and issues that are opinion. It does not pay to argue over fact; by definition, facts are provable. Do not fight; just find out the documentable answer. Similarly, it does not pay to fight over opinion; by definition, opinion can't be proven. If that is true, your opinion, even if it differs from mine, is of equal validity. The converse is likewise true - even if mine differs from yours, yours might also be true! While it is reasonable, and sometimes even enjoyable, to have a debate, where we each attempt to use reason and logic to emphasize the superior cogency of our point of view, in the end, it's helpful to realize it's just opinion and not provable. If people don't argue about fact and don't argue about opinion, it really doesn't leave them much to argue about. When people argue they are angry, and as you may recall when we previously spoke about anger, anger and the resulting arguments boil down to simply believing that you have to get your way.

With respect to lying, people tell four different kinds of lies.

1) People lie to ego-aggrandize, which means people like to make themselves look bigger in their own eyes and in the eyes of others. These types of lies are called fish stories. I'm sure we can all relate to catching a six-inch fish, and afterwards, telling people who weren't there about the huge fish we landed and the significant struggle we went through to bring home our prize.

2) People lie to get out of trouble and to avoid responsibility or blame. They may simply manipulate to get their own way. It is not a good idea, when your hand is caught in the cookie jar, to say that you were testing for freshness. A few times in my career, I did assessments in penitentiaries. It was quite amazing to me to meet so many honest men who guaranteed me they were innocent and had nothing to do with the reason they were in prison!

3) The third type of lie is often termed, white lie, and refers to not telling the truth to avoid hurting or distressing the other person. There is currently a commercial on television that shows Abraham Lincoln behind a somewhat short, plump woman, who asks him, *"Does my butt look big in this dress?"* Unfortunately, honest Abe says, "yes," and the woman marches off in a huff. Unlike Lincoln, when my bride of 40 plus years comes down the stairs in a new outfit and asks me how she looks, even if I am not thrilled, I do try to make a positive and supportive statement. I don't believe that makes me insincere or dishonest, just more aware of and sensitive to her feelings.

4) The fourth type of lying is akin to teasing. When friends meet, they often engage in a sport, where teasing is used to spar with the person being teased. There is no real desire to hurt the other person, and there is no attempt to put the other person down. The intention is to have a lively rejoinder that is seen as humorous and enjoyable to both parties. Making up stories can also fit into this category; it's done as a kind of jest and is usually corrected at some later time.

Ethics and Morality

Dr. Chapunoff: Howard, it appears to me, that if the woman in vignette #2 decided to lie, it might be labeled a white lie, wouldn't it? She would lie to avoid hurting his feelings. But, what if she lies because she's manipulative and wants to marry her fiancée, no matter what?

Dr. Paul: Ed, I think the way you ask the question makes it somewhat rhetorical. Many would understand her lying to spare him pain. However, if she lies, simply to gain her end desire, that is frank dishonesty. Getting back to your story as you presented it, one way for her to get out of this moral dilemma might be to say, "*We have promised each other to be honest. Are you really ready to hear my answer?*" She might also ask, "*What is motivating you to ask this question? Do we need to talk about this issue before you press on with your question?*"

Dr. Chapunoff: I like your way of dealing with the moral and ethical issues of being truthful, without exposing the raw truth first and causing unnecessary pain.

Dr. Paul: At this point, I hope you realize we are up against ethical and moral issues that have as much to do with absolute thinking as they do with honesty itself. When it comes to shades of gray, it seems important for everyone to develop a moral compass to help them through these kinds of issues. Sometimes, the truth hurts and the other person needs to hear it. Sometimes, there is simply no reason for purposefully being hurtful in the name of honesty.

Dr. Chapunoff: In my opinion, Howard, that is exactly what happened in vignette #1. The woman had no valid reason to relate her florid sexual past to him. This might be equated to dropping an atomic bomb on her lover's head. However, this reasoning does not apply to vignette #2, where the woman had made a formal commitment to always tell the truth. It's clear that being untruthful, when it's not necessary to be truthful, can be appropriate and wise. On the other hand, not telling the truth when one must is unethical or illegal, depending upon the circumstances. However, I do believe there are times when hiding the truth is the right thing to do. If I propose marriage to a girl and I tell her, "*I love your personality. However, your nose is so ugly, big, and deformed that just thinking about it makes me run to the nearest toilet I can find!*", that would be a cruel and unnecessary statement. There is no justification for this type of honesty. If I have such contempt for my girl's nose, I might recommend plastic surgery. If she refuses, perhaps I shouldn't think about living with her for the rest of my life.

Dr. Paul: I certainly agree Ed; sometimes not telling the truth, or giving more information than is required, can be unwise. I do think that it would be best for us to be careful of our own rigidities and absolutes. I could chide you for using the anger-producing word, *must*, in your question. When lying is seen as a black-and-white issue, and we utilize an all-or-none way of thinking, agreeing to a commitment to always be honest can brew trouble.

Dr. Chapunoff: That's what Albert Ellis referred to as musturbating, isn't it?

Dr. Paul: That's right, Ed. Values are best when based on good ideas. Truth telling is clearly one of those good ideas. Finding others who share our values is part of the process of keeping friends - friends with whom we can have a positive, long-term relationship.

Dr. Chapunoff: I agree with that! That is why in vignette #1, *Sex, Sex, Six,* the woman didn't have to be honest. He never asked her what kind of intercourse she had with previous partners. He never asked her how many lovers she had before him, and he never asked her other very intimate questions. In my opinion, she made a mistake and acted unwisely. Do you feel the same way or not?

I see vignette # 2 as a very different matter. There was a moral commitment, and an ethical issue, that, in my view, had to be honored regardless of the consequences. Am I wrong on this? Am I missing something? Don't ethics and morality matter?

I'd now like to elaborate on another point, and I need your help to know if I am right or wrong. Keep in mind that I am not a psychologist, and I may not have the flexibility in my character that is so important to understand these difficult issues. You were correct when you critically observed the tendency to absolutes in my character. Besides the pure honesty issue, I believe in vignette #2, when the man asked the woman about her past sex life, she should have told him the truth. In all probability, he would soon learn anyway that she had extensive experience with intimate contacts, and at that point, he would probably feel so frustrated and disappointed that he might not recover; the relationship would have a great chance of ending quickly. The way I see it, these two people were probably not made for each other, and telling the truth about her past would mean the avoidance of future divorce attorneys.

Dr. Paul: In vignette #1, the couple shared such an open and free physical relationship that the woman may have falsely believed this would extend to discussions of her past sexual experiences. I don't believe this would have been an unreasonable assumption. However, assumptions often can do us in. We all know the little phrase, "assume makes an ass of you and me." At some level, this could be more about communication difficulties between the two, paired with faulty assumptions about the other person's ability to hear and accept the truth. She may have thought he was secure enough to hear the truth. We must be cautious about expecting people to have a functional crystal ball and always know exactly the right thing to say.

Dr. Chapunoff: That is so true!

Dr. Paul: The other interesting feature of this little vignette is, even though your friend may have been sexually liberal, his attitude toward the woman he would marry appears to be far more parochial. There is a possibility that this gentleman had, perhaps unknowingly, a dual standard that he unfairly applied to this woman, and perhaps other women. If this is true, he may have deprived himself of an exciting and satisfying long-term relationship. The dual standard that men have of different principles for women to mess around with and women to marry, is pervasive in many societies, including ours.

Dr. Chapunoff: I remember that I asked him, *"Why did it bother you so much to learn she had anal intercourse with other men?"* And he told me, *"Ed, it isn't the fact that she had anal intercourse with other men before me, but the fact that she did it with five other guys. That revealed to me how open-minded and liberal she was about it. Maybe I'm wrong, but I associated her behavior to some kind of promiscuity."*

At this point, Howard, I'm beginning to understand why, at the beginning of this chapter you said that the problems we were going to face in these discussions could be more existential than real. In vignette # 1, it is clear to me that personal points of view can be more important than real life behaviors.

Dr. Paul: It sounds like your friend had a number of hidden beliefs about how a potential spouse should have acted in her past. Once again, imperatives create anger, and anger creates a denigration of the person who fails our demands.

It is probably important for any couple to have frank discussions about their sexual expectations. It is especially important for men to work with someone to gain an understanding of their own parochialisms and demands as they pertain to their partner. Women are not exempt from this either. When different levels of sexual exploration and comfort exist, it can create stress in the marriage or relationship. These problems are worked out best beforehand, not afterwards. As you mentioned before, anyone who has guilt about sexual fantasies could definitely be helped by consulting a competent therapist to explore that issue. Guilt is simply another way to be angry, only it's aimed at the self. Determining the inwardly directed demands causing it could prove very beneficial. There is an old line that goes, "When two people get married they become one." The problem with this adage is that they then fight about which one! When people become a couple, the two would best become three: you, me, and us. It is essential that each partner does something every day for themselves, for their partner, and for the unity that the couple has become. When anger enters a relationship, the balance and parity that exists is always upset. If I am angry with you, I believe that I am superior to you. Therefore, I will perceive you as inferior to me.

Let's speak again about the couple in vignette #2, who was ready to get married. There's a good rule of thumb that pertains to the question he asked her about her past sex life - never ask a question that you already know the answer to or are unable to hear the answer to.

Control issues are simply a variant of anger, with my belief that I can exert my will over you, and you must be compliant to me. At some level, the request to always be honest shows the antithesis of trust and is typically requested when there is distrust and insecurity. Ideally, each partner in any relationship has a sense that they have a separate area of self that is respected and honored by the other person.

Dr. Chapunoff: Howard, please forgive me for stretching your patience and asking you to help me with a yes or no answer to the question in vignette #2 when the man asks the woman about her intimate past. Do you think she should tell him about it, or not? And I'll tell you why I insist on that point: we are no longer talking about how convenient, beneficial, or smart it is to make such confessions on past sexual encounters. The issues now are strictly moral and ethical. We are speaking about principles. At this juncture, I'm not only interested in knowing what a great psychologist such as you thinks about this couple, but also what your opinion is about my way of thinking. When I say I feel the woman should tell the man the truth about her past relationships, am I too rigid, too inflexible, or too impractical? If morality and ethics are important, at what point do they become unimportant? Should convenience or practicality prevail over ethics and morality?

Dr. Paul: Ed, I think you are still looking for black and white, when the answer lies in shades of grey. As I said earlier, there are many ways the woman could have responded to possibly avert a disaster. If he finally said to her that he wanted the answer, given their commitment to each other to be forthright, it would have been best for her to simply answer truthfully.

Dr. Chapunoff: Great! I love that answer!

Dr. Paul: If he was so rigid that this would be a deal breaker, it might be better for both of them to part at that time.

Dr. Chapunoff: That was precisely my point!

Dr. Paul: You asked if there is a place for ethics and morality. The answer is clearly, YES! However, I approach it from the standpoint of a psychologist who actually believes in and tries to practice what I teach. I cannot agree to a statement that we *must* tell the truth. But I do endorse the statement: it's best and important to tell the truth.

7

CONFLICT WITH A HOMOSEXUAL SON
His son's homosexuality tormented him throughout life

Why?

Dr. Chapunoff: Henry was a prominent, retired attorney and a WW II veteran of the US Marines. An incident occurred in 1943 while his ship was cruising the Atlantic waters. After he and the other sailors went to sleep, Henry was awakened by what he thought was a *terrible nightmare*. But, it wasn't a nightmare at all. *It was a real life and, to Henry, a most disgusting experience.* A homosexual man had positioned himself sitting on Henry's face, with his penis and testicles rubbing Henry's lips. Henry was definitely heterosexual. Henry became so furious that he strangled the intruder with his bare hands. The crew members who were watching the scene did nothing to stop him. The captain arrived, and when he was told what happened, he ordered the cadaver of the offending marine thrown into the ocean. He stated that he was going to report the casualty as, *"Missing in action, and that's it!"* There was no penalty or disciplinary action against Henry. In fact, he was discreetly congratulated for what he had done. Since Henry was Jewish, and there was significant antisemitism in the armed forces of the United States during WWII, I asked him if he knew why he got away so easily with his crime. He told me, *"It is true that there was antisemitism in the armed forces, but the antihomosexuality hatred was far more pronounced."* And life went on. He survived the war, practiced law successfully, got married, and had kids. One of his sons was homosexual. He was well behaved, an A student in college, who became a professor, and by all measurable standards, an excellent human being. Nevertheless, when Henry's son became an adolescent and Henry learned about his son's homosexuality, the horrible memories of his traumatic incident in the Navy led to rejection of his son. Henry never told his son why he acted the way he did, and the son never understood why his father was so mean to him.

When Henry was 81, he related his past ordeal to me. At the age of 81, he was healthy and appeared much younger than his age. Henry continued suffering from *irreversible animosity* and nightmares. He told me that he never consulted a psychotherapist.

I have a question for you, Howard. If Henry had consulted you after learning about his son's homosexuality and had expressed his deep rejection of his son, how would you have managed this difficult situation? What would you do to reduce his perpetual torment?

Dr. Paul: Ed, this is a compelling, tragic, and interesting situation. Had Henry consulted me, I think one of the first things he and I would have discussed would have been his values regarding being a father and what sort of relationship he truly wished to have with his son. Keep in mind that for him to present for therapy might signify that he wished to deal with this issue. Our initial time together would have been spent clarifying the issues, sharpening his view of what was truly important to him, and deciding on what he wished to achieve and accomplish in treatment. I suspect we would have spent some time trying to get a sense of the pervasiveness of antihomosexual feelings and beliefs that existed in the mid 40s. I found your statement that antisemitism was prevalent in the military at that time but antihomosexual, homophobic ideation was even worse, to be quite interesting.

There is a zinger hidden in your portrayal of Henry's story, however. It is not that he awoke and was repulsed, or even that he awoke enraged and pummeled the offender, but that he *murdered* him!

Dr. Chapunoff: That is a big deal, indeed!

Dr. Paul: It certainly is! I believe we would have to explore whether he rejected his son because he was trying to deal with the fact that he killed someone, or whether it was a continuation of his own distress with homosexuals.

This might be a good time to look at historical and scientific perspectives on homosexuality. At the time of this incident in 1943, being gay (homosexual) was seen as a derangement, a crime, and a sin under the willful control of the individual. The first research on homosexuality was reported by Kinsey in 1948. He recognized that about four percent of men reported themselves as homosexual, exclusively. Even prior to that time, it was recognized that though seen as criminal and sinful, people who defined themselves as homosexual, often had higher than typical degrees of creativity and made significant contributions to art and literature.

Hans Christian Anderson, Sir Francis Bacon, Leonardo da Vinci, and Amelia Earhart, to name a few, are frequently cited among the many gay people who have made significant contributions to the world.

Dr. Chapunoff: It took centuries to redefine what homosexuality really is.

Dr. Paul: Yes, and it wasn't until the mid-1970s that scientists began to realize being gay was not a choice, a crime, or a derangement. As of the late 1970s, homosexuality is no longer in the *Diagnostic and Statistical Manual (DSM) of the American Psychiatric Association*; however, homosexual acts between consenting adults is still seen as a crime in many places. Ongoing research seems to suggest that at critical developmental stages, hormonal balances that exist in the brain of fetuses have impact on their developing sexual orientation. Let me be clear that by only briefly noting current research, I am not saying that being gay is pathological. There does appear to be a clear genetic component to homosexuality supported by twin studies, as well as prevalence studies within families to name just a couple. The notion that being homosexual is a choice is not supported by current scientific investigation.

Dr. Chapunoff: There are legions of people who never heard your latest statement or heard it and don't believe one word of it!

Dr. Paul: Interestingly, being homosexual may not be a choice, but, being homophobic certainly is a choice. There are many who are bisexual because they have overcome their homophobic aversions.

While science has made contributions toward correcting many of the misconceptions widely held about being gay, public policy and many laws still reflect views disproven by social and behavioral scientists. Strangely, this has led many religious and politically conservative individuals to see psychologists, psychiatrists, and other biobehavioral scientists as liberal, in order to discount the value of their research. Likewise, many religions cling to an unrealistic view of homosexuality and continue to see it as a sin. It is understandable why organizations that perceive their power and strength come from numbers would take such a position.

Unfortunately, due to the ongoing bias within many cultures, being gay can adversely affect custody and visiting rights, adoption, and job opportunities. While it is now seen as a bias crime to allow sexual orientation to influence decision-making, it still occurs in far too many places, including our own laws.

Dr. Chapunoff: The military included, right?

Dr. Paul: Definitely, there's an ongoing struggle within the military, which very recently grappled with the issue of, "don't ask, don't tell." The military has long been a bastion of homophobia. While it is clearly better today, one can only imagine what it might have been like when Henry provided service to his country.

Dr. Chapunoff: It must have been pure hell.

Dr. Paul: Yes, Ed, you may be very correct. Let's get back to Henry's particular case. One of the things that I would want to explore with Henry would be the feelings he had about the fact that he killed a man. While it clearly could be traumatic to wake up and find someone's genitals in your face, how Henry perceived and managed the murder that ensued would need careful exploration. Which created the bigger trauma? It may very well be that Henry needed to reject his son in order to avoid dealing with the murder that was on his hands.

Dr. Chapunoff: I find this reasoning provocative and fascinating!

Dr. Paul: Most therapy I conduct starts with something that is called psycho-education. This simply involves letting people know and understand what current thinking is, as it relates to what brings them to therapy. Part of psychoeducation is also about helping people understand that the expression of their emotional reactivity is modified and controlled by their internal beliefs; the core understanding of cognitive treatments. Helping Henry understand that these internal beliefs or schemas are often unheard and unknown to the person who owns them, creates an avenue through which change can occur. Helping him understand that not everything he came to believe were true may enable him to begin to look at his attitude toward being gay in a new and more constructive way.

Dr. Chapunoff: It is possible that he never thought he might have rejected his son because of the crime he committed.

Dr. Paul: That's right, Ed. If he had never addressed the fact that he had murdered someone, helping him understand its possible impact could be crucial to the outcome of treatment. By exploring with Henry the nature of any intrusive thoughts and feelings, and exploring any nightmares that may have persisted, we would be able to have more clarity regarding the key elements of this trauma and then begin to develop a treatment plan based on what emerged.

Ed, you described his circumstance as a recalcitrant nightmare. I would wish to determine how much of this nightmare reflected Post Traumatic Stress Disorder (PTSD). No one would disagree that the events you described represented a significantly traumatic event. If Henry continued to have intrusive thoughts and memories of this event, the treatment protocol for PTSD would need to be added to the treatment plan involving an exploration of his attitudes and feelings toward homosexuality, as well as exploring any guilt that might be present because of the murder.

PTSD has many faces and can present itself in many different ways, but the core symptoms remain the same. From some of our previous discussions, I know that we will be returning to this issue of PTSD as it relates to other wars and conflicts. It might be wise at this point, to further explain what PTSD really is.

For an individual to be diagnosed with PTSD, they must have undergone a traumatic event that involved almost being killed or seriously injured or seeing someone else almost being killed or seriously injured. Also included in this list are events that are a threat to one's physical or even psychological integrity, such as Henry's case. In all cases, the traumatic event must produce intense fear, helplessness, or horror, as it did in Henry's case. These traumatic events must be experienced over and over again and present themselves either through distressing dreams when asleep or intrusive recollections when awake. Some people relive the experience, including all the original feelings, and they have flashbacks that allow them to believe they returned to the original "scene of the crime." There is a reliving of the psychological distress and the physiological reactivity that occurred at the time of the original trauma. People with PTSD develop strategies to cope with these ongoing unpleasant experiences and too frequently try to avoid the thoughts and feelings that are related to the event. They avoid talking about it and avoid places or people that arouse recollections of it.

I would want to explore with Henry whether this was one active dynamic in his intense rejection of his son. People with PTSD often feel detached and have a sense of estrangement from others. They are often unable to recall important aspects of the trauma while others have perfect recollection of every painful detail. Some people develop a restricted range of emotional expression and others develop a negative outlook toward the future. They stay on guard for the rest of their life, believing that if they are always vigilant, they may be able to protect themselves against future trauma. Unfortunately, such hyper-vigilance only tends to increase anxiety as it makes it more difficult for people to concentrate. In addition, PTSD is often associated with an exaggerated startle response, so that even little things produce large reactions. Many people have difficulty with sleeping and therefore become irritable and angry.

Dr. Chapunoff: I find it interesting to see that Henry coped with his problems - his own experience with the homosexual marine during WW II and having a homosexual son. These are facts that caused him so much distress all of his life, and he still managed to be a successful attorney.

Dr. Paul: It appears that Henry was able to compensate fairly well and have a remarkably functional life except for the impact on his relationship with his son. While Henry was functional, I would wish to explore with him how much internal pain he kept secret from others.

Dr. Chapunoff: After interviewing him, I was under the impression he had suffered more than his share of internal pain. He also gave me the impression that he was a man in control of his actions. He had a serious facial expression, but at the same time, appeared very personable.

Dr. Paul: Ed, you mentioned that Henry was 81 years of age when he shared this information with you. As long as Henry was not suffering from significant dementia and was able to have good access to the part of his mind that still was able to think, I would be able to provide a service to him.

To review, his treatment plan would most likely consist of clarification of his values and goals combined with an attempt to provide him with good education and current scientific knowledge on homosexuality. I would also provide him with information on the cognitive behavioral approach to treatment. I would explore with him the potentially hidden impact of the fact that he killed someone. In addition, I would want to get a clear picture of the aspects of his nightmares and obtain a sense of how intrusive they really were.

If Henry valued having a relationship with his son more than he valued trying to escape the pain of his trauma, I am sure that I would be able to assist him in reaching toward his goals.

Dealing with PTSD does involve a good deal of effort on the part of the traumatized person, yet it is possible to get people past their avoidances. Often, the goal is to have people become better able to functionally tolerate distress rather than eliminate it. It is close to impossible to remove all reminders of trauma; teaching Henry strategies to endure and alter his reactivity would be more functional.

One aspect of treatment would be to determine if Henry continues to have nightmares. I would have Henry try to clearly develop the images in his nightmare and then ask him to write it out as a script. One strategy might be to have him read the script of his nightmare several times a day. This kind of chronic exposure over time, serves to reduce his reactivity and diffuse the anxiety depicted in his portrayal of events.

A second strategy that I enjoy using is to help people actually change the content of their nightmares.

Dr. Chapunoff: I need help to understand the last thing you said, Howard. Changing the content of nightmares, how in the world do you do that?

Dr. Paul: Ed, in New Zealand, there are indigenous Indians called Maoris. The Maoris are the only culture I am aware of that actively teach their children how to dream. They have only two rules: 1) never run away from anything in a dream, and 2) never leave a dream until you have fixed the ending and recaptured a sense of control. When people awaken from nightmares, I teach them to go back into the dream and come up with a better ending, where they demonstrate control or mastery. This works very well with children, especially when they have nightmares of monsters and wish to flee their bedrooms for the comfort of their parents. When children or adults have the same recurrent nightmare, I suggest to them that they make themselves relaxed and quiet a few times during the day, and practice the new ending to their chronic, anxiety-producing nightmare. It takes about two to three weeks before this new, more secure, and controlled ending begins to show up in dreams at night ending the nightmares.

Dreaming aside, I would help Henry understand that there is a clear absolute or set of demands in his head that is telling him his son could not be homosexual. In all probability, Henry also believed that if his son was homosexual, he was bad or evil. These misconceptions need to be discussed. Henry needs to decide whether he wants to modify these beliefs and bring them into the current century. To the extent that guilt played a role in Henry's rigidity, helping him understand the absolutes he aimed at himself is crucial to helping him become more accepting of his own actions and his son's behavior. As I noted before, getting people to understand is only the first part of treatment. For now, I am leaving the description of this more mundane part of treatment mostly out of our discussions because it's much drier and involves rehearsal and review. I do need to emphasize that it is the development and strengthening of these habits through creation of more functional, internal scripts that are the real heart of treatment - even if less interesting and less exciting than development of an understanding of the problem.

Dr. Chapunoff: Howard, will you please clarify your last comment for me? I'm referring to "the functional internal scripts that are the real heart of treatment." What exactly does this mean?

Dr. Paul: Ed, this goes back to the information I provided to you in our discussion in Chapter 4, titled, *A Method to your Madness*. I explained the basis of CBT. We all develop beliefs, which become habit. These beliefs turn into hidden internal scripts. If we are lucky, they will be functional and work for us. Often, the beliefs we learn when we are very young do not make sense when we examine them with an adult mind and understanding. These faulty beliefs become dysfunctional internal scripts. When I have people practice corrections to their faulty scripts, I hope they learn scripts that will work. That is why we call them functional internal scripts.

Dr. Chapunoff: Thank you so much for such a lucid explanation.

Dr. Paul: You are most welcome, Ed. Some say, "You cannot teach an old dog new tricks." This is usually said by people who are not good teachers. It is possible to make a difference and get people to a better and more comfortable place, as long as they are alive and capable of learning,

Dr. Chapunoff: Howard, you mentioned that Henry could benefit from understanding that homosexuality is influenced by genetics. If he understands that, he might conclude that homosexuality is unavoidable, that he murdered a man innocent of his sexual orientation, and the thing that caused his killing of the marine was not that the marine was homosexual, but that he made a repulsive contact of his genitals on Henry's lips.

Dr. Paul: Ed, there is every chance that Henry believed homosexuality was an aberration and that he also thought he was being sexually assaulted. We can never know exactly what his frame of mind was. However, we can both agree that Henry was shocked and traumatized. The trauma haunted him, and sadly, probably destroyed the relationship with his son.

Dr. Chapunoff: Wars cause many direct casualties and so-called, collateral damage. Henry exemplifies the latter.

8

OBSESSIVE-COMPULSIVE DISORDERS: A BASE OF ANXIETY

Dr. Chapunoff: Howard, when one practices cardiology (as I do) or internal medicine, one tends to focus on diabetes, hypertension, myocardial infarctions, abnormal blood lipid levels, and so forth. However, when I ask patients if they suffer from nerves, I infrequently come up with a suspected diagnosis of schizophrenia (hallucinations, hearing voices). Much more often, I see depression or some form of anxiety, such as an obsessive-compulsive disorder (OCD). It appears that many individuals who suffer from OCD don't tell anyone, or they may just mention it to a friend or family member; seldom do they seek specialized help. In my opinion, many people are prejudiced about consulting a psychotherapist and admitting that they have a psychological problem. It appears that suffering from any kind of emotional disorder is seen by some as less honorable than having a kidney or a gastrointestinal disease.

There are individuals with mild OCD who are not terribly disturbed because of it. Take the case of a woman who has to look at herself in the mirror five times to make sure that her hairdo looks okay. Although that's a nuisance, life goes on without major inconveniencies.

It's a different story when a person needs to check his car lights repeatedly to make sure they are turned off. If his car is parked in a garage, and he goes to his apartment by taking the elevator, and he then needs to go back to the car 10 to 15 times to verify that the lights are off, that would be very disrupting.

In one of his books, Albert Ellis describes the case of a woman who took from one to four hours to shower every morning. She could not hold regular jobs because of the time she took showering to get ready in the morning. Treatment for this obsession cut down her time in the shower to about 15 minutes a day, and she was then able to hold a regular 9 to 5 job.

Patients who suffer from OCD experience obsessions and repetitive, useless, self-defeating rituals, such as counting. This condition can be nasty.

I understand that many patients with OCD may be successfully treated. I'd like to raise the awareness of beneficial treatments available for those who suffer from OCD and perhaps persuade them to seek the help of a psychotherapist for possible correction or significant improvement of the disorder.

Howard, will you please explain what might be the origin of these irrational, unrealistic, illogical, and self-defeating thoughts? What kind of psychotherapeutic and pharmacological treatments are available to deal with OCD?

Dr. Paul: Ed, these are very good questions, and I appreciate your desire to help people with OCD understand that it is both understandable and treatable. OCD is an anxiety disorder. Therefore, I am going to take this opportunity to expand the topic and begin by speaking about anxiety in general and then OCD in particular.

Dr. Chapunoff: Before you continue your discussion, I'd like to ask you if anxiety is always an abnormal reaction.

Dr. Paul: Not really, Ed. Many people are under the false impression that anxiety is always pathological. Nothing could be farther from the truth!

Many, many years ago, when people started being people, there was always a chance that when you finally got back to your cave after a hard day's work, a saber toothed tiger might be waiting in the back. People in these situations, who failed to experience acute anxiety, were unfortunately called lunch. Those who were activated and experienced anxiety would run like crazy. Anxiety is adaptive, biologically necessary, and something that we do not want to eliminate.

If you recall from our earlier discussions, we can make anxiety worse by *awfulizing*. It is this amplification of anxiety that can be reduced. I explained that when we are confronted with noxious or threatening stimuli or events, we become activated. Our autonomic nervous system drives this activation. This was briefly described in a previous discussion. There are temperamental differences - some people have sympathetic arousal that is rapid and intense, while in others, the reaction is much more tempered.

These temperamental variables are difficult to alter. Change in reactivity can only be achieved in a limited way. It is actually quite fascinating how evolutionary principles fit well into an understanding of anxiety and why the body works as it does.

Dr. Chapunoff: Howard, please tell us what you mean by evolutionary principles?

Dr. Paul: Ed, changes that would lead to increased chances of survival and reproduction of the species would have a genetic advantage and tend to have an edge in being represented in the gene pool. This is a basic evolutionary principle. It goes back to Darwin's survival of the fittest. In the case of activation, it took two paths. Those attributes that made for the best warriors tended to be favored, while those attributes that made people react with fear and act to run and preserve them selves were likewise favored. People with highly reactive nervous systems actually were, many years ago, genetically advantaged. Today, with far fewer tigers around, this heightened reactivity is more problematic and manifests itself in increased false alarms and other anxiety problems.

It does not take medical training for people to understand that if they walk into their cave and a tiger is sitting there waiting to eat them, a number of physiological changes will need to take place in order to survive this circumstance. If they are running, they will need to increase blood flow to their muscles. That is done by shunting and diverting the blood from our brain, our gut, and other organs.

Dr. Chapunoff: What happens if we meet a tiger or have another situation where we respond with anxiety, and we decide not to run?

Dr. Paul: If we become sympathetically activated and we are not running, we tend to feel nervous, antsy and edgy, cannot sit still, and have a sense of dread and discomfort that can be coupled with a sense of doom and gloom. If there really is an unexpected tiger in the cave, one definitely feels better running than not.

The autonomic system has two major components that essentially run our body and control the functioning of our internal organs. This same autonomic nervous system has a significant impact on our emotions.

The parasympathetic nervous system (PNS) is the part of us that runs us when we feel calm, protected, and secure. Parasympathetic tone is typically what follows a good meal, good sex, or other activities that lead to comfort. It is behind having feelings of well being.

The sympathetic nervous system (SNS) is antagonistic to the PNS, meaning that it works in the opposite way. Rather than comfort when activated, it produces the fight or flight response.

Suppose that you are sitting in your cave munching on a delightful roast loin of mastodon. You are feeling sated, there is good company around you, and both you and your belly are happy. You would, no doubt, be parasympathetically toned. At this point, a tiger walks into your cave. It would be helpful, in fact necessary, to go from calm and mellow to rather scared and activated instantly. The designer of our body was quite ingenious in that the chemicals that transmit the signal from the brain down our nerves, called neurotransmitters, are very different in the PNS versus the SNS.

The PNS produces acetylcholine, the substance that is secreted into the spaces existing between the endings of the nerves. When acetylcholine fills this inter-nerve gap, the receiving neuron fires and immediately secretes an agent called cholinesterase, a chemical off-switch that turns off the signal. If this off-switch system did not exist, we would be sluggish and not able to change rapidly from calm to activated.

In the SNS, the neurotransmitter is primarily norepinephrine. Here there is *no* off switch! The effects of norepinephrine last about 20 minutes. This piece of information is very important for people to understand. **Once aroused, this state persists, even if we understand that we are in no danger and that there is no threat. The state of arousal and associated anxious feelings do not go away immediately.** This happens even when we positively talk to ourselves and look to produce our own reassurance.

Roughly, our brain is divided into three different major layers. The layer on the outside is the neocortex. This is where thinking takes place. The neocortex is the part of our brain that helps us make decisions and understand what is going on around us. This area of the brain can make anxiety worsen, but it is not where anxiety comes from.

The middle layer is the mesocortex (middle brain). It is involved with some emotions, but is not directly involved with the onset of anxiety. It is involved in the continuation of anxiety, and it can unplug the neocortex, so that we cannot think straight or remember things well.

The oldest part of our brain is the paleocortex, which means *old brain*. Anxiety is paleocortical in origin. When information from the world is transmitted to the brain, it first goes to low-level, signal-processing areas of the brain, then to the hypothalamus, and then messages are sent to the pituitary and adrenal glands for the release of hormones. It is within this hypothalamic–adrenal-pituitary axis that anxiety and physiological activation is initiated, and it is at this point that individual differences begin to emerge. Depending on temperament - the result of neurotransmitter balance - we will react by either preparing to fight or to flee.

Dr. Chapunoff: This internal arousal system exists in every person. Evidently, anxiety can exist when people are preoccupied, disgusted, or even happy. It seems to be a ubiquitous component of the human psyche.

Dr. Paul: That is right, Ed. Some people enjoy acute anxiety, which really represents sympathetic activation and pay a price in dollars to become panicked. When people attend an amusement park and ride thrill rides, such as roller coasters, they are paying to become sympathetically aroused, and they love it! Of course, not everybody enjoys this kind of activation.

There is something called the James-Lange theory of emotion, which essentially says, *"If I'm running, I must be scared."* We can become scared before we even confirm that there is a tiger (something really to be afraid of)! The signal to be frightened finally makes it up to the part of our brain that thinks after we are already activated. Our thinking brain often agrees that we are scared, simply because we feel scared, even when there is nothing scary around us. This explains why many anxiety problems do not seem to make real sense.

Dr. Chapunoff: Howard, do you mean to tell us that our brains react to false alarms?

Dr. Paul: Exactly, they sure do! Many people are prone to false alarms. To deal with these alarms, they can be taught that if they believe they are about to be eaten by a tiger, it pays to look around and see if there really is a tiger there! If there is no tiger, then there has been an error in our low-level signal processing system that has created our activation. It becomes important not to listen to it and accept the fact that we will have uncomfortable activation feelings for a while.

Dr. Chapunoff: What do people do, without the help of a psychotherapist, to rid themselves of anxiety?

Dr. Paul: Many people adopt magical behaviors. If these magical or superstitious actions happen to work, they teach themselves to do these rituals repeatedly. This is how superstitions, rituals, and obsessive behaviors, including OCD, form and get stronger. This process is negative reinforcement. If I am anxious, and I believe that repeatedly turning on and off the light will reduce anxiety and allow me to feel better, the ritual is reinforced and strengthened.

There is an old joke that tells of a man walking down the street in the middle of Manhattan snapping his fingers every minute or two. A passerby asked him, *"Why do you repeatedly snap your fingers?"* The person responded, *"It keeps the elephants away!"* The passerby was taken aback and said to this individual, *"That's really foolish. There are no elephants within a few thousand miles of here!"* The snapping man then responded, *"See, it works."*

Dr. Chapunoff: I like the joke. It's cute!

Dr. Paul: I am glad you like it, Ed. People have often seen a cardiologist, endocrinologist, neurologist, or gastroenterologist, before seeing a psychiatrist, a psychologist, or other mental health worker.

Dr. Chapunoff: Howard, is it important for a patient with anxiety to see a physician along with a psychologist?

Dr. Paul: Ed, as you know, anxiety can sometimes be caused by an underlying medical condition. A good history and careful diagnosis is very important. Many anxiety symptoms, such as shortness of breath, chest pain, dizziness, feeling faint, palpitations, sweating, flushing, numbness, tingling, nausea, and a myriad of other somatic complaints can have a physical basis that must be ruled out. Frequently, such anxiety symptoms lead patients to visit their physician or utilize the emergency room. Sometimes after many such trips, when it is finally seen as a psychological problem, will the person correctly be referred for mental health treatment.

In my practice, there have been many cases, where medical problems were not diagnosed or drug side effects were central to the presenting anxiety. It can be dangerous to presume that patients were thoroughly diagnosed without a medical component to their problem. Thyroid and other endocrine and hormonal issues must always be considered and ruled out.

Dr. Chapunoff: Howard, if there are no medical conditions to explain the strong contribution to anxiety or OCD, what drugs can be used to treat them?

Dr. Paul: From a medical management perspective, since almost all of our neurotransmitters are involved in either the creation of or enhancement of anxiety, there is a rather broad range of prescriptive options available.

Typically, most of the drugs used for short-term and acute management of anxiety are benzodiazepines, such as Xanax®, Klonopin®, and Ativan®. These drugs have different characteristics in terms of how fast they work and how long they last. This information helps the doctor decide which one to use. They are very effective. However, for prolonged use, especially if the dose is high, they can become addictive. As such, there has been a growing trend to be very conservative in the dosing of these drugs; primary care physicians frequently prescribe them and underdosing is a common finding.

For chronic anxiety, antidepressant medications are the gold standard with selective serotonin reuptake inhibitors (SSRI's) and selective norepinephrine reuptake inhibitors (SNRI's) as the most frequently prescribed. In some cases, beta-blockers are used to make sure that the heart rate does not unduly rise when the flight or fight response takes place.

Dr. Chapunoff: From a behavioral perspective, how do you approach the treatment of anxiety disorders?

Dr. Paul: Cognitive therapy, when combined with exposure treatments, has been well demonstrated to be effective.

Dr. Chapunoff: Howard, please remind us what the essence of cognitive therapy is.

Dr. Paul: Sure, Ed. Cognitive therapy is about increasing understanding of what anxiety is, especially the fact that once people are aroused, they will have feelings in their body long past when their thinking head clarifies that there is no real danger. It also involves identifying false beliefs and correcting them. This is coupled with the gold standard of anxiety treatment, which is exposure, and in OCD, exposure coupled with response prevention.

Dr. Chapunoff: How do you do that? Can you be a little more explicit about the technique of "exposure coupled with response prevention"?

Dr. Paul: Helping people tolerate these physical sensations becomes very important. After providing education, there are a number of strategies currently proven to be effective:

1) Exposure is another way of saying having the individual confront the trigger of their fear coupled with helping the person not escape and not do their rituals

2) Relaxation skills, especially when combined with exposure and desensitization. One way to decrease anxiety is to assist people in learning better relaxation skills

3) Cognitive restructuring, which is teaching people to increase realistic appraisal of things and adopt more realistic ideas about the way people operate

Dr. Chapunoff: Howard, please tell me what relaxation skills are?

Dr. Paul: Of course, Ed. Relaxation techniques fall into four basic categories:

1) Diaphragmatic breathing

2) Hypnotic relaxation inductions

3) Muscular relaxation exercises

4) Other relaxation exercises, some of which use imagery

With respect to diaphragmatic breathing, the diaphragm is the muscle that separates the thorax from the abdomen and helps us breathe. Most people, when they are anxious, do what is called thoracic breathing, rather than diaphragmatic breathing. Thoracic breathing is what gets them into trouble.

Dr. Chapunoff: Howard, please tell us why?

Dr. Paul: With thoracic breathing, people use a lot of muscle activity to inhale and to expand their chest. Surrounding our chest is very hard tissue. Because we displace our ribs and sternum, it takes more effort to breathe in. This extra effort translates into increasing sympathetic tone, which can lead to anxiety and even panic.

Dr. Chapunoff: Why is diaphragmatic breathing useful to control anxiety?

Dr. Paul: In diaphragmatic breathing, people are taught to avoid thoracic breathing and only use their diaphragm, spending more time breathing out than breathing in.

The instructions I give people are to, at first, lie down, get a heavy book, and place it on their navel. I then instruct them to cross their arms and put their hands on their chest, and then, breathe. When people put their hands on their chest, they are able to feel if they are moving their chest. When we breathe correctly, our chest does not move much if we are lying down. When we are sitting up, our chest will move more. This is the reason for starting these exercises lying down. Not only should our chest not move, the book on our belly button should be slowly moving up and down. Most importantly, we should not be utilizing our abdominal musculature to make this happen.

When learned correctly, this style of breathing should feel effortless. Once people are able to get a sense of how it feels to breathe diaphragmatically, it is no longer necessary to use the book on the abdomen that initially serves as a visual cue and helps us feel what our muscles are doing, so we know that we are breathing correctly.

Once people can breathe diaphragmatically, they are asked to spend twice as much time breathing out as breathing in. With expertise, people are able comfortably to bring their respiratory rate down to six per minute with three seconds spent breathing in and six seconds being spent breathing out, with a one-second rest.

The exact timing is ultimately less important than simply spending more time breathing out than breathing in. Breathing is a key to all relaxation, which is why I have chosen to spend a little extra time on it.

Dr. Chapunoff: What about muscle relaxation exercises, Howard?

Dr. Paul: With muscle-focused relaxation, people are trained to sense which muscles are tense. They are then taught how to let the tension go. This can be done with equipment, such as electromyographic biofeedback or simply done as a self-control exercise without instrumentation; both are effective. Muscles have a process called habituation - when they are tense for a long period, the brain gets bored with the signal and recalibrates that new level of tension to zero - we are actually no longer aware of the tension. Over time, the difference between not feeling our muscles tense and feeling pain diminishes.

Once muscles become chronically tense, it is very difficult for individuals to release that tension, even if they are aware that it is present.

Well-done muscle retraining relaxation exercises start with only slight increases in muscle tension. One common mistake many people make is to start by asking people to take a muscle or muscle group and *significantly* increase the tension within that area. This is wrong, as it leads to rebound and ultimately more tension. In order to do muscle retraining correctly, one must begin by introducing the slightest amount of muscle tension that can be felt, then hold that amount of tension and pay attention to what it feels like. After a clear picture of that slight increase in tension is perceived, the person is asked to let it go. Next, one is asked to introduce only half as much tension as on the first effort. After this instruction of introducing only half as much tension, people are better able to feel the tension. For the third trial, one is asked to think about increasing muscle tension with no active volitional increase in muscle tension, and by only thinking about it, they are often able to sense increases in tension. In each case, they are asked to let it go only after they sense the tension.

Typically, if you ask someone to let go of tension, he or she will not be able to do it. If you take them through this three-step process, they can learn to do it.

Dr. Chapunoff: Howard, you previously mentioned exercises using imagery. Will you please explain what imagery consists of?

Dr. Paul: Imaginal procedures involve mentally visiting a favorite spot coupled with thoughts of safety and self-guided instructions of comfort, especially warmth. This can be enhanced by using some hypnotic induction techniques and teaching people self-hypnosis.

Dr. Chapunoff: What about anxiety associated with fear?

Dr. Paul: Just as muscles develop habituation and our senses become immune to tension, a similar process exists when we sense fear. When behaviorally trained therapists treat anxiety, they try to help anxious people maintain contact with feared objects or circumstances for a long enough time to allow arousal to diminish. People who are anxious and fearful wish to avoid what frightens them at all costs. Unfortunately, avoidance worsens the problem, leading to increases in anxiety. Exposure is what reduces anxious reactivity. It is important to teach people relaxation and distress tolerance skills first to help them have the capacity and desire to do exposure.

Dr. Chapunoff: Most people know that OCD stands for obsessive-compulsive disorder. However, many are not so clear on the difference between obsessions and compulsions. Can you please explain to us what they are?

Dr. Paul: Obsessions are thoughts that serve to provoke increases in anxiety. These thoughts tend to impose themselves in a very unwanted way, and people often feel powerless to control them, leading to constant worry and rumination, both about the thoughts themselves and about the worry that they produce.

Compulsions represent an individual's attempt to control and reduce anxiety, often by performing some repetitive, ritualized behavior. Obsessions and compulsions exist with different levels of severity and represent a continuum. Repetitive hair pulling, skin picking and nail biting, compulsive gambling, compulsive shopping, for some, eating, hoarding, fixations, and excessive, unrealistic dissatisfactions with body image, as well as preoccupations with health and other similar challenges are included in obsessive-compulsive spectrum disorder. People can have an obsessive-compulsive personality without having OCD.

Dr. Chapunoff: That's very interesting. Can you explain this further?

Dr. Paul: Here it is. Individuals with obsessive-compulsive personality are often preoccupied with details and rules. They tend to be perfectionists or workaholics, or can often be overly conscientious and rigid on ethical issues. Such people frequently insist on doing things their way only and can easily become angry when things are not done to their standards. Psychoanalytically, these folks are termed *anal*. OCD itself has a number of different presentations. Most people are somewhat familiar with those who are *crazy clean* and wash themselves and everything around them many, many times. The example you mentioned of the patient from Albert Ellis fits well into this category. Closely related are people who fear germs and fear that they, themselves, will spread contamination or be the recipient of contamination wherever they go.

There are many people who look for that *just right* feeling, and when things do not feel that way, they develop compensatory rituals (compulsions) to offset their anxiety. Key OCD categories break down into several presentations: people who fear that they are responsible for harm and mistakes, people who fear contamination, and people who are preoccupied with order and symmetry and have difficulty with unwanted thoughts, often about violence, sex, or morality. Compulsive rituals are developed to cope with anxiety by using behaviors, such as counting, checking, not stepping on cracks when walking, and seeking reassurance in a driven and unhealthy way.

Reassurance, when it has an OCD base, is meant to decrease anxiety. However, it never satisfies the person and leads to increases in anxiety and an increased need to seek more reassurance. If you know someone with OCD who constantly asks you for reassurance, please do not oblige. It just makes things worse, even though they will tell you it makes them feel better.

There have been many studies done on OCD and validated treatments have emerged utilizing a cognitive behavioral approach coupled with exposure and response prevention. Avoidance strategies need to be understood; rituals, whether overt or mental, need to be catalogued, and plans need to be developed to deal with both obsessions and compulsions.

Dr. Chapunoff: Will you please elaborate a little bit on avoidance strategies?

Dr. Paul: I will be happy to, Ed. The key to dealing with OCD involves exposure and response prevention. Teaching people to understand the irrationality of their thoughts is sometimes not necessary, as they already know it is silly. We need to teach people to expose themselves to what they fear and then prevent (avoid) the ritual they believe will save them and make them comfortable. This is the trap of OCD, in that the ritual makes them comfortable in the short run, but makes things worse in the end. It takes a good deal of work and support to get people to face their fears; however, this is the best way to deal with them.

With OCD, it takes a great deal of work to achieve gains and comfort but, with what we know now, it is very achievable. If anyone happens to be reading this, who suffers from any of these problems or knows someone who fits into this category, please, let them know that effective treatment is available.

9

HUMAN CRUELTY

Dr. Chapunoff: Is cruelty a sport, a selective absence of feelings, human idiocy, a personality disorder, a mental derangement, the revenge of the unsuccessful, a way of asserting authority, none of the above, some of the above, or a combination of all of the above? I've been struggling with these questions for many years, and I've never come close to answering them. I am hoping that the readers have a better understanding of what I'm about to ask you, if I introduce the subject matter through basic, historical information about cruel events and the executioners.

Cruelty is evil, but there is a broad perception of human cruelty. In some instances, an act not viewed as cruel by some, is defined as barbaric by others.

An attempt to provide a complete description of human cruelty might take thousands of thick volumes, and even then, the collection would be incomplete.

We can define cruelty as the deliberate, unnecessary, malicious, and often joyous, infliction of mental or physical pain upon others.

Men and women can be good, bad, and anything in between. Persons with destructive inclinations appear to be an inspiration to others whose minds are screwed up with limited hope of improvement.

Francois de la Rochefoucauld, a French writer (1613-1680), wisely said, *"Evil, like good, has its own heroes."* True! Very true!

In order to present clearly my questions on the subject of cruelty, I will touch on four examples:

1) Hitler, Stalin

2) The Roman Circus and the Inquisition

3) Christopher Columbus and Napoleon Bonaparte

4) Bullfighting and other blood sports

The order in which I will discuss these examples has nothing to do with the historical timing of their occurrence; it has to do with the particular aspects of cruelty these examples display.

Hitler, Stalin

These monsters, so well-known for the disasters they caused, were so cruel to humanity that I will not discuss them any further. As they pertain to my questions that follow, they are technically unimportant. It doesn't take much brain power to classify them as cruel.

The Roman Circus and the Inquisition

Julius Caesar is considered the father of the Roman Circus. He made it a national institution. The blood spilled by the gladiators in combat during the circus, while fighting animals and other men, was unspeakable. Pompey had 600 lions, 20 elephants, and 400 leopards; all fighting men were armed with darts. In 10 AD, Augustus boasted that he had 10,000 men who were killed in eight circuses. Nero and Caligula were notoriously cruel, but because they presented the bloodiest shows, where men and animals killed each other without mercy, a large part of the populace were sad when these emperors died.

The Inquisition was a Spanish tribunal, established in 1478 by the Catholic monarch, Ferdinand II of Aragon, and Isabella I of Castile. The Inquisition was abolished in 1834, even though the last trial took place in 1818. Other European countries had their own Inquisition tribunals.

In Spain, the monarch wanted to take control of the Inquisition, which was under Papal authority. The purposes were to convert Jews and Muslims to Catholicism and deport them or kill them. These people were called conversos. Many Jews underwent conversion, but privately continued to practice their Jewish faith. These persons were called crypto Jews. People accused of being crypto Jews were judged by the tribunal and presided over by Tomas de Torquemada, a very sadistic fellow. If the tribunal found the conversos guilty, but they expressed repentance, they were given the privilege of death by the garrote and then burned. Those found guilty who didn't express repentance, were burned at the stake alive. Both the Roman Circus and the Inquisition are buried in the shadows of history.

I have exposed examples of human cruelty (Hitler, Stalin, the Roman Circus, and the Inquisition); all of which are generally seen as unacceptable by most in our contemporary society.

What follows next particularly disturbs me because the persons involved were cruel and killed many innocent people. Today, they are honored and respected. I'm referring to Christopher Columbus and Napoleon Bonaparte. On October 12, 1492, Christopher Columbus was sailing aboard the Santa Maria, financed by the Spanish crown, when a sailor on the boat sighted land. There was a reward of 10,000 maravedis (US $540), a large amount in those days; more than one year's wages for a typical sailor. The Spanish crown offered this reward to the sailor on board who first sighted land. Columbus stole the reward from the sailor. The man was so upset and distraught by the rapacious action of his boss that he abandoned Christianity and became a Muslim.

Columbus thought he had reached Asia. After three voyages to America, he continued to think that he had landed close to China and Japan. He never knew that he had landed in America. During his first discovery, he stumbled upon the island of Guanahani - believed to be San Salvador - in the Caribbean region. He described the natives as *friendly, happy, and well dispositioned;* Columbus and his men never received a hostile reception. He was obsessed with gold, and he made 75 written references to it in the first five weeks, despite the fact that he found very little gold on any of the islands he visited. This greed for gold led him to introduce severe penalties to the Indian population, who refused to cooperate with him by accepting slavery and working as hard as he demanded. He ordered his men to cut off the Indian's noses and ear lobes or kill them mercilessly. He used various methods to kill natives, including specially trained, large dogs, such as mastiffs and greyhounds, and then he used the cadavers to feed these animals.

Since gold was almost nonexistent, and Columbus had to repay the Spanish monarchs the borrowed capital that financed his expedition, he sold slaves, which he named human gold.

Samuel Elliott Morison, a Harvard historian and the most distinguished writer on Columbus, was the author of a multivolume biography about the man. Morison was also a sailor and retraced Columbus' route across the Atlantic. In his popular book, *Christopher Columbus, Mariner*, written in 1954, Morison tells us about the enslavements and the killings, stating, *"The cruel policy initiated by Columbus and his successors resulted in complete genocide."*

Over the last several years, the story of Columbus has finally undergone a historical revision, and his crimes and methods have been shown by some historians to be what they actually were. Nevertheless, there are still many Columbus' Day celebrations - the White House celebrates it in his honor, and elementary school students continue to be brainwashed about him. Then we have Columbia University, such a prestigious institution, carrying his name. Unbelievable!

Howard, please explain to me why Americans continue to honor the memory of a greedy, avaricious, and cruel man? From your learned perspective, does it mean that *we* are also as greedy, as avaricious, and as cruel as Christopher Columbus? In addition, if it doesn't mean that, can you tell me what it does mean?

Now, I'd like to deal with another jewel, the number 1 French hero, Napoleon Bonaparte.

The French hate comparing Napoleon to Hitler. It's true Hitler was more evil than Napoleon and did evil on a far greater scale. Napoleon created modern France, while little remains of Hitler's Germany except the ruins of the concentration camps. However, the resemblances between the two men are inescapable. Both achieved military domination of Europe, both were tyrannical, both had contempt for human life, and both were megalomaniacs. In 1941, Professor Pieter Geyl of the University of

Utrecht, published a book on Napoleon and stated that the similarities between him and Hitler were *too striking* to be ignored.

Three days after the fall of France in 1940, lying in his marble tomb in Paris, Napoleon received a visit from his greatest admirer, Adolph Hitler. He removed his cap in deference and remained silent for a long while watching the remains of the one he so admired. This was the only visit Hitler ever made to the French capital. Throughout the war, Hitler placed sand bags around Napoleon's tomb to guard it against bomb damage.

Napoleon presided over mass atrocities. During his reign as emperor, concentration camps were set up, and gas was used to massacre large groups of people. Claude Ribbe, a respected historian, philosopher, and member of the French government's Human Rights Commission, has been researching Napoleon's bloody record for some years. He accuses Napoleon of being a racist - an antisemite who persecuted Jews and reintroduced widespread slavery, shortly after it was abolished by the French government. In Ribbe's words, *"Napoleon was the first man, who for the first time in history asked himself rationally the question of how to eliminate, in as short a time as possible and with a minimum of cost and personnel, a maximum of people described as scientifically inferior."*

Haiti was a French colony at the end of the 19th century. During that time, Napoleon attempted a massacre of the entire Haitian population over the age of 12. In those days, Haiti was the world's richest colony, with a factory of slaves for export. It produced 43 percent of the world's coffee and almost half of its sugar. When the slaves who worked at the plantations were punished, they were roasted with slow fires or filled with gunpowder and blown to pieces.

Howard, please discuss my following questions about the psychological makeup of those who admire and love Napoleon, even though they know who he was. Why is Napoleon's memory revered in France? Did the French like what he did? Is it because they are as callous and indifferent to human suffering as their master was? Is it because countries and the populace need heroes, and there are none better to show?

HOWARD PAUL, PhD, ABPP, FAClinP and EDUARDO CHAPUNOFF, MD, FACP, FACC

Bullfighting

Bullfighting is a traditional spectacle of Spain, Portugal, Mexico, Colombia, Venezuela, Peru, and Ecuador. In France, they have corrida de toros - a benign version of bullfighting, where there is no killing or tormenting of the bull. For a period of 15 to 20 minutes, men compete to snatch rosettes tied between the bulls' horns.

In Spain and Latin American countries, the bull is repeatedly lanced by the bullfighter's assistants; some on foot and others on horses. The matador uses his cape to attract the bull in a series of passes. When the animal is exhausted and confused, the torero finalizes his performance by stabbing the bull with a sword in between its shoulder blades, through the aorta and the heart. Quite often, several attempts are needed by the bullfighter to kill the bull. Only the bull knows the suffering involved in the process.

A 2002 Gallup poll found that 68.8 percent of Spaniards expressed no interest in bullfighting, 20.6 percent expressed some interest, and 10.4 percent expressed a lot of interest. The popularity of bullfights varies in different regions of Spain. It is least popular in Galicia and Catalonia with 80 percent of those polled expressing no interest. In a poll conducted by the Sports Marketing Group of Atlanta, Georgia, in 2003, 46.2 percent of Americans polled hated or strongly disliked bull fighting. In July 2010, a ban on bullfighting was passed by the legislation in Catalonia; it will take effect in January 2012. Hurrah, for the Catalonians! I have closely observed the Spanish society for a number of years, and I admire many features of that country. Spain is technologically advanced. It has prominent thinkers, philosophers, artists, writers, scientists, and one of the largest numbers of volunteers who travel to the poorest regions of the world to assist people in need of medicines, basic education, and who are often in danger of starvation. In a few short years, Spain showed an enormous capacity to recover from the dark days under Franco's dictatorship. It now has an excellent judicial system and a democratic society.

Spain's King Juan Carlos I attends bullfights. His wife, Queen Sophia, repudiated them publicly. He is a gentle, refined, and a politically, excellent monarch - Why is he watching and enjoying such an uncivilized spectacle? Does he do it because it is a Spanish tradition? The King should inspire good traditions, not bloody and cruel traditions. Howard, how is it possible that a country with such extraordinary qualities continues to have bullfights with millions of enthusiastic followers enjoying the savage treatment of the bull?

I read a torero's description of a bullfight, and he equated bullfighting to an art, such as ballet dancing. This fellow is nuts. He dared to compare the sadistic killing of an animal with Tchaikovsky's, *Nutcracker Suite*. The insanity and the stupidity of that statement are unbelievable.

I badly need the judgment of an expert psychologist like you. I beg you to explain to me what animal cruelty means. Is it just a personal opinion by people who try to justify the unjustifiable, an excellent business (some make a lot of money with bullfighting), a bloody show that never overcame the embryonic development of its tradition, a proof of people's emotional dysfunction, or collective social idiocy? Is the joy of causing suffering to an animal part of a normal psyche or an abnormal psyche? Is anyone who enjoys the suffering of an animal, a normal person?

Sigmund Freud (1915) specifically related cruelty to egotism. Egotistic and cruel impulses pave the way for a *destructive drive*. Rebellious by nature toward what is nevertheless the power of civilization, the human being is always able to display a *cruel aggressiveness*.

In today's world, Roman and medieval carnivals of death are perpetuated in movies and electronic media and in gladiatorial contests, such as boxing and kick-boxing; violently inflicted cruelty is presented in smash-hit novels, films, most video games for children, and many TV series. The torture of animals for entertainment was prohibited in England and the United States in the 19th century, but it continues clandestinely in many countries. There are about 30 blood sports: dog fighting, cock fighting, canary fighting, lion baiting, donkey baiting, Chilean rodeo, bear baiting, fox tossing, rat baiting, among others.

Where does evil originate in aberrations like Hitler and Stalin?

How do people who are excellent parents, hard-working, law-abiding citizens, sensitive about family affairs, and superb artists in various disciplines, who can show affection and tenderness, still be fervent admirers of bullfights and other blood sports and derive immense pleasure from watching the suffering and the barbaric treatment of animals?

Please, help me to make sense of this, Howard!

Dr. Paul: Ed, it is very clear to me that this is a topic you are very passionate about, and you are not alone in struggling with these issues. In explaining the little we do know, I would like to make it clear that I am not supportive of the behavior nor am I making excuses for the behavior of those who display such cruelty.

Dr. Chapunoff: I clearly understand that, Howard.

Dr. Paul: You are quite correct that cruelty exists on a continuum, and you have cited some of the poster children for cruelty. They serve as the worst examples of cruelty and sit at the farthest end of the continuum. More importantly, you are also correct in your statement that acts defined by some as barbaric will not even be defined as cruel by others. There are clear sociological factors that are best appreciated when discerning why things are seen as cruel in one culture and not in another.

Let's take sacrifice as an example. In biblical times, sacrificing animals was commonly practiced as a way of thanking God or appeasing God. Somewhere along the line, someone decided that if a goat were a good sacrifice, a human would be a better one. Humans of all ages were sacrificed, and no one thought this was cruel or unusual. In some cultures, losers of sport contests were sacrificed. In the Mayan culture, the captain of the winning team was sacrificed as were their aristocrats. People can be taught to believe almost anything!

Dr. Chapunoff: That is the most accurate statement I've ever heard in my life! Howard, do you agree with the definition of human cruelty, as I presented it at the beginning of this dialogue?

Dr. Paul: Yes, Ed. I do agree that we can define cruelty as the deliberate, seemingly (I am adding this word to your definition) unnecessary, malicious, and often joyous, infliction of mental or physical pain upon others.

Dr. Chapunoff: Howard, can you please give me an idea about the mental origin of cruelty? What is the substratum that delivers it, the basis from which it departs?

Dr. Paul: Cruelty has a few related bases, one of the big ones is anger and the second is insecurity. If you recall from our previous discussions, the agenda of anger is pain. It makes sense that where there is the purposeful infliction of pain, we can trace the problem back to the unreasonable demands of the individual who is inflicting pain. I also mentioned that where anger is involved, even if it is latent, the angry person feels justified in what is being done and believes that the person who is being punished is a lesser being. This then reduces their moral conflict, as there is no sense of parity or equality between the two.

Dr. Chapunoff: From many observations of human behavior, it seems that cruelty has different origins and involves personal, sociological, and psychological points of departure. When some of these origins act in combination, a most explosive cocktail can result.

Dr. Paul: That is correct, Ed. This is an issue that has been addressed by countless thinkers and concerned individuals over the years. I am sure that I can add some information for you, but it is doubtless I can answer all of the questions. Our knowledge is incomplete, and some of what I say will be speculative. However, I will respond by looking at psychological, sociological, cultural, and biological issues, as they relate to cruelty.

Dr. Chapunoff: All the issues you mentioned related to cruelty are extraordinarily important, but I have a particular curiosity about the psychological ones. I'd like to know what kind of stew is being cooked in the brain of a cruel person.

Dr. Paul: Since all humans are capable of anger, all humans are capable of cruelty. The range of this dimension is exceedingly broad. Past a certain point, cruelty becomes pathological, and individuals are seen as psychopathic. Unfortunately, cruelty exists well within the range of normal limits.

Dr. Chapunoff: Sometimes, cruelty mingles with laughter. Some forms of teasing can be cruel.

Dr. Paul: Yes, indeed. Bullying and teasing are inescapable, and in some places, forms of cruelty are rampant. Behavior is always supported by its consequences; what is the payoff for bullying or teasing? The mechanism here is very straightforward. If I can make you feel bad, then I will feel superior to you and sense that I have more power and potency than you have. One can ask what kind of person tries to make him or herself feel good by making someone else feel bad. The answer, which by no means serves as an excuse for this behavior, is that someone who tries to make him or herself feel good by making someone else feel bad, starts out not feeling good about themself to begin with. Teasing or bullying is simply an easy and often far too effective, way of instantly providing self-gratification and a sense of superiority. It is typically borne by a sense of inferiority.

Dr. Chapunoff: Is there any special connection between anxiety and cruelty?

Dr. Paul: Yes, Ed, and I will explain what it is. In our discussion on obsessive-compulsive disorders (OCD), I expanded the section to include anxiety as an important factor in OCD. There are some people who are easily made anxious, while others seem almost impervious to it. Anxious individuals are individuals who tend to be more interpersonally sympathetic and sensitive. This group tends to abhor and avoid violence and gore. Individuals who seem impervious to anxiety are sometimes less sympathetic to others and can be far less sensitive to the pain and concerns of others.

There have been a number of studies done on individuals at this end of the reactivity dimension. These individuals tend to be difficult to stimulate and arouse and are sometimes drawn like magnets to high-energy or highly exciting activities. They seem impervious to punishment and are driven by reinforcing behaviors or circumstances that highly stimulate their brains. Such highly stimulating behaviors are frequently illegal, often immoral, and can easily involve being turned on by the suffering of others, especially if it happens at the hand of the person wishing to be excited. Many criminals fit into this category. Our criminal justice system tends to focus on punishment. For this group, punishment has diminished success. There are many individuals who are able to take this brain state and make it functional, finding occupations that keep them moving and constantly challenged; not everyone can do this.

Dr. Chapunoff: What about the state of mind of a warrior when approaching the *decisive moment* or the fighting experience?

Dr. Paul: Biologically, the distinction between individuals that are more anxious and less anxious individuals has adaptive value. Successful warriors needed to be in the nonanxious group. They do best when energized by combat. If we go back in time, but not that far back, combat was a gruesome, bloody event where the distinction between cruelty and being the superior fighter was often blurred.

Dr. Chapunoff: On many occasions, a decapitation yielded more cheers than horror! When you think about famous warriors like Alexander the Great, you might think that this fever to conquer and kill hundreds of thousands was like an addiction.

Dr. Paul: I am glad you raised the point, Ed. There is an element of truth in what you are saying. In many cases, battle produces excesses of endorphins, leading to a state of euphoria, which for many is addicting. Some people believe that this process goes back to when people split into meat hunters versus gatherers and farmers, who engaged in less violent and nonpredatory behavior. Early on, pursuing, killing, and finally eating prey were exciting and altogether rewarding experiences. This same basic process operates in battle and, for some, serves as a basis for cruelty.

Sociologically, whoever controlled the meat, gained the power in that society. Such power gave hunters increased access to status and sex. Those involved in the hunt were typically given a larger share of the bounty. As humankind developed, the search for food (meat) morphed into the search for power, with all the same benefits. The conquest of others became sought after. Cruelty and predation have their roots in this dynamic. For some, the sight and smell of blood and the sound of screaming during hunting or fighting can activate internal biological systems leading to the release of endorphins, which can be addicting and produce both a mental and physical high, just like morphine can.

Domination of others can also release potent chemicals that are highly reinforcing. If a person who lacks empathy can make you suffer, it can serve as a positive experience that the person will wish to repeat. Good socialization is necessary to tame this biological base. There are a number of factors that contribute to the disruption of the normal socialization process. Child abuse, traumatic life experiences, early parental rejection or separation, school failure, and a history of family violence are all factors that increase vulnerability and can produce a lack of empathy and increased risk for cruelty.

I am sure you can see in some of your examples, Ed, that bullfighting and other blood sports have a cultural and societally supported base. From the little that I have said, it might make sense now to discuss why these blood sports only appeal to a certain segment of the population. The sights and sounds of blood sports - dog fighting, cockfighting, bullfighting, or even people fighting provide a thrill for some. We are linked to our biological past, which goes back to the need to hunt for survival. Blood sports pay homage to this aspect of human development.

With respect to Christopher Columbus, the sad fact is that most people are not taught the very facts you detail. Instead, a romanticized and factually emasculated version of Christopher Columbus is presented to school students. As you noted, the tale of Columbus has undergone a historical revision, and most of his crimes and cruel, self-serving methods are simply left out of the chronicles of history.

Dr. Chapunoff: I believe that celebrating Columbus is a travesty of history and does not allow people to judge this man the way he deserves to be judged.

Dr. Paul: I do think that the celebration of Columbus Day has far more to do with the celebration of heritage than history. Columbia University most likely received its name, not in celebration of Christopher Columbus, but in celebration of the United States of America, which early on was also known as Columbia. I do agree with you that this does pay homage to Columbus, but takes it one step away from him and lets the blurred truth of his cruelty fade into a secondary role. This last statement is a pure guess and would require someone actually to do the research to prove or disprove this notion.

Dr. Chapunoff: Howard, I have nothing but the utmost respect for your opinions and intellect, but my feeling on the Columbia University issue is different from yours. I believe the name of the university honors Columbus, not the United States. Otherwise, I presume that this prestigious institution would have been named the United States of America University. However, as you said, we have not researched this issue, and we're only expressing our personal opinions.

You made a very important statement when you suggested that the celebration of Columbus Day was more related to heritage than history. For educational purposes and a sense of patriotism, heritage is often projected as more important than history. Many historical aberrations and the misdeeds of heroic leaders of a country are not mentioned at all, particularly in history textbooks. Glorifying stupidity can make heroes out of villains.

Dr. Paul: Ed, you carefully detailed the Roman Circus and the Inquisition. I have already addressed the Roman Circus as a blood sport combined with the corruption of power. An adage says power corrupts and absolute power corrupts absolutely. There are, unfortunately, too many proofs for this statement.

On the other hand, the Inquisition combines power with anger and fear; some see this as a most dangerous combination. We previously discussed how when people view things in terms of absolutes, such as commandments, denigration and punishment of disbelievers seem to follow naturally. Even when this is toned down with some modicum of socialization, it leads to bias, racism, and hatred of others. Those involved in the Inquisition actually felt they were on the side of God and truly believed they were more than justified to carry out their cruelty. If behavior is to be understood, it needs to be seen in context, even if the context is horrific. At times, even religion is subject to corruption by power, and that corruption can be amplified by fear. I have said before that one reason for religion is to attempt to have people choose the rational and empathic over the cruel. Even religion sometimes fails this ideal. The struggle between good and evil is never-ending.

Hitler fits well into exemplifying the additive component of fear when combined with power and anger. He is frequently described as an individual fraught with insecurity about his own adequacy. One overused mechanism to make us feel big is to make someone else feel small. Anger imbues us with a sense of strength, righteousness, and correctness. Hitler understood that if he generated anger across his nation, he would provide a mechanism for lifting his own insecurities, as well as his country's insecurities. Hatred is also a base for group cohesiveness, as providing a scapegoat produces a seemingly sensible plan of attack that far too many people can rally behind.

I hope my explanations are sufficient to give you a bit more understanding of how these things can occur. We are all capable of anger; therefore, we are all capable of cruelty. When taken to the extreme, genocides, in the minds of those doing it, actually seem reasonable!

We live in a world of polarities. If there is yin, there must be yang. There are individuals in the world who are wonderful examples of kindness, charity, empathy, and caring. Some even reach the point of sainthood. For better or for worse, the other end of this continuum is cruelty; that strange mixture of fear and power that has existed since the beginning of humanity.

Until we devise better ways to raise our children with good attachments, with a positive sense of personal value, and with good instruction regarding giving, empathy, and charity, there will always be an unending list of perpetrators of cruelty. This notion is sad, but I am afraid true.

Dr. Chapunoff: Howard, I know that not all the questions I asked you in this book have easy answers. This applies particularly to this chapter on human cruelty. You said most of what can reasonably be said about the mechanisms that originate and perpetuate cruelty. Cruelty is an inherent part of the human psyche. It always existed, and it will never disappear. It is an obvious fact, although, as we noted, opinions about it vary according to moral, religious, family, social, and genetic backgrounds. At times, whether something is seen as good or bad depends on the eyes of the beholder. Some good people favor the death penalty, and yet that is considered by many to be cruel and unusual punishment.

The cruelty phenomenon has plagued the world since its inception, and evidence supports its eternal continuity.

In this discussion, you suggested that people could realistically and practically reduce cruelty by avoiding child abuse, traumatic life experiences, early parental rejection or separation, school failure, and family violence; all of which increase vulnerability by producing anger, disenfranchisement, and a lack of empathy. All of this increases the risk for cruelty. You also stressed the importance of having parents develop healthy, early attachments with their children, providing them with the proper attention, care, support, moral-ethical values, and the avoidance, of psychological-emotional traumas that have the potential to create cruel ideas and the implementation of them.

10

GUILT, RELIGION, AND A
COMPROMISING OATH

Dr. Chapunoff: Joseph was 48. He was a successful, handsome, and healthy, businessman. He was fortunate to have had a great upbringing and education, great parents, well-behaved children, and a wonderful wife. He and his wife were both fervent Evangelists. They did not have any sexual experience between themselves or with other people prior to their wedding. Every day, Joseph thought he was the luckiest man on earth. That is, until one day his wife was diagnosed with a terrible form of leukemia. She died in a few months. He was devastated. His grief was so intense that he thought his whole life had fallen apart without hope of recovery. Nevertheless, he did recover fairly well. After three years of mourning, he began to think that he was too young to live alone for the rest of his life and wondered about the possibility of meeting a woman for a serious, committed relationship. Due to his spiritual background and education, he was not prepared for informal or casual affairs. Joseph was well connected socially. Beautiful single women were eager to have a date with him, and why not marry him. All he could do was to invite them for a cocktail, dinner, and occasionally, dancing. He was particularly attracted to, as he described, a gorgeous, beautiful, intelligent, and sweet lady. She was also a devoted Evangelist, and she thought she qualified to be his second wife. However, life is not so simple, as we all know. Joseph felt *guilty as hell* and thought he was being disloyal to his deceased wife. To make matters worse, he was distressed by a few words he had pronounced to answer one of his deceased wife's questions, *"Joe, when I die, I'll be waiting for you in Heaven. You're not going to marry another woman, are you?"*

He answered, *"No, my love, I sure will not."* She answered, *"Do you swear?"*

"Yes, darling, I swear!" he said. Now, he was not only confronting a feeling of disloyalty toward his dead wife but also the oath that forbade him ever to have another relationship. He felt he was irreversibly and irrevocably tied to his oath and that he *would be offending the Lord* if he didn't fulfill his promise and honor his *sacred religious commitment.*

Howard, my question to you is: What technical principles would you deploy to deal with Joseph's guilt that is stopping him from achieving happiness and peace of mind? He and his wife were faithful Evangelists. They were raised and educated to follow their religious faith, without displaying any human weakness that would offend the Lord. If Joseph consulted with you, how would you handle his counseling? It seems that we have here one example of the absolutes you referred to in previous discussions, where people are forced to deal with the *"I must do it" without an alternative* or option. Rigid things break more easily than flexible things. You were so right when you suggested that absolutes create all kinds of troubles! In cases like this one, is it possible that an Evangelic pastor might have a better chance of solving his problems than a psychologist? If a psychologist had any chance of helping him, don't you think the professional should be one of his own religious affiliations? I don't believe that a Jewish or a Catholic psychologist would be a desirable therapist for him. Am I wrong?

Dr. Paul: Ed, I will start with the part of your question that is easiest to answer. It is not necessary to be of the same faith as the people you are working with to be able to assist them. I do not have to have cancer to deal with a cancer patient. If I had to have the same experience as the people consulting me, I would not be able to see many people! Psychologists, if they are doing their job properly, do not impose their own value system or beliefs on the people they are working with. My job is to assist people clarify their values and decide what matters to them.

Dr. Chapunoff: Howard, I see your point. You just said that psychologists, who do their job properly, do not impose their own value system onto their patients. Realistically, how many professionals of your specialty act like that? I have known highly opinionated psychologists who very straightforwardly and assertively, instruct their patients to take a particular course of action. I'd like to know if that approach is always inappropriate.

As far as the religious orientation of psychotherapists, I've known liberal Evangelists, ultraconservative Evangelists, Jews, and Catholics, who disagreed on crucial issues, such as abortion. Some were pro-life and others accepted abortion. What percentage of psychotherapists do you estimate are able to put aside any personal bias when they counsel their clients? What percentage of psychologists strongly delineate guidelines of therapy that are quite direct instead of a broader variety of acceptable options?

Dr. Paul: I only know what goes on in my sessions, Ed, and in the sessions of those I supervise. If anyone in therapy is being told how to live their life by their doctor, they might want to look for another doctor. When I do tell people what to do, it involves circumstances where I provide directions on child management or detail a treatment plan, where individuals would best follow certain procedures, such as exposure, in order to overcome their difficulties. When it is about values, being directive is a no-no.

Ed, you were able to explain Joseph's dilemma quite clearly, so I was able to understand the problem. The solution would not come from me or be based upon my beliefs, religion, or value system; it would come from the person sitting across from me.

I find it interesting that you pose the question in a way that suggests you expect me to extricate Joseph from his dilemma. I would not see that as my job. I do believe my job would be to assist him in clarifying his values and help him decide what his oath means to him. It may very well be that if he truly believes his oath was solemn and sacred, and if he truly believes that he will reunite with his first wife in the hereafter, to be consistent with his values, his decision may well be to remain true to her for the rest of his life on earth. I would feel no sense that I had to rescue him from his dilemma. *Happiness is, at some level, making peace with what we do not have.*

Dr. Chapunoff: I never forget what Hubert Humphrey said when he was running for president of the United States and lost the election, *"I finally decided that I do not need to be president to be happy."*

Dr. Paul: He was right, and that was a wise conclusion!

With respect to Joseph, it would be best for him to decide what the meaning of his oath to his first wife was. If he chose to honor it, as he well might, my conversation with him will be more about standing behind his decision and discussing what accommodations he might be willing to make to live without a partner. We will deal with him taking responsibility for his words and then work to help him stand firmly behind his decision. He will be better able to tolerate the loneliness of being without a partner if he recognizes that this was a committed choice and does not represent a circumstance in which he is helpless. We will have to deal with issues of entitlement and make sure he doesn't feel that, because he is a good person, he is entitled to happiness, and happiness means having a partner. If that is his operating ideation, he will have little choice but to be depressed and unhappy. He will have to have his faith sustain him and take comfort in the fact that he is living his life in congruence with his beliefs. One can only hope that someday, he will reunite with his wife and enjoy happiness. For the rest of his life on earth, he will need to find happiness in activities that do not include a new relationship. He will need to adopt the mindset that he is still in a continuing, committed relationship - now with his first wife who is looking down from above. If he is able to adopt this mindset, there will be no guilt, and it will not be an issue to address. However, he may still have guilt if he thinks his thoughts have to be pure.

The reality is that people often have thoughts that are at crossed purposes to their committed religious beliefs. If this were the case, we would help Joseph understand that it is normal to have longings, wishes, and thoughts that go against his commitment to stay faithful to his wife.

When people behave badly, feeling remorse is quite appropriate. Once again, we are dealing with the vagaries of language, and many would agree that when people behave poorly, it is quite okay for them to feel guilty.

Dr. Chapunoff: You said that others might agree that it's quite okay to feel guilty. Guilt might be a redeeming feeling, but emotionally it causes damage. Would it be reasonable to conclude, Howard, that guilt might be an appropriate response, but not a beneficial one? Is guilt a first step in a healing process that works its way toward the achievement of peace of mind?

Dr. Paul: When I work with individuals, we try to develop a clear understanding of language, so that we are better able to communicate. Remorse and feeling bad about our poor choices is a requirement of a socialized individual. To me, guilt is what happens when we add anger to the mix and denigrate our self. This seldom leads to growth or learning, as the agenda of anger takes us away from growing and puts us in the mindset of having to induce pain, with the mistaken notion that it will somehow be good for us. Self-induced pain and suffering is often antithetical to growth and learning.

The sticky part of this example will come from Joseph, if he decides that his oath to his wife didn't count because of the circumstances in which it was made. There is every probability that this would lead to a good deal of ambivalence on his part. I believe there would be a sizable part of him that would not believe his own subterfuge, and he would come to understand that he reached this conclusion simply to increase the likelihood of having more pleasure in his current life. This is where guilt would come from. This is where our discussion of the pitfalls of absolutes would probably come into play. It also brings up another interesting point. Many people believe that if they drop demands, they are left with nothing to control themselves. If it is not true that I must obey my own vows, people often believe that they then have no responsibility to be truthful, honest, and to exert self-control.

Dr. Chapunoff: When is the responsibility factor more important - during the absolute terms of an oath or when the oath is somehow bypassed and replaced by a more flexible spiritual posture?

Dr. Paul: Elimination of the absolute actually increases our responsibility, as it puts it squarely into the realm of a personal and committed choice, rather than blind obedience. Psychologically, I would work to help transmute Joseph's, *"I must honor the vow to my wife,"* into, *"I think it is important to be a man of my word."* I would do this, not to get him off the hook, but to have him accept the responsibility of his own values and convictions.

Dr. Chapunoff: How can you transmute his oath without getting him off the hook? In other words, how can you release his spiritual duty and at the same time ask him to be connected to it?

Dr. Paul: I would work to help him decide if he truly believes it would be best for him to honor this oath or not. My sense is, that given his commitment to his religion and his own value system, he would ultimately choose to honor his vow.

Dr. Chapunoff: As I know this person better than you do, Howard, since you never met him, I think your expectation about his ultimate choice is most likely correct.

Dr. Paul: In your question to me you state, it seems that here we have one example of the absolutes you referred to in previous chapters, where people are forced to deal with the, *I must do it,* without an alternative option. I would like to point out that there are rarely times where we have no alternative option, unless we are thinking in terms of *musts,* which eliminate options. Even if we can eliminate the should, there are many times when the alternative option is so unpleasant that it seems like it does not represent a choice. Joe has a choice; he can stay true to his vow and commitment to his first wife, or he can act in a way that may be against his value and belief system. Just because we do not like our options, does not mean we do not have any.

Dr. Chapunoff: I presume that having a bad option is preferable to having no option.

Dr. Paul: Ed, you raise an interesting point. People are confronted with three different types of choices. In the first instance, we are in a position to choose between two things that are each positive. In the second instance, one is positive and one negative or at least it is not as positive, and in the third instance, both options are negative. The first instance is difficult (two positives); when we get close to deciding on one, the other begins to look better.

Dr. Chapunoff: Howard, I'm thinking about what you just referred to regarding the choice between two positive things.

Dr. Paul: What is it, Ed?

Dr. Chapunoff: You stated that the choice between two positive things is difficult. At first, one would tend to think that it's wonderful to have two positive options and that it should be easy to decide which one to choose. But you're right; it's difficult to decide between two good things. In addition, I'll provide one example of such dilemma:

Imagine a person who falls in love with two different individuals, both are considered ideal candidates for marriage. It would be most difficult for one to have to make a choice between the two.

Dr. Paul: You've got it, Ed, but the psychologically interesting part is that as soon as we choose one, the other begins to look better, creating a great deal of potential ambivalence.

The second choice circumstance, where one is positive and one is negative, looks easier, but even though there are times when the positive option is the easiest or most fun choice, it may not be the best choice.

The third is the antithesis of the first, and when we are able to make peace with the lesser of the two evils, the other begins to look better.

In any situation of choice, even when both appear not to be what we wish, it is always best to be driven by our values. Therapy is about helping people make value-based choices with the values emanating from the patient, not the therapist.

11

MARRIAGE: IS IT GOOD FOR YOU, OR NOT?
Our dreams and realities sometimes clash

Dr. Chapunoff: Howard, the institution of marriage has been around for thousands of years. That fact alone would make you think that people have learned enough about marriage to avoid making gross mistakes when they formalize that crucial commitment. Obviously, that is not the case. In Western civilization, the incidence of divorce is over 50 percent. About 25 percent of couples who remain married do so for reasons that have nothing to do with marital happiness. Other factors intervene: religion, tradition, family values, fear of loneliness, uncertainty, insecurity about future relationships, depression, disruption of family ties, negative reactions, the feared impact of divorce on a couple's children, financial losses or fear of losses, and disruption of social and family connections, to name but a few.

As far as economics are concerned, an unsuccessful marriage is just about the worst investment anyone can make. In the United States, the person who earned the bulk of the couple's capital and made it substantial after 20 years of hard work may lose almost everything (and often does) with a divorce. It's difficult to find a good businessperson who might invest 100 percent of their own capital and effort, (that's what a married man or woman usually does), knowing they have a 50 percent chance of losing everything.

When a marriage or sustained relationship is successful, it is an extraordinary experience. There is harmony, understanding, tolerance, companionship, deep friendship between partners, sexual chemistry, shared moral-ethical values, loyalty, unlimited spiritual resources, AND love. The children are typically well behaved, respectful, and responsible. What a beauty!

BUT, when the union is unsuccessful, and everything or most everything goes wrong, marriage becomes stressful, deceptive, sour, sad, and an incredibly messy and exhausting torment. Still, many people compromise and find ways to live within an unhappy marriage. Apparently, they find it easier to digest their marital conflicts with the help of an antacid than survive the difficult situations created by a divorce. Tranquilizers and antidepressants often help to control the distress. Each affected person must decide what to do. Some negotiate the situation with resignation. This reminds me of a joke. Howard, do you mind if I tell it to you now?

Dr. Paul: No, not at all, Ed, go right ahead.

Dr. Chapunoff: A very poor man, who lives with his family in the poorest section of Brooklyn, is unhappily married. He shares a moment with his 16-year-old son. The boy asks him, *"Dad, what would you do if you win the $40-million Lotto this weekend?"* Dad answers, *"My son, you're quite mature for your age, and you're beginning to understand things. If I tell you frankly what I'd do with so much money, will you promise me that you won't tell anyone?"* His son says, *"Of course Dad, tell me!"* Dad tells his son, *"It would be champagne, Paris, women!"* The son then remarks, *"But Dad, what are you going to do **if you don't** win the lottery?"*

"Okay my boy," says Dad, *"in that case, it'll have to be Brooklyn, Coca-Cola, and your mother!"*

Dr. Paul: That's a cute one, Ed.

Dr. Chapunoff: And now, let's resume our discussion. In general, the process of a prospective marriage, generally - not always - begins by falling in love. A man or a woman is convinced that they have found their perfect match. It really doesn't matter if they have premarital sex. It doesn't matter if they get along very well during intimacy or playing Ping-Pong. The reason why it does not matter is that things may change as time passes by. In addition, more often than not, things do change. There may be a subtle change or a drastic and rapid change in behavior and attitudes. Some discoveries of a spouse's character may quickly surface but others take months or years to release their toxicity. A spouse may undergo a metamorphosis that is difficult to explain. Did the person really change and intentionally or subconsciously hide their real personality? In the therapeutic approach of whether a couple should seek a divorce or work out tentative solutions to avoid divorce, how often do you find that the couple used a premarital evaluation to help analyze each of their individual proclivities and potential roles in causing future marital trouble? It's easier to get married than get a divorce. In one second, or less, a person will say, *"Yes, I do,"* and commit his or her entire life and whatever they have to another person. Getting married is indeed, a huge decision. Taking into consideration the number of marriages that end in divorce, the aggravation, frustration, deception, and financial hardships that this legal separation causes, I wonder if it would be a good idea to have the process leading to marriage be more difficult, and the process of getting a divorce, easier?

Howard, do you agree with me or not about the potential benefits to a couple if, they took a premarital questionnaire like the one I will present to you? The questionnaire may be an idea that not everyone is willing or able to deal with. When people fall in love, the mind loses part of its rationality. You said something like that in another discussion, and I think you were very correct. You also stated in another section, *"No person is completely normal,"* psychologically speaking. I found the phrase appealing that you used to discuss the status of being in love, *"Love is the only madness sanctioned (authorized) by psychologists."*

Many people would be offended by the suggestion of completing a premarital questionnaire. If the other person is the *perfect match,* who in this world needs to ask so many questions, some of them being indelicate and dealing with issues of intimacy, various sexual acts, and other *irreverent propositions?* Only those who learned from a bad marriage and experienced living the drama themselves or having observed what happened to others will understand what I am saying.

Ignorance of the prospective husband's or wife's character, sensitivity, flexibility, sense of responsibility, readiness, willingness and capacity to share a life where all kinds of problems may occur, predilections on sexuality, and other situations that will surely surface when sharing life together, may turn out to be disastrous.

In the following questionnaire, the questions I suggest should be answered YES, NO, or I DON'T KNOW.

1) Do you like a home with warm room temperatures or cold temperatures?

2) Do you like to eat at home, or do you prefer to go to restaurants several times a week?

3) Do you like to socialize a lot, have parties at home, or go to parties elsewhere?

4) Do you like to read? Do you like to read about US news, world news, history, biographies, classical music, jazz, country music, rock and roll, movies, nutrition, pet care, philosophy, actors, politics, or other subjects? Are you curious about events in the world or do you prefer not to bother with them?

5) Would you object to my mother coming home and staying with us for six months?

6) Do you like pets? I would like to have two cats and two dogs. Do you have any objection?

7) If I ever have a serious accident and lose my two legs, do you feel that you are the kind of person who could cope with that situation? Do you believe you could live with me for the rest of your life? On the other hand, do you honestly feel that you do not have the character or temperament to do that if that should occur?

8) How many children would you like to have? I would not like to have more than one child. Would that be okay with you?

9) Are you a jealous person? If so, how jealous do you think you can be, a little jealous or a lot jealous?

10) How many times a week or a month, do you feel you would be motivated to engage in lovemaking?

11) Would you like to engage in oral genital sex (fellatio and cunnilingus), the 69 position, the rear entry position, or any other creative variants of sexual positions? I like

them. Do you find any of these positions and techniques acceptable? Do you find them unpleasant, unacceptable, or abominable?

12) Would you mind having mirrors on the walls to heighten the stimulation while having sex?

13) Would you mind watching X-rated videos, or do you consider them unpleasant, useless, or disgusting?

14) Would you like to make love during the day or during the night?

15) Would you like to travel during vacation time?

16) Do you like to go dancing? Would you like to participate in sporting activities or games like chess, pool, table tennis, poker, or others? Do you find any or most of the above attractive?

17) If we need to make an important decision and we disagree, how would we solve the problem?

18) If your parents or other relatives become intrusive in our marriage, how would you react and approach them?

19) Are you pro-life or pro-abortion?

There are more questions one could ask, but those listed above represent a good beginning.

I believe that this sort of premarital questionnaire might help couples gain a better understanding of each other, intellectually, spiritually, emotionally, and physically.

Howard, please help me with the following:

a) What do you think about my suggestions? Are they good, bad, or good and bad at the same time?

b) How do you approach couples who have little in common,

have children, and the husband wants a divorce and the wife does not or vice versa?

c)   Do you ever recommend that a couple divorce or help the couple make their own decision about divorce?

d)   Do you find that with appropriate marital counseling, couples truly get to love and understand each other, or do they act and feel like they saved the marriage but not their happiness?

e)   Do you find that children are better off watching their parents in conflict every day while the family stays together, or do children feel better when their parents get a divorce?

f)   Do children resent the parent who wanted the divorce?

Dr. Paul: Wow, Ed, what a list of good questions! It seems like this is an issue you have given quite a bit of thought to. You have proposed some very substantial and important questions.

I mentioned this before, but when I gave my little talk at my daughter's wedding, I used a story that goes like this. It is said that when two people become married, they become one. The problem is that they then will often fight about which one! The reality is that when two people marry they would best become three - you, me, and us. It is important that each one of these components of any relationship is nurtured, honored, and protected in order for the relationship to survive and thrive. As you point out, marriage can be a sublime and beautiful thing. Simply from a health standpoint, recent studies continue to point out that married people are less likely to get pneumonia, have surgery, develop cancer, or have heart attacks. There is even a lower risk for dementia. As a rule, when *all* causes of death are factored into the equation, it is safer to be married than not married. Newer research has looked more closely at the quality of marriage, and not surprisingly, has shown that the advantage of marriage does not extend to those whose relationships are challenged. Actually, people who have never married may be better off than those who are in bad marriages. Stressful marriages can be as bad for someone's heart as smoking. While marriage may be sacred, it appears that the benefits of marriage rest in the quality of the relationship, rather than in the institution of marriage itself.

Ed, you cited the sobering statistic that half of all marriages end in divorce. That figure only holds for first marriages. Two thirds of all individuals in a second marriage land up in divorce court, and three quarters of all people in a third marriage are unsuccessful and again seek divorce. Of everyone who is married and then divorced, two thirds of individuals who marry before the age of 25 will end up being divorced. For those who marry between the ages of 25 and 35, the frequency of divorce is cut in half. For those that marry after the age of 35, over 90 percent will remain married. These numbers are for first marriages rather than subsequent marriages.

You and so many others have asked, *"If marriage is such a risky business, why do so many people do it?"* The answer is, for better or for worse, people fall in love.

You quoted a previous statement of mine, where I said that love is the only sanctioned psychosis. You slightly changed that, stating that it was only sanctioned by psychologists, but that is not quite accurate, as it really is approved of by society in general.

The original purpose of marriage had nothing to do with love, but everything to do with keeping tribes strong by increasing their number. Marriage was initially about having children, as strength came from numbers. Marriage by love and by personal selection is actually a recent addition to the history of people uniting. Arranged marriages were more the rule than the exception. Love had a tendency to mess up the works, and while it was often seen as romantic and intense, it tends to be presented in older literature as more of a tragedy. Romeo and Juliet is one fine example.

When marriages were arranged, the divorce rate was remarkably low. This was in part because there was no such thing as divorce, or if there was, it was difficult to get. King Henry VIII determined it was far easier to banish or behead his spouses; divorce was too much of a hassle!

Dr. Chapunoff: Yeah! Just thinking about the rolling heads of Anne Boleyn and Catherine Howard gives me the chills!

Dr. Paul: Before too many women hate me, I must say that, as the song goes, love is a many splendored thing. I am not trying to be unromantic in my comments nor am I in any way against romantic love. The problem is, from my professional standpoint, it keeps me far too busy with the chaos it can create. While love can create euphoria, it can also create remarkable despair.

Dr. Chapunoff: You're not kidding!

Dr. Paul: Perspective tends to be lost, and the proverbial rose-colored glasses people unwittingly wear when they are in love, make it very difficult for anyone in love to accurately understand or appreciate the foibles of their partner. When people are high on love they believe that their partner is the best thing in the universe; that the positive feelings they share will last forever; that there is no insurmountable problem, big or small; and that nothing can ever split them apart. The mind-altering effect of being in love typically fades over the first few years of marriage, and for some, they wake up in shock one day asking themselves, who is this person laying next to me?

Ed, you took the time to put together a questionnaire that might be helpful for people to take prior to marriage. I'm not sure if you did this alone or if you used some other source, as your questions are quite comprehensive.

Dr. Chapunoff: I did it alone, but I'm almost certain that I'm not the first one who produced a premarital questionnaire.

Dr. Paul: There are prepackaged premarital inventories that are available; all meant to avoid what is termed, *posthoneymoon shock syndrome*. These questionnaires, like yours, try to initiate discussions regarding expectations, communication styles, level of commitment, desire for children, how many children, financial management, sex in all its aspects and variations, career goals, relationships with friends, family, and religious preferences.

Previously, you identified one of the problems with the use of questionnaires, specifically with young individuals (people under 25), who are deeply in love and feel no need to use them.

Dr. Chapunoff: Yes, and I think they make a big mistake!

Dr. Paul: Sadly, love is wasted on the young. One reason that maturation leads to a reduction in divorce rate is that love tends to be less intense, meaning that people can be in love and still have some access to their sanity.

Dr. Chapunoff: You said it so well, Howard.

Dr. Paul: As we mature, our executive functioning, which is the ability to remain logical and suppress the impulse to behave in entirely emotional ways, is enhanced. The full maturation of our frontal lobes does not occur until we are about 25 years of age. This may be one reason why the divorce rate begins to reduce after age 25. Those who take the time, no matter what their age, to go comprehensively through your set of questions, either by themselves or with a trained counselor, will probably greatly increase the odds that their marriage will be successful. You asked if I thought your suggestions were good: I don't. I think they're great! I have had the good fortune to do premarital counseling, and the questions you pose are very similar to the questions that I ask. As I observe individuals deal with these questions, I gain insight into their communication style and their ability with their current skill sets to engage in problem solving, compromise, and perspective, taking as well, other skills necessary to maintain a healthy marriage. I also look to see if one partner is controlling and the other passive. When I see imbalances in power, I often point them out to the couple, explain the risks to them, and attempt to have them deal with these issues before they tie the knot.

Ed, in other discussions, we have spoken at length about anger. Anger is the poison pill of marriage. I do spend time helping people understand the destructive power of anger and provide them with communication strategies that help maintain the parity necessary in any quality relationship.

Dr. Chapunoff: That's right, Howard! Anger in a married couple is equivalent to shooting poisonous darts aimed at the opponent's retina!

Dr. Paul: Actually, the darts are aimed at each other's heart and sense of wellbeing. I often ask couples to take two chairs, put them about eight inches apart, sit with their knees interwoven, and hold hands. I ask them to hold all important conversations in this position. I am not sure if you are aware of this, but when people are holding hands and then become angry, one or the other of them will back away. When people become angry, their agenda is no longer to fix anything or communicate in a positive way, but to begin punishing or hurting the other person, even if done subtly, passively, or unconsciously.

Dr. Chapunoff: I presume that when two angry people hold hands, the only thing that would prevent their separation is crazy glue!

Dr. Paul: I make it very clear to couples, that no constructive communication will arise when people are angry at each other. When couples are angry, what they say comes from their anger and is meant to inflict punishment and pain on their partner. If couples are able to keep anger out of their communication, they are in a much better position to discuss each other's frustration and behavior. I do need to mention that being upset leads to somatic activation and feelings in our body. I am using the term anger to mean the expression of our upset that is contaminated by our unreasonable demands.

I have mentioned that it is important we learn to **talk only when we have a pair of ears ready to listen**. When people are angry, they are not typically in a place where they are capable of good listening. One of the strong suggestions I give to people is that as soon as one backs away, communication would best stop. Whoever becomes angry or has to back away has 24 hours to recompose themselves, and it is their responsibility to return to the talking position and work to finish the conversation. The person, who is the one being pulled away from, is strongly counseled to suppress the urge to continue the conversation. I try to make it clear that it is important to let the other person have space in which to try to recompose themself. Too many partners in this kind of circumstance demand that the other person stay and *have it out*. This does not usually lead to resolution but to increases in marital distress.

Ed, you did point out earlier that the marital knot is one of the easiest to tie and one of the hardest and most costly to undo. Good communication skills are comparatively cheap to learn and can save a bundle.

One of your questions asked what I do when couples, who have children, reach a point where they have little else in common, and one partner wants a divorce and the other does not. In any situation like this, no matter who wants the divorce and who does not want the divorce, what I do depends on how absolute the person is who has made the decision to end the relationship.

If they are willing to come in and speak with me, we explore such things as what led to their initial attraction, what positive attributes they still see existing in their spouse, and what particular things create frustration and anger. We then explore the strategies that the individual has tried, to make things better. Where I find that ineffective strategies have been used, and I usually do find this, we explore their commitment to leave. If there is any ambivalence, I usually suggest that the person give it another try under professional guidance, as it may lead to a more positive outcome. When the partner is dead set on leaving, I ask the couple if they have any desire to spend time with me to work on an amicable split, especially when children are involved. Unfortunately, there are times when one partner is so angry, that everyone, even the children, end up being punished.

You asked if I ever recommend that a couple split. I honestly do not think it is wise for me to make such important choices for people when they come to me for professional guidance. I present a plan to the couple that I believe is worth putting effort into to repair the relationship. Either it will be effective for them, or it will make it very clear that there is little left in the relationship to rescue.

You asked a very interesting question as to whether couples in distress can ever restore their relationship to the point where it is warm and loving. The answer is a very clear yes! If couples are able to improve their communication, be less demanding and punitive toward each other, work on the you, me, and us rubric that I mentioned earlier, and spend time being more positive toward each other, it is possible to strengthen and improve relationships and to restore them to a more acceptable, satisfactory, and even sought-for circumstance.

Another important question you asked is whether it is beneficial for children to have their parents remain together yet be in conflict. Somehow, the notion has been promulgated that it is bad for children to see their parents disagree. This is not exactly the case. It is bad for children to see their parents being hostile toward each other, as it teaches children to be mean and vindictive. However, it is not bad for children to see disagreement, as long as what follows the disagreements are attempts at problem solving and resolution.

Parents are indeed teachers to their children. Children are mirrors that reflect back to parent all of their foibles. If parents yell, children will yell back. If parents are angry, children will learn to attack (in all of its different guises). If parents disagree and children see good problem solving skills, perspective taking, compassion, flexibility, compromise, and the maintenance of caring, children will grow to be more successful in their own interpersonal capacity, and be able to handle what comes their way.

You also asked if children resent the parent who wanted the divorce more than the parent who did not. The answer is, sometimes. The damage to children is often related to their age and vulnerability. It is also related to their particular bonding and relationship with parents. I have seen situations where one partner in the relationship was aggressive and demeaning to the spouse. That same person had a high identification and a strong bond with one of the children. That child, who was very much aligned with the aggressor, had a strained relationship with the other parent, who was clearly being unreasonably attacked. There are too many variables in how children will react to make this a black-and-white situation. As a rule, when conflict bleeds through to the children, it is not a good thing.

In truth, as long as individuals marry when young, the current sad state of affairs will continue. One can only hope that people see the light and extend courtships, use premarital questionnaires, become involved in premarital counseling, and learn good communication and anger resolution skills prior to marrying.

Dr. Chapunoff: Do you find that couples in trouble often consult you late, rather than early, about their conflicts? There's something called the right timing for almost everything. A wounded marriage is like a hemorrhage - if you don't stop it in time, the damage may become irreversible.

Dr. Paul: That's right, Ed. Timing is indeed, important. One can hope that people seek out a trained professional, a psychologist, social worker, or marital therapist, when signs of trouble are beginning to emerge, rather than when it is almost too late. Too many people do not understand that love, that joyous yet often temporary state of affairs, changes in any relationship. The intensity of love often reduces, and if the giddiness and high are replaced with dedication, caring, and a daily commitment to stay with the other person, the relationship will probably thrive.

The best relationships exist when people stay together, not because they have a paper that says they are married, but because they make a daily commitment to honor the vows they gave to their partner, and they continue to make the personal choice to be with them. As people age, they change; health changes, interests change, libido changes. Maintaining the quality of any relationship is an ongoing effort.

Dr. Chapunoff: I don't remember who defined love as daily hard labor.

Dr. Paul: For some people, little effort is required. For others, maintaining the quality of any relationship takes effort and cannot be taken for granted.

Dr. Chapunoff: I hope that our readers who are in love will remember what you explained in this chapter, Howard. There is nothing more beautiful than love and nothing more preoccupying than the lack of love. I don't believe there is anything more disgusting than the ugliness that results from relationships that should never have existed to begin with.

Dr. Paul: Dreams about love, as well as being in love, are wonderfully romantic. However, love creates illusions that are best handled by substituting the illusions with an appreciation of what is real.

Dr. Chapunoff: That's right! The race between reality and dreams is always won by the former.

12

PERSONALITY: WHAT IS IT REALLY?

Dr. Chapunoff: Howard, I'd like to offer the following examples of my experiences with different personalities and a question or two that you might answer for me.

The first vignette is about George. George fell deeply in love with a woman who seemed to be a devoted daughter. Her mother had a postpartum psychosis after one of her brothers was born and remained mentally deranged for the rest of her life. The woman took wonderful care of her mother and loved her father dearly; she pleased him constantly. Her brothers insisted that she was the best sister anyone could have. George found her to be sweet and affectionate. She projected an adorable disposition. He married her. From the very beginning, starting with the wedding night, he noticed she wasn't exactly the person he thought she was. The marriage produced two children. After a few years of dealing with her stubbornness and irrationality, she became impossible, and as George described it she acted *like a demon*. They divorced. During and after the divorce she was vindictive, cruel, irrational, and destructive. What kind of personality did this woman really have? She displayed two very different expressions of character. Which was the real one? Or, did she have more than one personality?

For my second example, I'd like to tell you about a 40-year-old, distinguished radiologist, who worked at a major medical center and enjoyed an excellent reputation. His manners were refined - always ready to help others, sensitive about human suffering, charming, and engaged in conversation with a great sense of humor. One day, I asked him, *"John, I've been seeing you at the hospital for quite a while, and I marvel at your attitude and disposition toward people. You're so nice, so warm, and so special. What happened in your life that led you to be such a noble human being?"* He replied, *"Ed, please follow me. I'll answer your question, but we need more privacy."* After making sure that nobody was around, he told me, *"Ed, I think you're a fine man, and I appreciate very much all the praise you have for me. However, I want you to know that you're wrong. I consider myself a bitter, obnoxious man, quite insensitive about a number of things and not very loyal. What you've been seeing is a total camouflage of my real personality. Why do I act so well when I'm so bad? I'll tell you: I do it because I'm weak and need others to adulate me, to tell me how wonderful I am. Since my real personality would never inspire that, I decided to act as a perfect gentleman. What's the result? People respect me and most of them, even like me."*

My third example is about Albert. Albert was a 20-year-old man who presented to me because of chest pains that had nothing to do with his heart. He had a distinguished physical appearance. His hair was well done and his beard trimmed to perfection. He wore a fine suit with a beautiful tie and gave the impression of being an interesting and amiable personality. He told me that he was studying law at the University of Miami. We communicated very well and after dealing with the medical issues, we engaged in conversations about history, politics, and other subjects.

A day later, his parents, who were my regular patients, came to the office for a routine follow-up visit. They were very pleasant, family-devoted, and had three sons and two daughters. I took the opportunity to congratulate them for the wonderful son they had. Both parents assured me that the young man was not the kind of person I thought he was. The father said to me, *"This young man is a regular cocaine and alcohol abuser, obnoxious, offensive, insensitive, abusive, and a notorious liar. He told you that he's studying law? This is one of his typical lies. Since childhood, he was the black sheep of the family, always tyrannical, domineering, and disruptive."* One of his sisters, who I had also seen as a patient, confirmed to me that her parents and all her siblings, except Albert, were normal, pleasant, and lovely. She told me that Albert had always been *the most erratic, insolent, and manipulative person you ever saw.*

In the book, *Multimodal Behavior Therapy,* by Arnold Lazarus, he discussed the question, *Why do people behave as they do?* His discussion of personality issues intrigued me. I always had trouble defining personality, and it seems I wasn't the only one. In his book, Arnold

Lazarus mentioned that Gordon Allport listed 50 different definitions of personality. Even today, the term has different abstract meanings, such as one's popular appeal, one's outward appearance (as distinct from how one really is), one's style of life, one's characteristic adjustment to environmental conditions, and so forth. Later on in that chapter he said, *"The term personality is employed as an abstraction to express these regularities and continuities of behavior."*

At a personal level, I've been fooled numerous times and believed that Albert had a certain personality. Later on, I was proved wrong.

It seems that the person who is best positioned to understand a subject's personality is the psychotherapist, who has the opportunity to analyze an individual's mind in depth. However, most people are not psychotherapists and do not have the time, the opportunity, or the knowledge to proceed with a mind exploration of that sort.

Using the examples I provided at the beginning of this conversation, I concluded that one cannot reliably identify a personality based upon what an individual thinks, says, or does. What they think, we do not know, what they say may mean something very different from what they intend to do. Moreover, what a person does might be the expression of a manipulative idea that perfectly disguises deep-seated, sinister intentions.

I admit that more often than not, I do not know whom I am dealing with. I try to solve the problem by not trusting people implicitly or believing everything I hear or see. I do not have to believe that a nice person is as nice as he or she looks or sounds. A gradual, progressive testing of an individual's personality and the accumulation and verification of what he or she says and does, seems a more reliable methodology and proves itself to work better, at least, for me.

Howard, I'd appreciate your opinion about personality and what is the best way to get to know people and learn how to deal with them, if that is at all possible.

Dr. Paul: Ed, you are in very good company regarding your curiosity about the concept of personality. The founders of modern medicine, first Hippocrates at about 450 BC and then Galen at about 150 AD, delved into this issue. They developed the notion of humors and categorized people into groupings:

Groupings of Humors	Humors Associated With	Body Fluids That Account for Humors	Corresponding Traits
Choleric	Irritable	Yellow Bile	Agreeable
Melancholic	Depressed	Black Bile	Neurotic
Sanguine	Optimistic	Blood	Open to Experience
Phlegmatic	Calm	Phlegm	Neurotic

Much later, in the 1940s, William Sheldon developed his theory of somatotypes - separating people into body types of endomorphic, mesomorphic, and ectomorphic. The somatotypes were taken from Ayurvedic Doshas, stemming from Indian medicine. Vata equated to the ectomorphic slender shape, and Pita equated to the mesomorphic shape that represented individuals of medium build, who were strong and had endurance. Kapha equated to the endomorphic build that had a tendency toward being overweight. Different personality styles were attributed to each of these different categories.

Jung described four typologies of personality traits and arranged them along dimensions of introversion–extroversion - those who rely on intuition and those who rely on observation, those who rely on thinking as opposed to those who rely on feeling, and those who tend to set schedules and be organized versus those who tend to leave their options open and simply see what happens.

Dr. Chapunoff: Howard, where does the word temperament fit into the broader concept of personality?

Dr. Paul: Temperament is another word that is a part of personality as it relates to an innate, genetically influenced propensity to behave in certain ways.

Dr. Chapunoff: I presume that genetically induced, temperamental markers may be detected in the very early stages of our lives.

Dr. Paul: That is true, Ed. Differences in the ease with which babies are aroused and soothed can be seen as early as infancy. There are infants who cry intensely and do not soothe easily; there are infants who are not easily distressed and do not cry much, yet they do not soothe easily; and there are infants who are minimally distressed, cry infrequently, and are easily soothed. Some infants become alert and active when they are presented with new stimuli that are not painful or frustrating, while others will cry or remain motionless. Since these differences are present at birth, it is clear that there is a genetic component to our reactivity.

Dr. Chapunoff: It seems apparent that both genetic and environmental factors influence personality. I guess that it would be a more challenging issue to estimate which of these two factors is the more powerful to shape an individual's temperament and personality.

Dr. Paul: In the ongoing battle over which is preeminent, nature or nurture, the real answer is – it's a tie!

Dr. Chapunoff: Why do people show marked behavioral changes and inconsistent behavioral patterns?

Dr. Paul: Ed, I would like to introduce another concept I think might be helpful in explaining the dilemma of personality. There are two viewpoints people take when trying to understand personality: the single person framework versus the two-person framework. If you and I are speaking, and I am acting as if my presence in the room has no influence over you, and what you do simply emerges from your personality, your learning, and your habits, then I am adopting a single-person framework. In a two-person framework, I work under the assumption that my presence in the room has an effect on your behavior, and the transactions that occur between us are influenced, not only by internal learning (personality), but also by my reactions to you. This reciprocal, transpersonal, and interactive conceptualization greatly expands our understanding of why people are not universally consistent in their behavior and why behavioral differences emerge, given different settings and circumstances.

Dr. Chapunoff: Howard, if I ask you to define personality with a few words, what would you say?

Dr. Paul: Personality represents the sum total of the reactive style we were born with, plus all that we have learned about how to behave.

Dr. Chapunoff: I like your definition. It's very precise!

Dr. Paul: One would suspect that as you get deeper into the exploration of an individual's mind, you will learn more about their personality, to the point that what you find at the surface will turn out to be totally different from what you discover at the bottom. With the one-person framework, personality is seen in what has been termed an archaeological fashion, where at the top of a person's mind are superficial behaviors and traits, and as we dig down, we unearth more and more important and core structures. With a two-person framework, this conceptualization gives way to thinking that people can have more than one way of reacting, depending upon the circumstances that surround them and the way people are reacting to them. To my way of thinking, the two-person framework gives a much more realistic view of how things really operate.

Dr. Chapunoff: I guess that sometimes, when people adopt and put into practice different behavior and personality changes, they may be operating under the umbrella of the multiple personality disorder (MPD).

Dr. Paul: That is true, Ed. It is also called, dissociative identity disorder (DID). In this disturbance, people can have multiple selves.

Dr. Chapunoff: This is disturbing, Howard, because quite often you really don't know what sort of individual you are dealing with.

Dr. Paul: It is not always easy to know the personality of the people we know or the people who we think we know. While the monolithic way of looking at personality is called archaeological, the more modern conceptualization is called dissociative. We do have more than one way of behaving, reflecting the notion that personality is not singular. This is different from the notion of DID that I just mentioned. DID is pathological, while seeing personality as transactional is not.

Dr. Chapunoff: You mentioned that those who have a MPD have multiple selves. How do you know which one is the true one?

Dr. Paul: Ed, they are all true. Earlier, in one of your examples, you posed the conundrum that you can only know what people do, but not what they think.

Dr. Chapunoff: The more I talk to you and to myself, the more convinced I am that statement is indisputably correct! What people say or even what people think seems to have little value in getting to know a person. There's no substitute for objective reality.

Dr. Paul: That is true. The reality is that what people do is paramount. Even our past President Jimmy Carter joked that he had *"lust in my heart!"*

Dr. Chapunoff: I remember Jimmy Carter's incident. He smiled when he said that, but I believe he was truthful when he admitted he had *"lust in my heart."* I also remember he said, *"This is part of being human."* He was more serious when he said these last words.

Dr. Paul: What we think is of secondary importance compared to what we actually do, although, how we think does significantly affect what we do. Everyone, at one time or another has negative thoughts, while they're doing something positive. Judge people by what they do, period.

Dr. Chapunoff: I love that conclusion!

Dr. Paul: There are too many people that feel guilty or ashamed, while they are busy leading a positive and good life. They harbor negative thoughts. Thoughts are just that - thoughts. Actions do speak louder than words or thoughts, as the case may be.

Dr. Chapunoff: I don't believe there is anyone in this world better positioned to know an individual's personality than a psychotherapist. I'd like to know if people could fool you as much as they can fool me.

Dr. Paul: Ed, many people have notions similar to yours and believe that by virtue of our training, psychologists have x-ray eyes and can see deeply into people's psyche and have a better than normal understanding of someone's personality. It is one of the reasons that when people become aware that I am a psychologist, they begin to worry about what they are saying, believing that it will be analyzed and that I will somehow *know* something about them that they would prefer to remain secret. This is a popularly held notion, but it is not true. Personally, I can think of no better way to mess up friendships than to always be working and not simply accept people as they present themselves. As to being fooled, if psychologists are to have a positive rapport with their patients, it is important that they extend a certain amount of trust and act as if what they hear is true or at least is believed by the person saying it. I can only see the world through the eyes of my patients, and I am just as vulnerable to being fooled as the next person.

Dr. Chapunoff: That is very interesting!

Dr. Paul: One other issue that makes knowing someone's personality difficult is that I do not believe we have a singular personality that is so overarching that it defines behavior under all circumstances. When people come to me and say they wish to find their true self, I tell them it will be a fool's journey, in that they must look to find their many selves and the situations that bring them to the fore. Then it is important to decide which ones they wish to support and which ones they need to be mindful of and allow less access to people around them.

I tell people that who they are is of less importance than who they wish to be.

We spend time defining values and then try to let values lead choices and behaviors. I am more interested in what people wish to be, and I work to help them become that person.

Personality is defined by what is inside of us, but it is also influenced by what is happening outside of us. Personality is part personal, but also part transpersonal, and it is controlled by external stimuli. A good example of how external stimuli influence our behavior is the marital couple, who when at home fight bitterly and have difficulty being in the same room with each other. Some couples, when they are away on vacation, are able to spend a glorious week with each other with little distress and little negativity happening between them. Often, within a few minutes of arriving home, they will be back behaving as if they had never left.

As learning organisms, we are influenced by consequences, and we are also influenced by setting circumstances and other relevant external conditions.

Dr. Chapunoff: When we interact with people we know, we show some features of our personality that are different from those we display when we have exchanges with individuals we do not know.

Dr. Paul: That is correct. When we meet new people we wish to influence, we often behave in ways different from how we behave when we are with our close friends. People may behave one way in their church, temple, mosque, or synagogue and in a very different way when they are in a social club or professional organization. Most of the time, these differences are small and benign, but in some cases they can be of larger proportion. Often, how secure or insecure we are has an influential role in determining these differences.

Earlier we discussed honesty and lying. I explained that one form of lying is meant to self-aggrandize and makes the person telling the mistruths feel better in their own eyes. In your last example involving the wayward son, there is little doubt that this individual had enough insecurity that he felt the need to present himself as someone other than whom he feared he really was. One problem with lying is that the more we do it, the more we become comfortable doing it. Ultimately, the line between truth and lie becomes blurred in the person's mind.

Dr. Chapunoff: This young man would be defined as a pathological liar, right?

Dr. Paul: Yes, Ed, you might call him that. However, doing so tends to blur the dynamics behind such behavior, and it is a blame statement. I prefer not to call people names, even if it is a diagnosis, and deal with the behaviors.

In the example of your physician colleague, there is every probability that this individual had a poor self-image, and he was unable to see that if he behaved in a kind, charitable, and equitable fashion toward everyone, that _was_ real. Seeing himself positively probably created a dissonance between his real way of acting and his distorted, internal, damaged belief about himself. His overt actions represented a truth about himself, but due to whatever circumstance injured his psyche, he clung to a distorted and negative image of himself.

Dr. Chapunoff: I think you're right about what you said about the radiologist. I truly thought he was more of the good man he projected than the bad guy he believed he was.

Dr. Paul: Your first example of the woman who did an apparent flip-flop when she became married and changed from a kind and caring person to a driven and demanding shrew, would require more information to accurately take a guess at what went on there. I would certainly wish to explore what her mother was like and whether some of these behaviors were taught to her as a child, representing the model she learned about how mothers are supposed to act. When she was dating and before her marriage, she acted according to the sweetheart role she had come to believe was correct. After she became married, she probably switched into her mother role, portraying the behaviors she believed appropriate for that new role.

While I tend to try to make things simple in my explanations, seeing personality as a more dynamic, interactive, and contextual process gives more clarity to this sometimes perplexing issue.

Dr. Chapunoff: Howard, I don't think that anyone could have explained the personality challenge better than you did. Getting to know the intricacies of the human mind may be an impossible task, even for a psychologist of your caliber. Observing a person's actions appears to be a far easier proposition.

13

RAPE AND INCEST

Dr. Chapunoff: Susan is a 50-year-old, American woman of Italian extraction. She was in the US Army for a number of years, and now she is a disabled veteran. Her past, traumatic experiences led her to a life of seclusion. She told me that she *never* leaves her apartment, except to see her psychiatrist and her cardiologist. When she was a teenager, her boyfriend wanted to have sex with her; it would have been her first time. She resisted, and he then had violent intercourse with her against her will. The act was painful, and he bruised her while forcing himself on her.

A few years later she married, had two daughters and soon after got a divorce. She remarried, and years later learned that the girls' stepfather had been having regular sexual encounters with both of them. She divorced him. To Susan's dismay, when her daughters reached adulthood they continued to have sex with their stepfather. Gifts went regularly from the girls to their stepfather on his birthday and other celebrations. He in turn, lavishly reciprocated. The trio seemed to have a ball with their relationship, including their intimate experiences. The girls *love him*, Susan told me.

While in the US Army, Susan was again raped. Her ex-husband (the girls' lover) threatened to kill her. He belonged to a Mafia family. I asked her if she lived in fear. She said, *"Not at all."* I next inquired, *"Why are you not afraid if you have a death threat like that?"* She told me, *"I'm fine and secure. I also belong to a Mafiosi family, and he was told that if something happens to me, he's a dead man. So, trust me, that SOB won't do anything to me!"* This is obviously a complex case because Susan was raped twice, and her daughters had long-lasting sexual relations with her husband, while she was married to him and after they were divorced. She told me, *"I would not even think about having any kind of relationship with any man. I also had a reaction against human beings in general.*" She thought, "*We live in a rotten world.*"

I'd like to ask your thoughts about this disturbing case and how you might deal with it. Also, I would like to know how you deal with cases of rape and incest.

In the case I just described, the man who had sex with the two girls was their stepfather. I've been aware of situations where the biological father had sex with his own biological daughter for several years; the girl's mother knew about it and never did anything to stop it.

Dr. Paul: Ed, unfortunately, you are correct, "We live in a messy world." It is amazing to me that in a world with so much love and beauty, there can also be so much pain, depravity, and suffering. The world is full of polarities, and as the song goes, you can't have one without the other. Rape is a sexual crime that has far more to do with power and abuse and nothing to do with anything intimate. In reality, it's an assault, a sexual assault. When sex is consensual it can be beautiful, intimate, and a sublimely positive experience. Within the context of an assault, it is none of these. Instead it is too often painful, psychologically hurtful, demeaning, and traumatic.

Ed, when you discussed this case, you mentioned that the act was painful and resulted in bruising. You also noted that it led to the development of clear, psychologically traumatic overtones that resulted in a complete agoraphobic condition where Susan feared leaving her home. She told you that she never left her apartment, except for specific medical appointments.

Dr. Chapunoff: When you approach a psychological evaluation and therapy of a rape victim like Susan, who was raped twice, I presume you have to deal with the rape episodes and the additional damage these actions produced.

Dr. Paul: That's true, Ed. I would begin (but not necessarily in the order presented here) by treating the trauma of the first sexual assault, as well as the second rape, the emerging distrust of men in relationships, and then her escape into the perceived safety of staying at home. Any time anyone tries to diminish fear with avoidance, as is clearly the case here, problems will typically grow, rather than become resolved.

Dr. Chapunoff: Howard, when you take into consideration the number of psychological and emotional wounds Susan sustained that resulted from the rape episodes, where would you first focus your attention when treating her?

Dr. Paul: In Susan's case, I would start with her avoidance of life, as it may be the easiest of all the components to address here.

Dr. Chapunoff: This type of isolation seems to be the result of an intense fear. Am I correct in assuming that?

Dr. Paul: Yes, Ed, you are, and the best treatment for fear that I can offer Susan is to assist her in facing it by getting her to be more comfortable with regularly leaving her apartment; adding *life* to her life would most likely be an initial goal. I might also speak to her about what she misses and what are the things she wishes to add back into her life. I would work with her to create a hierarchy, encourage her to organize her motivation, and begin to re-experience living.

Dr. Chapunoff: If she shows some positive response to that, what would you do next?

Dr. Paul: When some success is achieved and we establish a positive and comfortable rapport, I will begin to explore with her the meaning and effects of her first and second rapes; you mentioned that the second one occurred when she was in the US Army. In reality, I have no idea how this will unfold. Do you have a guess?

Dr. Chapunoff: No, Howard, I don't.

Dr. Paul: The person sitting in front of me will have significant input into my understanding of how things unfolded.

Dr. Chapunoff: The personal rapport between patient and therapist is always important, but in cases of rape like this one, I think that good chemistry and trust between patient and psychotherapist is important!

Dr. Paul: That's true, Ed. I can honestly say that establishing a good therapeutic relationship would be my primary goal, no matter what topics we decided to approach first. It is my belief that if Susan and I were able to begin with definable and achievable behavioral goals, our working relationship will be solidified. Dealing with more emotionally laden, potentially painful, and important material will then go a bit more easily.

Before I progress any further with my management of rape, I would like to talk a little bit about rape itself. Rape involves sexual intercourse that is not consensual and is both aversive and coercive. It is illegal, and it is about power, control, possession, and self-satisfaction, where little concern exists for the well-being, either physical or psychological, of the other person.

Dr. Chapunoff: What is the legal definition of rape? Can a husband be accused of raping his wife?

Dr. Paul: The legal definition of rape has changed over the years as society's view of it has matured and altered. Historically, and up until recently, a husband could never be convicted of raping his wife. The way rape was viewed began to change in the 1970s from involving only a man against a woman. By early 2000, the definition was modified to involve any forced sexual contact with penetration between any two people, not only a man and woman.

Dr. Chapunoff: A woman can rape a man too.

Dr. Paul: Yes, indeed, although it is far less probable. In today's understanding, it is possible for a woman to rape a man, as well as a man to rape a woman. How is that for equality? It is difficult to get real data on rape frequency because historically, it is underreported.

Dr. Chapunoff: I'm sure embarrassment is one reason that explains the underreporting of this crime. Are there other reasons?

Dr. Paul: Underreporting may be related to the cold, often blame-based and embarrassing way women were and in many places still are treated when they report being raped. Women are often made to spend long hours in an unsupportive, sterile hospital emergency room with no privacy and little real concern shown for their emotional well-being. In more recent years, specially trained nurses became available in newly created hospital interview facilities existing only in some locations to help make this a less onerous process for the rape victim.

Dr. Chapunoff: Howard, what is the estimated frequency of rape?

Dr. Paul: Statistically, some studies indicate that almost one out of every six women may have been either raped or subjected to attempted rape. According to studies in certain countries, the reporting of frequency of rape varies significantly. Lesotho has the highest reported frequency of rape; Sweden and New Zealand come in second and third, and Belgium and the United States share the honor of being almost tied for fourth and fifth. Muslim countries have the lowest reported frequencies of rape. These statistics come from data garnered by the United Nations. There is no cultural commentary given as to why these differences exist.

Dr. Chapunoff: What does a person do to attempt the recovery from rape? It is such a terrible ordeal!

Dr. Paul: Yes, Ed, it is not easy, to be sure. To answer your question, I would like to introduce the concept of resilience that is very important when dealing with any trauma, even rape. It was believed that no one could survive being raped without being traumatized, and those raped would have lasting psychological scars. The reality is that only one out of four individuals experiencing trauma, including rape, have significant negative alterations to their adjustment. Current psychological research has identified key elements of resilience that increase the likelihood of people surviving trauma and coming out of it with minimal or no damage.

Dr. Chapunoff: Howard, please give us a psychologist's definition of resilience?

Dr. Paul: Resilience is the capacity to withstand stress without acquiring mental illness or a persistent negative mood. It is a person's psychological capacity to withstand duress, even when it is significant, such as rape.

Dr. Chapunoff: What is the anatomy of resilience? In other words, what is resilience made of?

Dr. Paul: The components of resilience include good coping skills, strong attachments, a can-do attitude, optimism, the ability to take multiple perspectives, a good ability to control anger, a long fuse as it relates to frustration, a limited sense of entitlement, positive relationships leading to a strong and present support group, and a strong, positive work ethic.

Dr. Chapunoff: Howard, please tell us what you mean by a limited sense of entitlement. Does this refer to the reduced expectation of help or assistance that others can provide to the victim?

Dr. Paul: Yes, it does Ed, but it means even more. People with a sense of entitlement believe they are due nurturance, revenge or compensation for their pain. They tend to believe that it is someone else's responsibility to take care of them and make up for their pain. People with a more limited sense of entitlement look internally for management. They rely on their own strengths and do not expect rescue. Their ideation is more self-reliant. I'm sure you can understand how exploring with individuals their own elements of resilience and working with them on enhancing attitude and coping skills can be a powerful tool when working with trauma, especially rape.

Let me recap the key treatment elements I would probably follow in a case such as Susans. I would try to:

A) Establish a caring, safe, supportive, and understanding therapeutic relationship

B) Understand the circumstances, meaning, and impact of both the first and second rapes

C) Explore the person's strengths, as well as their vulnerabilities

D) Enhance coping skills, optimism, and a positive attitude, as well as deal with rage, both directed at the rapist and, even more importantly, against the self

Dr. Chapunoff: In cases of rape that carry disabling emotional scars, how can a person assemble the pieces of a broken soul and hope to find life meaningful again?

Dr. Paul: Something I work toward is putting *life* back into a woman's life after such trauma. In this particular example, one most important area to delve into is exploring whether this woman is ready to take the enormous risk of trusting others.

I would like to shift gears and move on to your example of the woman whose children were having an ongoing incestuous relationship with their stepfather. Incest is a taboo that typically leads people to have horrific and gut-wrenching reactions to the very thought of it; sex with a close relative!

Dr. Chapunoff: Yes, just the mention of it generates great repulsion!

Dr. Paul: Incest is universally prohibited. When anthropologists study cultures around the world, incest is one of the very few prohibitions found in almost every culture going back to the dawn of humanity.

Dr. Chapunoff: Incest appears to be nearly always a form of child abuse.

Dr. Paul: Absolutely! Today, incest is considered the most heinous form of child abuse. It is typically done coercively. Until recently, when children brought forth complaints of sexual molestation and incest, they were disbelieved and often blamed or ignored. When the incidence of child sexual molestation by relatives is studied, some researchers come up with the shocking figure depending on the research you are reading that it can occur to almost 25 percent to 60 percent of all girls and 20 percent to 45 percent of all boys!

Dr. Chapunoff: Frankly Howard, I would never have imagined that the statistics on incest were so impressive and this kind of crime so prevalent. What's the average age of the victimized children?

Dr. Paul: Research reports that most abuse occurs when children are quite young under seven years of age and often when they are three or four years of age. With girls, uncles account for 25 percent of the incidence of incest, fathers 15 percent, brothers 10 percent, and stepfathers eight percent. Other studies report sibling incest occurring at a rate equal to or higher than all other instances and note that it is occasionally consensual and seen as part of adolescent exploration.

As is usually the case, trauma, even incest, causes damage when it is coercive. In cases where it is non-coercive, children often emerge unscathed.

Dr. Chapunoff: I find it intriguing what you just said about the incidence of sibling incest. That should give parents a cautionary message.

Dr. Paul: The amount of sibling sexual activity is much higher than most people would like to admit.

Dr. Chapunoff: Howard, what can you tell us about the incidence of adult-child incest in non-Western civilizations?

Dr. Paul: In Middle Eastern and far eastern cultures, incidence rates of adult-child incest are much higher. Unfortunately, like so many of the other issues we are speaking about, people can convince themselves that almost anything is legitimate, and they inure themselves to almost any negative consequence. In part, this skill is utilitarian. Physicians and surgeons learn to be nonreactive to gore, undertakers learn to be unfazed by dead bodies, honey dippers (septic tank cleaners) learn to see what they do as sweet, and porn stars come to see what they do without guilt or anxiety; they see their activities as a profession done without embarrassment.

Ed, in the particular case of incest you mentioned, the girls apparently came to believe that the payoff of their behavior (remember, stepfather was the Candy Man, who showered them with gifts), coupled with the fact that there may have actually been genuine, positive affection between the partners, overcame any learned societal objections to their behavior. Clearly, without speaking to any of the individuals involved, what I am saying here is speculative. Could there have been psychological wounds that came from these acts? Certainly! However, similarly, individuals can, and often do, reframe their negative behavior in such a way that it becomes acceptable to them and causes no psychological duress.

Many muggers have little remorse after they beat someone and take money from the person they assaulted. Too many people engage in cruel acts with little remorse. As with so many things that are psychological, people get used to accepting as okay their own behaviors that are outside of the mainstream of society and are viewed by most as unacceptable.

14

POSTTRAUMATIC STRESS DISORDER
It wasn't the killing that bothered me so much, but the laughing

Dr. Chapunoff: I was interviewing a 30-year-old veteran, who fought in the Gulf War in Iraq. From the outset of our meeting, he was crying, and he didn't stop until the interview was over. He came to me for medical reasons, but his depression was so severe that we first had to talk about it. When he was in the Gulf War, he belonged to a tank division. While in the Iraqi desert, he and his crew drove their tank over bodies, some were dead, but some were alive. He and the tank crew burned the bodies to death with the tank flame-thrower.

To try to help him relieve his torment from the war experience, I told him that cruel and terrible things happen in wars and that in a way, he was another victim of the ordeal. Up until this point in our conversation, everything was awful but understandable. However, there was something else. He laughed his head off as his tank kept running over the bodies of enemy soldiers and converting them into human torches. I asked him why he laughed when he saw people suffering so much. He said that he saw what the enemy did to prisoners - the tortures and the killing - and he wanted to seek revenge. He took revenge all right, but he felt so guilty about his own laughing and celebrating of his victims' torment that he suffered a major depression that caused him to be disabled at the age of 27.

Howard, in cases like this, of severe posttraumatic stress disorder (PTSD), is there any chance of significant improvement with long-term therapy? Or, does the outlook for rehabilitation remain dismally poor?

I dealt with many war veterans and saw plenty of them suffering permanent disability. The psychiatrists had a hard time trying to keep them under control. Some of these veterans told me directly that they wanted to shoot people that they did not even know from their apartment balcony. Their wives had to step in to change the direction of the rifle and then take them quickly to the nearest Veterans Administration (VA) facility. The veteran we are speaking about in this example was one of them. I asked him, *"Johnny, why did you want to shoot innocent people from your balcony?"* He answered, *"We are all guilty."*

Dr. Paul: Ed, there is a bumper sticker that simply says; *"War is not healthy for children and other living things."* As is sadly exemplified by your example, this bumper sticker is true, even for trained combat troops. In a previous discussion, I outlined the definition and criteria needed for one to be diagnosed with PTSD. Your example clearly highlights PTSD, but also poignantly details how debilitating and devastating it can be, both for the sufferer and for the community at large.

You ask if significant cases of PTSD can be treated, or is the sufferer relegated to a life of pain? The clear answer is, yes, people with PTSD can be helped. We may not be able to eliminate all of the effects of PTSD, but PTSD sufferers can often be returned to a more functional life.

Trauma can create permanent changes in the way our brain works. The trauma does not have to be as devastating as the one you identified and can be something as simple as being bitten by a dog, being mugged, or being in a car accident. It's as if we are all born surrounded by a bubble of invulnerability that protects us and helps to keep us calm and less anxious. When something breaks that bubble, indelible changes occur within us that, at some level, and are irreversible.

I treat many people who have been traumatized, and they do successful work to reduce their anxieties and diminish their tendency to avoid and withdraw. When treatment with me is complete, they will be significantly more functional, even though there may always be residuals. By the way, the bubble of invulnerability and invincibility is only issued once in life. Once ruptured, it's gone forever. I may be making things seem overly bleak. However, it's very possible to help people reduce their anxious reactivity, so they can return to a more fulfilling and enriching life. I am saying, however, that often it is not possible to get back to 100 percent, but we may get very close.

HOWARD PAUL, PhD, ABPP, FAClinP and EDUARDO CHAPUNOFF, MD, FACP, FACC

There is an interesting procedure, Eye Movement Desensitization Reprocessing (EMDR), that has proven to be helpful in some instances of PTSD. About 25 years ago, I received a manuscript to review for a professional journal. In psychology, as in medicine and many other professions, there are journals that do a blind review of all articles submitted. These articles are sent to experts in the professional field for review and comment, including a determination of their worthiness of publication. The reviewer is not told who the author of the article is or who initially performed the study and the submitter of the article is not told who the reviewer is. One particular article I opened had the authors' names blanked out, as was the rule at the time. I read the study and remember thinking that it was unique and unusual, as well as somewhat *outside-the-box*. The section on procedures noted the following: If you work with someone with PTSD, sit in front of the person, have the person stare at your finger tip that is held approximately 12 to 18 inches in front of their eyes, and then wave your finger back and forth while the person tries to vividly imagine one of the scenes that causes them repulsion and fear. At the time, this suggestion seemed rather strange and a bit preposterous to me. As fate would have it, my next patient was a Vietnam veteran who presented with PTSD. Since I had just read the manuscript, I proceeded to go through the entire suggested procedure (only one particular highlight of it is mentioned above). At the end of the session, this man was much relieved and reported that his dread and sense of panic was significantly reduced. I saw him a few more times during which I repeated the procedure. It produced a rather dramatic positive change, leading to a significant increase in his comfort level. At that point, I suggested that the manuscript be published! This EMDR procedure is now widely used, even if the particular neurological mechanisms behind its effectiveness are not well understood. One part of the effectiveness of the procedure rests with exposing the person to fearful images; the other part of the procedure rests with the component that replaces images of fear with images of coping and efficacy.

Dr. Chapunoff: Howard, I find this to be amazing!

We just mentioned a case of PTSD in the military environment, but PTSD in the general population is not rare at all. Just living with the wrong mother-in-law can certainly cause it!

Dr. Paul: Ed, while this example represents PTSD emerging from the military, as you suggest, PTSD can be generated by all sorts of different traumas. It is actually a relatively common, psychiatric condition with estimates of those with PTSD reaching as high as 15 percent. This is a reflection of our uneasy world, with a troubling amount of potentially life-threatening and life-upsetting events. Some estimates note that *more than half* of all people have been exposed at least once, to some event traumatic enough to qualify for producing PTSD. Some events are more likely to create PTSD than others; torture leads the list.

Dr. Chapunoff: Your explanation reminds me of traumatic events I had over the course of my life. My military experience was one of them, but certainly not the only one. Three seconds ago, I concluded that I probably suffered, at one point or another, from some degree of PTSD. I hope that I managed to overcome it. I do not believe that most doctors think about the diagnosis of PTSD in the civilian population as often as they should. I suspect that many cases of depression and anxiety have the full spectrum of PTSD symptoms.

Dr. Paul: Ed, you are probably correct. PTSD estimates run as high as 30 percent, among those who have been involved in combat. The more someone is exposed to trauma, such as prolonged abuse or combat, the higher the likelihood that PTSD will emerge. Without treatment, PTSD can last quite a long time. Almost 50 percent of a sample of individuals with PTSD reported symptoms that occurred a few times a week and lasted for years. In about half of all people with PTSD, symptoms subside after about five years, but they are often replaced by depression, anxiety, substance abuse, or personality disorders. When one treats PTSD, it is important to discriminate between core PTSD symptoms and associated mood and anxiety problems, as well as other associated negative behaviors. PTSD is well studied and there is good evidence that both psychopharmacology and psychotherapy can make a positive impact. Two forms of cognitive behavioral therapy are recognized as effective for treating PTSD within the Veterans Administration, and they involve prolonged exposure and cognitive reprocessing.

The core of any effective PTSD treatment begins with establishing a positive rapport and a good therapeutic relationship with the patient.

From the technique standpoint, use of exposure, cognitive restructuring, stress-inoculation, skill building, and sometimes, EMDR are typical elements that make a constructive difference.

Dr. Chapunoff: Do you find a significant difference between the Gulf War veteran I presented to you and other cases of PTSD? Do you think that due to the nature of the severity of his war trauma, he belongs to a special PTSD category that poses a particularly difficult therapeutic challenge?

Dr. Paul: Ed, this particular example is set apart from most situations of PTSD. Rather than having life-threatening events happening to the person who develops the problem, this individual was directly involved in committing offenses, including immolation and probably murder. Because of these offenses, this individual was wracked with guilt, further compounding the effects of his PTSD. You do not mention whether or not he has ongoing nightmares and flashbacks. It would be necessary to do a careful diagnosis and make sure that this was PTSD and not a major depression because of his guilt and self-torment.

Dr. Chapunoff: Human cruelty exerted on a victim, sometimes ends with self-retribution and self-punishment. The guilt, depression, and terrible nightmares that some executioners suffer for the rest of their lives appear to corroborate that.

Dr. Paul: That is right, Ed. I previously noted that people can become immune or inured to cruelty. They can come to look at other human beings as the enemy - people who are considered less than human and less than worthy of compassion. With sufficient anger, the enemy can be seen as deserving of punishment and the angry person can come to see him or herself as being righteous and correct in their desire to punish and avenge.

Just as exposure and desensitization can be used to help people therapeutically reduce anxiety, exposure, in the wrong circumstances, can reduce anxieties to the point where people can inflict pain and behave in ways they would not behave under other circumstances.

Dr. Chapunoff: You mean the exposure and training that those serving in the military receive (techniques to fight and kill) can desensitize them and allow the warriors to do killing without remorse?

Dr. Paul: That is correct.

Dr. Chapunoff: What I find interesting about the killings and other atrocities seen during wars is that many people who commit them are truly good people.

Dr. Paul: That is right, Ed. This is not to make excuses for committing war crimes; it is an attempt to take a nonjudgmental look at the circumstances that can lead good people to do very bad things. There is little doubt, that through the twisted lens of war, people do things that they would never do under circumstances that are more normal. Exposure to war does lead to an alteration in normal anxiety, which protects them from killing and being cruel.

Dr. Chapunoff: What do you make of this veteran's laughter? Why did he laugh while he was killing his enemies?

Dr. Paul: I suspect that the laughter he described, that now haunts him, represented not only his desire for revenge, but the residual anxiety he felt when he was encouraged to behave in ways that he knew were wrong.

Dr. Chapunoff: Do you mean to tell me that anxious people laugh when they have a bout of anxiety?

Dr. Paul: Yes Ed, people often laugh when anxious, and there is every probability that the veteran's laughter represented his inability to quell fully his own aversion to what he was doing.

Dr. Chapunoff: You see, I could never have figured that out without the help of a good psychologist!

Dr. Paul: Managing this case would have a moral-ethical component. I would not be sitting in judgment over this person's behavior, but helping him explore his own values within the circumstance of war and now. In many of our discussions, Ed, I will return to the same basic themes I discussed earlier to explain the processes provoking your questions and curiosities. You mention here that this person was very guilty. Guilt is a way individuals have of being angry and wishing to punish themselves. Behind guilt, there is always a core of anger. It may be interesting to explore this area, assisting this individual to recognize the absolutes he was using without regards to circumstance or the particular context, which led to his self-hatred. Clearly, it would have been better had he not committed these acts, but he did. Freeing him from this anger might put him in touch with sorrow and remorse. It may also enable him to explore areas of restitution or other acts that will have a positive, prosocial effect on both him and the families of those he fears he victimized.

When people err, two mutually exclusive things ensue:

1) Learning and associated growth

2) Punishment, suffering, and pain, which can often be very chronic

The soldier was right - we all are guilty. We all are guilty of being human and we all have the foibles that go along with that. His statement, *"We are all guilty,"* shows a lack of acceptance that serves to damn him, rather than to damn everyone else.

Dr. Chapunoff: Governments send people to war all the time, Howard. I am not being judgmental about the righteousness or incorrectness of these decisions, but I do wonder if veterans receive adequate preventive training to avoid or minimize PTSD. Do they receive the treatment and attention they deserve after returning from hell?

Dr. Paul: The lack of attention to PTSD in the military and to troops who have experienced combat, points out the sad state of affairs regarding the way psychological interventions take a back seat in public policy. There are far too many soldiers who have PTSD and far too few trained practitioners to deal with them. Too little money is put into effective postwar treatment, not only within the VA, but also throughout all of the mental health centers in the United States. One day, and let's hope our discussions contribute to it, people will put a higher priority on mental health services and be willing to develop public policy that supports it, rather than making it more difficult for people to obtain.

Managed care has made it a challenge for people to gain access to quality mental health treatment with behavioral health professionals. Unfortunately, the need for easily accessed mental health care is undervalued. In the example you mentioned above, the soldier was fortunate enough to have his wife push the gun barrel aside so that no one was killed or injured. Often there is no one there.

15

GREED AND THE
BERNARD MADOFF SYNDROME

Greed is like the universe: it seems to have no end

Dr. Chapunoff: Bernard Madoff's story is a recent one and is known by almost everybody in our society who reads the news.

This man was a multibillionaire who pleaded guilty to stealing huge amounts of money from people and organizations, some of them charitable, by taking their money and placing it in a Ponzi scheme. Some foreign countries invested so heavily in his scheme, that their ability to pay pensions and national benefits was seriously compromised.

His fraudulent scheme follows the typical Ponzi plan: Madoff pretends that the money given to him by his clients is invested in the stock market, but in reality it is not. The money is used for his own benefit and purposes. He promises substantial profits, so people are willing to invest more and more. He pays the nonexistent profits with money that keeps on arriving at his corporate quarters and falsely reports great profits, so many people think he is a financial genius. Because he pays well, clients feel he's the finest stockbroker in history.

Bernard Madoff practiced his Ponzi scheme for over two decades, making many millions with it. Investors had the delusion that their money was safe and that they were getting richer by the minute.

Wrong! On March 12, 2009, Madoff pleaded guilty to all federal charges filed against him: 11 felony counts, including securities fraud, money laundering, and perjury, which resulted in a prison sentence of 150 years.

The single most important factor that caused his scheme to collapse was the crash of the stock market. People became fearful of making further investments and wanted their money back. The requests for withdrawal came so quickly that Madoff was unable to proceed with the refunds. When it was obvious that he had no way out, he told his two sons that the entire operation was *a big lie,* and the next day his two boys reported him to the police. One of his two sons recently committed suicide.

Bernard Madoff's behavior qualifies him as the biggest swindler in the history of humanity. He ruined the lives of thousands because so many individuals and charitable corporations dealt with him personally and trusted him completely. Even some countries and many municipal governments invested heavily with him are now in dire financial straights. For far too many, their lifetime savings suffered a process of evaporation, as had never been seen before. His callous indifference to the suffering of so many people is beyond description.

Here is my question: How can a person be so greedy, so insensitive, and destructive? What is behind this sociopathic performance? Why did he act the way he did? Was he born with the wrong genes? Did he have a life experience in his childhood or adolescence that provoked this kind of behavior? Did his parents or other people do anything to him aberrant enough to create such a monster?

He was the master of greed. What makes a person who already earned billions pursue the gain of more billions?

Madoff knew how to spend money: he acquired the most luxurious items life can offer. However, there are multimillionaires who live comfortably, but without spending that much. Some of them seem to enjoy making money and not spending it.

I would also like to know, what is the best way to recognize greed in a very young person? How do parents uncover disguised sociopathic, manipulative, and selfish tendencies? In addition, most significantly, if this kind of behavior is detected early in a person's life, are there ways to modify it and prevent it from reaching a truly sociopathic level?

Dr. Paul: Ed, I am sure, as is the case with all of us, you can remember cartoons in which someone struggling with an issue is portrayed with the devil sitting on one shoulder and an angel sitting on the other, each trying to persuade the person to choose either the moral or amoral choice. Many different religions have tried to deal with this very same struggle. In Eastern religions there is yin and yang. Within Judaism, there is the concept of yetzer (pronounced yeah-tsir) that stands for tendencies within each of us to act in either good or evil ways. We are all thought to have yetzer tov, or good side and a yetzer ra, or dark side. I may have mentioned previously that one legitimate goal of all religions is to have our good side win out over our dark side.

The struggle between good and evil is as old as humanity itself. Metaphorically, much of what we watch on TV reflects this struggle. When I was growing up, I watched Westerns on TV. The good people wore white hats; the bad people wore black hats. In those more naïve days, good always won out over evil. The movie, "Star Wars," was one of the best Westerns I ever saw, with Darth Vader dressed all in black, epitomizing evil and Luke Skywalker, dressed in white, epitomizing good. By then, we were no longer so innocent, and even the force represented both the good and the dark side in all of us.

You ask if Bernie Madoff was born with the wrong genes. He was born with human genes, and the reality is he lost the struggle to the dark side. This is not a genetic issue; it is a human issue. We have this tendency to view pathology as somehow discreetly different from the norm. I do believe that it is wisest to see pathology as the end of a spectrum, rather than as something separate from what most normal people do.

Did Bernie Madoff's parents do something that so damaged him that he was relegated to his life of greed? When parents ask me what they did wrong, I wryly respond that they simply decided to have children.

I honestly cannot tell you about the parenting style used by Madoff's mother and father, but I hesitate to blame them for causing his greed. It is clear that Bernie Madoff never outgrew his childhood and never became a properly socialized, caring, and socially responsible human being.

It is the responsibility of all adults finally to outgrow their childhoods. I previously mentioned that this really means outgrowing being a two-year-old! (The *terrible twos* we discussed earlier.)

There are three crucial ideas that parents would best work on diligently to teach their children. Firstly, it is highly important that we all learn that we do not run the world, that things do not have to work out the way we want, that we cannot always win, and that we do not always have to have our own way or have everything that we like. These all really represent the same idea. Secondly, it is highly important that parents teach children that if we do not have our own way, do not win, or do not get exactly what we want, it is not catastrophic or terrible, only disappointing, frustrating, or irritating. Lastly, it is important to teach that we are capable of handling disappointment and that we all have within us the capacity to cope.

The next important lesson for us all to learn is that there is a difference between what we do (and what we have) and what we are. If you look at children in kindergarten, they often believe that if they are at the front of the line, then they are somehow the best and everyone behind them is of lesser value. The idea that our value is not related to our position in-line or in life, is unfortunately poorly taught and little embraced. If I win a race, it does not make me a better person than those behind me. It does make me a good racer, which gives me pleasure and a sense of accomplishment, but it truly does not add to my personal value or self worth. Those behind me in position are of equal value on a humanistic level.

When the founding fathers of the United States stated that, "all men are created equal," they were talking about the humanistic notion that simply being human makes us of equal value. They were not talking about contributing to society; they were talking about a philosophical ideal of equality. I am not changing the language used historically in order to be politically correct, and I am hoping that you and anyone reading this understand that there is no desire here to be sexist. The word, *men,* in "all men are created equal" is generic, and I am using it to refer to all people.

Bernie Madoff and far too many others like him, believe that the more they have the better and more important they are. They are often driven by a sense of superiority that all too frequently, is fueled by a hidden sense of inadequacy.

Greed is in all of us. At one time or another, we have all had difficulty sharing, we have all lost sight of the concept of charity, and we have all had difficulty playing well with others. If we are lucky, we outgrow these childish tendencies and move on to become mature adults with a good sense of community, who value and respect others.

Greed is simply one example of the failure of this kind of socialization. Many of the other discussions that we will have, or have had, reflect variants of this failure.

Ed, you ask if this kind of greed can be identified when children are young. The answer is, of course. Most parents are very sensitive to when their children are being greedy, are unable to share, and always put themselves first. There is a developmental component here in that all children go through these phases. Sadly, some have more trouble than others in outgrowing the phases. The best way for parents to teach children is to be good models for them. Parents need to demonstrate compassion, altruism, generosity, and actively teach the balance between taking care of yourself and taking care of others.

Hillel, one of the most famous ancient Jewish rabbis, developed the question, *"If I am only for myself, then what am I, but if I'm not for myself, who will be for me?"*

As is often the case, life reflects polarities. Life is about balance. In this case, the balance is between self-interest and respecting and caring for others. In Madoff's example, that balance was wildly distorted. He, no doubt, believed that the person with the most toys (or in this case, money) wins. He truly did not understand what makes someone a winner. To me, a loser is someone who believes that they must always win. Winners are those who understand that even if they lose, they are still worthy human beings.

Dr. Chapunoff: If what you are saying is true, and it does make sense, then Madoff had a sense of inadequacy. You have made that very clear. Can you explain to me what he was trying to prove?

Dr. Paul: Madoff was caught up in a lie. When we discussed lying, I noted that the two types of lies that are most disrespected are those that self-aggrandize and those that shirk responsibility or try to avoid punishment (or both).

In Madoff's case, both of these are underlying factors. If you try to prove that you are an okay person by what you do, you are bound to fail. Even if you have a great day and feel on top of the world, when you wake up the next morning, you are back to feeling no good and have to prove it all over again. If Madoff thought that money would make him feel adequate, no matter how much he made, every day he woke up, he would have to make more because of his warped sense of what adequacy truly represented.

Dr. Chapunoff: Does a great desire for power affect behaviors, such as Madoff's does?

Dr. Paul: People in situations, such as Madoff's, typically have a need for power and control. Money, unfortunately, does give people a false sense of power, which again is confused with a sense of self-worth.

Dr. Chapunoff: This is a very important concept: the fact that people who suffer from a sense of inadequacy try to feel adequate by achieving power explains the rise to power of many politicians and dictators.

Dr. Paul: Exactly! Bullies try to prove that they are superior by pushing people around. Power hungry people have the same internal mechanism - their own sense of inferiority is the driving force behind their quest for power.

Madoff was a financial bully. Making all that money fed his need for power and superiority. Since it was a fool's mission (trying to prove self-worth with money) it could never be enough. As is often the case with empires built on fraud, they ultimately collapse, leaving the person who craved fame, adoration, power, and control with the antithesis of that: spending the rest of their lives being reviled while losing everything.

Dr. Chapunoff: A while ago, you suggested that you were not inclined to blame Madoff's parents for his greed. However, is there anything that parents can do to prevent or minimize their child's greedy, toxic development?

Dr. Paul: While I do believe that it is not wise to blame parents for causing such debacles, good parenting can certainly help to decrease the odds that such a lack of human concern will occur. When good parenting has failed, the opportunity of being involved with peers who are positive role models, combined with a willingness to grow, can be very helpful. Strangely enough, crisis may be just what is needed to make a difference. If a greedy person suffers a major life-changing crisis, and this crisis causes enough pain, a window of opportunity often opens, leading to the possibility of change. People fear crises; however, they often are necessary to make a difference, when people have adopted self-defeating habits.

In one Eastern tradition, I believe that the written symbol for crisis is the combination of symbols for pain and opportunity. Sometimes, as I said, a crisis can be just what the doctor ordered, to activate the motivation to change entrenched negative behaviors.

Dr. Chapunoff: What do you think of people who produce great fortunes and spend very little money? What is behind that curious behavior?

Dr. Paul: In your introduction, you noted that some people with money, especially those born into it, are able to live comfortably without having to be extravagant or a show-off with their money. It may be that people who are new to having lots of money want to prove their adequacy by having the most and making sure everyone knows it. People born into money may not have this same desire or need.

Dr. Chapunoff: We keep on coming back to the issue of adequacy. Some people are desperate to show their adequacy, particularly when they believe that they do not have it. Inadequacy seems to be like a shadow that follows some people wherever they go. They go out of their way, often in destructive ways, to hide their fear of being identified as inadequate from the world.

Dr. Paul: Ed, that is exactly right. The notion that adequacy must be proved is behind so much psychopathology; greed is only one example. So many of the things that we will discuss, boil down to this same mechanism. All too commonly, a sense of personal inadequacy leads people to try to prove their worth. Since worth can never be proven, these strategies always fail.

Dr. Chapunoff: I find it to be quite remarkable that people who seek power or richness, repeatedly try to reach their objectives by using the same failed strategies and go through a lot of trouble in their attempts to get what they want.

Dr. Paul: Yes, Ed, they do. It is uniquely human that whenever strategies fail, what some people often do is simply try to repeat their failed strategies with more vigor! Greed, bullying, even anxiety and depression often boil down to people being unable to accept the notion that they are worthy simply because they are human.

Dr. Chapunoff: Howard, once again, you clearly answered my questions. The Madoff syndrome and the unspeakable suffering of so many of his victims that resulted from it left me with a heavy, dark cloud on top of my head! I am going for a bike ride. I need fresh air. I'll talk to you soon.

16

NONSURGICAL CASTRATION
Maternal Dependency that Lasts Forever

Dr. Chapunoff: Fred was a 45-year-old attorney who always loved his mother deeply. He had an excellent relationship with his father until he became 16. At that time, his father divorced his mother. His mother had a number of serious mental/emotional dysfunctions, as well as personality challenges, which included marked stubbornness, irrational ideas, poor judgment, and no capacity to accept self-criticism, corrections, or mistakes. Intellectually, she was a lightweight. She was also manipulative and vindictive. During and after the divorce, she began a never-ending campaign of character assassination targeting her ex-husband. Her audience for this smear campaign was not only her four children, but also the social and professional connections of her ex-espouse. She concocted a psychiatric diagnosis of bipolar disorder for her ex, the father of her children. He seemed to be a mentally normal man. One of her characteristic sentences offered for public consumption was, *"My husband had to be crazy to divorce a woman like me."* Twenty years later, she remained single, bitter, and frustrated. Her husband was the happiest man in the world with his second wife.

Fred always listened to his mother's marital grievances in detail but refused to do the same with his father, siding with his mother on everything. Their relationship was very good. After the divorce and during parties, Fred and his mother danced together. She would not dance with another man. He would not dance with another woman.

Until Fred was in his mid-30s he didn't have a steady relationship with any woman. He almost never had any intimate contact with women. He characteristically went out to parties with friends (couples in general), but he joined them alone. Nobody ever saw him accompanied by a girlfriend. By the age of 38, he engaged in what appeared to be a satisfactory relationship with a woman several years his senior. During this time, he refused to deal with his father's new wife. He did meet her once and agreed that she was *"a wonderful person,"* although he never wanted to see her or talk to her again because he felt he *"was being disloyal to his mother."* Fred's mother said to him that she would consider it *high treason* if Fred interacted with his father's new wife, ordering him never to see *that woman.* He gladly obliged. Fred's father felt deeply hurt and offended by this attitude. The father-son relationship deteriorated until it terminated a few years later.

Now, would you please help me with these questions?

In this case, is Fred a man psychologically castrated by his mother? That's my diagnosis, but I'm not a psychologist. He always showed ambivalent feelings of love and hate toward his father. The father perceived these feelings to be more about hate than love, although disguised and repressed.

Is it possible that Fred represents an Oedipus case? Can you give us some insight on this syndrome?

What is the prevalence of maternal castration cases that do not have the Oedipus' sexual components?

Would you tell us a bit about Oedipus and syndromes that are not, but bear a suspicious resemblance to it? I have seen men castrated by their mother on different occasions. They were told what to do with their unfortunate wives and they gladly, or grudgingly, invariably obliged. These men's marriages were total failures.

From a therapeutic standpoint and assuming that Fred was receptive to professional help, what would it take to deal with the stubborn resistance of an emotional umbilical cord that is so hard to cut?

Is there any way of detecting an ongoing process of maternal castration during childhood that might prevent or minimize the devastating effects during adulthood? What can one do to prevent the progression of a man's loss of character and independence from a mother who effectively controls it?

Dr. Paul: Ed, this is another sad but very interesting situation. You ask quite a number of very good questions, and I will do my best to answer them. Part of what makes this question interesting is that I suspect when you had your psychiatric rotation, you were trained within a Freudian/psychoanalytic model. As we previously discussed, I was trained within a behavioral and cognitive school and do not really think in terms of Oedipal complexes. I look more at issues of attachment, processes of individuation (even if it is a term developed by Jung), underlying belief systems, and modeled social behaviors.

As to whether or not Fred's behavior represented an Oedipal sexual attachment to his mother, my best answer is that it could be! However you look at this, it is very clear that Fred was damaged by an over-enmeshed relationship with his mother. He was never able to go through the proper process of individuation and maturation that would allow him to become his own person and then form attachments to others, as would be necessary for normal growing up.

Even though I do not normally use this frame of reference, I will take a minute and talk about the origins of the Oedipal complex. The term originally was used by Freud and taken from Sophocles' character Oedipus Rex. Oedipus, the king of Thebes, accidentally kills his father and marries his mother. The tragedy ends with Oedipus being banished after he blinds himself, in order to save the people of Thebes, who were being punished because of his transgressions. Freud believed males between the age of three and five secretly wish to possess their mother and kill their father, so he named this complex the Oedipal complex. Freud also believed that for a male to become a successful adult with a healthy identity, he must have some identification with a same-sex parent. We actually know that this is not true because boys who are adopted by a single woman or a gay female couple actually can grow up to be healthy individuals without a strong male role model. As to whether Fred really wished to possess his mother sexually, I would have to talk with him to be able to answer that particular part of your question. In addition, since this dynamic starts before the age of five, there is every chance that he would deny it, even if it were true!

You may be unaware of it, but there are some interesting sociological issues behind your question. Long before the time of Freud and up to the 70s and 80s, traditional families consisted of a stay-at-home mom and a father who could often be absent due to working. Then, most families only had one wage earner and one parent who primarily did child care, typically the mother. It was not unusual for mothers to be blamed for the psychopathology of their children. Autism is a good example, where the cause of autism was once felt to be the "refrigerator mom" or the mother who was cold, distant, and aloof. This notion has been soundly disproved, as it is very clear that warm, caring, and very involved mothers can still have a child with autism.

The notion of the castrating mother, which is to some extent explicit in your question, is another viewpoint to which modern social learning psychologists, and especially feminist psychologists, would take umbrage. Some men might joke, in order to mask their serious intent, that as feminism has strengthened, women have become more assertive and some would say, castrating. Many men have become intimidated and do not like this newer state of affairs and, pejoratively, have returned to using the castrating woman notion. As with any pendulum swing, some women have taken their new role to the extreme. While many men now do not use the term castrating women, many do see women as looking down on men or seeing them as clueless and always in the wrong. This has been a more and more prevalent theme when I do marital therapy. Men and women are truly different. They differ in how information is stored, how they perceive things, and how problems are solved. Men often do not understand women and some do not wish to, preferring to stay angry with them, in order to preserve their own sense of being correct. The converse is also true. Many women see their way of looking at things as the only true and correct way. There is a sense that, today, too many women see men as *always* wrong! It is, however, important that we not paint with too broad a brush. While there are some mothers who are smothering and promote unhealthy attachments, there are thank heavens so many that are not. We are back to acknowledging that there is typically a continuum, which ranges from proper to pathological.

The flipside of the coin is that, from the way you present the story, we are led to believe that all was well between this father and son up until the son's 16th birthday. I have some difficulty with that idea, and if I were to become involved in the situation, I would wish to get much more information regarding the father's role in this circumstance. Some questions might be how did he deal with his wife? Did he passively sit back while he saw his wife behave in controlling and demeaning ways? I am sure these, as well as other questions, would be important to ask.

These questions do not take away from your knowledge that the mother behaved in unhealthy ways and did her son a disservice; it just evens the playing field by trying to be more realistic as to the causes of some of the problems and look at all contributing factors.

Part of working with Fred, if he came to me and he was motivated to deal with this issue, would not only be to determine what he learned from his mother but to determine if his father was also a poor role model and inadvertently provided him instruction on being passive or contributed to Fred's strong attachment to his mother, producing his difficulty establishing his own independent ties outside of the family.

Without gunning for moms, I suspect the real question is, can mothers create disturbed attachments, which foster excessive parental attachment and dependence, leading to failing future relationships? The unfortunate answer is clearly, yes. Parents can affect their children's growth by teaching them that it is disloyal to leave the family and to have outside attachments.

One of the reasons adolescence is a challenge is that this is the time when teenagers need to grow away from their family in order to begin to create their own independent lives. The balancing act is to create new extra familial relationships, while not abandoning the family. Clearly, that balancing act failed in Fred's case. Another interesting factor is the impact of the divorce, not only on Fred, but also on children in general. I have frequently seen cases where children do align with one of their parents, and interestingly this alignment is often influenced by the genetic predisposition of the children. Children who are more genetically like their father will often align with the father, while the same is true for the mother. This is true even when one of the parents tends to be aggressive and even somewhat abusive. It may very well be that Fred was more genetically like his mother than his father, leading (among other things) to his affinity to be with her. It may also be true that since Fred's father was often gone, there may not have been sufficient opportunity for a strong relationship to be created. As I said earlier, without really knowing more information about this family, it would be difficult for me to comment on the probable determiners of Fred's behavior.

You are quite right that when individuals fail *teenagehood* and remain tangled with one of their parents, the probability of healthy future relationships is reduced. In some of the cases of failed marriages that I have been involved with, it has not always been the mother who has created this unhealthy attachment. Sometimes both parents simultaneously create such strong dependence that their children's future marriages fail or are severely strained.

Therapeutically, if someone is able to recognize their unhealthy attachment to one or both of their parents and wanted to go into therapy, we would probably start by trying to understand what this individual believed and what fueled their guilt, making it difficult to leave and maintaining their unhealthy attachment.

The difficult part in dealing with this kind of circumstance is helping the person become psychologically strong enough to deal with the anger that came from the affected parent or parents. In Fred's case, he lived many years with the potency of his mother's anger and would have to be willing to have his relationship with her disrupted and face a possible emotional cutoff and attack from her. The reality is that few people are willing to take this risk. This is one of those clear circumstances where knowing what to do is the easy part. Trying to help the person understand healthy attitudes and beliefs would fit well into the material I have presented to you in our discussions.

I just mentioned that knowing what to do is often the easy part. Getting people to do what might be best is the hard part. In this particular case, it sadly might not be possible. If the individual was motivated, I would certainly be more than happy to work with him or her, but I would also make it very clear what the risks might be, so that I did not lead them blindly into a place they really did not wish and were not prepared to be.

Ed, you ask if there is some way to detect that a parent or parents may not be supporting the emotional development of their children, such that there is an overdependence and unhealthy attachment to one or both parents. Unfortunately, I do not think there is a way to see this until it is too late. There would have to be a trained person observing the interactions between the child and their parents and parents willing to take direction. The probability of this happening is very low. If the child were lucky enough to have some additional, collateral problem and was fortunate enough to be in a facility where they could view the family interactions, this might be identifiable. I do not think this is likely, and it would be very difficult to identify this type of destructive parent interaction. As we have said in so many of our other conversations, building healthy attachments, having positive and reinforcing parents, who have the psychological integrity and capacity to support healthy individuation and growth of their children, is key for future mental health.

One has to take a test in order to drive a car, but there is no such requisite training for being a parent. I doubt that this situation will ever change, leaving us with too many Freds and too many failed marriages.

Dr. Chapunoff: Howard, the questions I asked you about this case were presented at the beginning of our discussion. You unfolded your points in such an organized and lucid manner that there was no need for me to interrupt you with additional questions. I'll talk to you later.

17

SELF-ESTEEM AND THE IMPORTANCE OF NOT LOSING IT

Dr. Chapunoff: Howard, self-esteem is a treasure of the soul. When it is lost, the consequences become apparent, and those affected do not have the consolation of finding an easy solution.

We know that the term self-esteem is used to describe a person's overall evaluation of his or her own self. It is also a measure of an individual's self-respect and self-confidence.

I have known people who were good professionals, good husbands and wives, and good parents, and yet they always felt diminished and continued to believe that they were never good enough. They were plagued by feelings of inadequacy and worthlessness and could never be satisfied with their accomplishments. You could clearly hear their excessive self-criticism, *"I'll never play the piano well, no matter how hard I practice,"* or *"I don't have any ability to be a good executive, a good father, or a good teacher,"* or their hypersensitivity to criticism, indecisiveness (fear of making a mistake), and their perfectionistic tendencies (if something they did, didn't come up perfect, they'd feel frustrated). On the other hand, they show a tendency to please other people excessively out of fear of any kind of reprisal or disapproval from the person who might be criticizing them. Their outlook on life, in general, tends to be pessimistic.

Howard, will you please tell us about the indicators that show a healthy level of self-esteem? I'd also like to know how poor self-esteem develops and grows with steady perversity. Where do these negative feelings and thoughts originate? What may have triggered their appearance?

Finally, can you teach us how parents can recognize early signs of poor self-esteem in their children and deal with it quickly and effectively in order to avoid the development of neurotic individuals, who most likely will create numerous problems for themselves and others.

Dr. Paul: Ed, this really is a very important discussion. As you just pointed out, the concept of self-worth is central to having good adjustment. I think we need to start with a definition of what self-esteem and self-worth might be and more importantly, what they are not.

Self-esteem, self-worth, and self-confidence are all related. Importantly, they have more to do with faith than with fact.

Confidence comes from two Latin words: con, meaning with, and fide, meaning faith. Far too many people have the idea that self-esteem and a positive sense of self-worth come only from successes or winning. The sad fact is that not everyone is capable of being a high achiever, and not everyone can always win or be successful. If self-esteem only comes from successes, which would relegate a vast number of people to the less successful category, everyone not in the top category would be at risk to have a poor self-image. The problem is that this is exactly the way it is.

Even successful people can have a poor self-image, if their standards are unrealistically high. To use a metaphor, not everyone in school can get A's all the time. Sometimes, those that do get A's come to demand A+'s!

Using that metaphor, let me pose a conundrum for you: You and I go into a school, and we take all the children who get A's and put them in a big pile. Next to them, we make a bigger pile by putting all the students who get B's in it. In the next pile, which unfortunately will also be of a fair size, we will put all the kids that get C's, all other lower grades, and even failures. After we have sorted all the children into these piles, I turn to you and ask, Ed, where are all the worthy children? I would hope that you would say to me, Howard, they are all worthy. The A pile contains the children who are the best students, but the worthy children are in all the piles.

Dr. Chapunoff: What you just said is a point frequently neglected by educators and parents alike. Too much emphasis is placed on achievement. Children who are not able to perform according to their teachers or parents' expectations are poorly treated, and their emotional development can produce all kinds of neurotic behaviors.

Dr. Paul: Ed, self-worth, self-esteem, or self-confidence, however you wish to describe our inner sense of worth, works best when it is understood as being separate from achievement. It is a given. We start with all the value we need, which is also all that we will ever get. Then, everyone slowly loses it due to the faulty teachings of parents, schools, and even our own misinterpretations of how we think things must be. These teachings are mostly inadvertent, in that very few people, on purpose, set out to destroy children's self-confidence, but in far too many instances this is exactly what happens.

Dr. Chapunoff: Howard, would it be logical to think that the faulty teaching you are referring to effectively promotes inadequacy?

Dr. Paul: In a previous conversation, I spoke to you about one of the prime ways messages of inadequacy are taught. If you recall our chat on anger, I explained that the message of anger is inadequacy. When I ask parents, "Would you purposively tell your child that they are of little value?" Most say that they would not. Some, if they were to be very honest, might admit that when they are very angry, they do say mean and destructive things to their children.

The reality is, even if they do not overtly tell their child that they are not worthy, I point out to them that when there are angry exchanges, *you are no good,* is exactly what their child hears. No child grows up without its parents occasionally being angry with him or her; therefore, no adult exists who has not heard the message that they are inadequate.

The second way that messages of inadequacy are inadvertently taught is when parents reward product, not process. Let me explain this. Children are often rewarded for good performance rather than good effort. When children are doing homework, parents often spend far too much time making sure that it is perfect and that there are no errors. It is important that parents spend time catching children being neat, organized, and focused, and not giving up when things are challenging, and then, reinforce children for positive work habits and effort. When children are rewarded for getting A's, they often come to believe that anything less than an A is unsatisfactory. They can create their own self-demand to get A's, *so they can be an A person*. Their demand-based belief becomes *I must be an A person*. Once this demand is in place, any time that child does not reach their own level of performance; they will be angry with themselves and deliver their own message of inadequacy. I see so many students (of all ages) where this is the case.

Dr. Chapunoff: What you just said reminds me of a 14-year-old boy with whom I shared my high school education. He was an A+ achiever. He was the best, not only in our class, but also in the school. One day, an English teacher gave him a C. He cried so much and felt so miserable that all the kids, including me, felt deeply sorry for him. I don't remember seeing any human being cry so intensely about anything! I'm sure this boy felt that his world had come to an end!

Dr. Paul: Many parents inadvertently reinforce perfectionism and teach that if you do not get A's, you are not a valuable person. Many children, even without their parents requiring them to be perfect, adopt perfectionistic standards.

Dr. Chapunoff: It seems that those striving for perfection are still disappointed even when they reach it. The word satisfactory doesn't appear to exist in their vocabulary.

Dr. Paul: Let me make this clear, **striving for perfection is marvelous. Demanding perfection is a curse.**

With unrealistically high demands (and all demands are unrealistic) no matter how good you are, there will always be the demand to be better. When this is so, the psychological baseline will always be one of inadequacy, instead of competence. I have literally had world-renowned scientists sitting across from me being depressed and feeling that they had no self-value. Why? Because they did not have a publication in the last six months! This overly rigid, perfectionistic demand system never allowed for the generation of a lasting and stable sense of self-esteem and self-worth. There are so many individuals, who on the surface are functioning satisfactorily and sometimes, even meritoriously, who are ably contributing to society, yet they see themselves as frauds and have anxiety about being *found out*. They fear that their true, even if successfully hidden, inadequacy will someday be exposed.

Dr. Chapunoff: I can't help having the impression that some children in school are in the wrong place, certainly the wrong place for them. How is a child with modest performance going to feel when he has to compete with other children, who have more capacity and a better achievement record?

Dr. Paul: I just briefly mentioned that schools are a breeding ground for the erosion of self-worth. Schools work very well for the academically talented. For those with learning challenges or those who have been endowed with only average intelligence, school can be a savage place, where feelings of disenfranchisement and lack of reinforcement are the rule not the exception.

It is crucial that schools do a better job taking care of all of their students, not just those who are academically talented. The message that you must be in the A pile in order to be valued needs to be challenged from kindergarten on. When children are unable to see themselves as academically successful, it produces a cascade of personally damaging events.

Dr. Chapunoff: How do children with poor or insufficient performance at school interact with the achievers?

Dr. Paul: Few nonachieving students are able to maintain friendships and identifications with those that achieve. In too many cases, this leads students to reject achievement as a goal, as they think that it is impossible to attain. Far too many students then look to nonachieving peers to gain acceptance. This group is at risk for drug abuse, alcoholism, and antisocial behavior.

I cannot emphasize how important this issue is, as it is the root cause of so many social ills that beset teenagers and then carry over into adult life. White-collar crime aside, most criminals in our penitentiaries will report a sense of disenfranchisement with school and a belief that they were unable to succeed within that venue.

About 35 years ago, before I went into full-time private practice, I was the director of special services at a nearby New Jersey school system. I managed to be appointed as the head of the report card committee and charged the committee with the task of developing an entirely new report card system. Using my guidance, we scrapped the A-F-system based upon academic achievement and developed an effort-based and curriculum-focused system. For the first and third marking periods, grades were given, not based on achievement, but on effort. Suddenly, students who would regularly get A's, but never really worked hard for them, were getting C's, and students, especially those in the younger grades who were still working hard and not getting A's, were bringing home A's. For the second and fourth marking period, the report card represented the scope and sequence of the school's curriculum. Teachers were asked to tell parents what material was being taught to each child and whether the material was just introduced, whether it was in the process of being learned, or if it had been mastered. This served to individualize each youngster's program, in that, once a youngster had mastered an element of the curriculum, he or she needed to be taught the next element. In effect, this individualizes teaching and bases it upon the learning capacity of each child and not upon what grade they happened to be in. It also gave parents a tool to be able to show the next teacher what material had been taught and mastered, so that youngsters would be able to move on and not simply receive the same information again because the class was being taught that. Obviously, the parents loved this. My understanding is that a few years after I left, the teachers reinstated the old system, which is sad.

Other ways poor self-image may be inadvertently taught can come from parents, who try to console their children when others do better than they do in anything from sports to school. Too often, parents try to point out the strong points and accomplishments of the child, who is feeling less worthy and who feels that others are better than they are. Most parents do not understand that it can be a trap to point out strong points and achievements because children can misinterpret it to mean that they must do well at something to feel good about themselves.

It is crucial right from the start, that parents teach children that they are the equal to anyone, irrespective of capacity and talent. This does not mean of equal power within the family or talent in school or on a playing field, but really is a more philosophical notion of human equality.

Dr. Chapunoff: Are you saying, Howard, that what you are and what you do are two different things that bear no connection with each other, as far as the value concept of the individual?

Dr. Paul: Absolutely correct! Ed, what you are worth is different from what you do. This equality is a conceptual ideal and can only be believed as opposed to proven. Strangely enough, we lose self-worth as soon as we believe we must prove it by what we do.

The only way to keep self-worth and self-esteem is to understand that we have it, that we always have had it, and that it does not have to be proven, simply accepted.

Dr. Chapunoff: If people assimilated that concept, the world would immediately become a different and better place for all of us to live in.

Dr. Paul: Confidence and its related sense of self-esteem really do mean with faith, not with fact. People, who believe that they are worthy and believe in their own capacity, simply do better than those who fret and worry about whether they are okay, worthy and acceptable and whether others might be better. Someone, eventually, will be better than you at something. Some people may have more value to society by their stellar contributions. That does not mean they have more human value.

Dr. Chapunoff: Feeling human is indeed better that feeling successful, and **being** human is better than being an achiever. Admittedly, it's difficult for many people to swallow that pill.

Dr. Paul: Yes, it is, Ed. A secondary complication of losing self-esteem is something that we have spoken about at length before, but because of the importance of the topic, it is certainly worth reemphasizing here. Everyone does two kinds of thinking. We do straight thinking, and we do crooked thinking. Straight thinking lets us manage things more comfortably and accurately, while crooked thinking leads to increases in negative emotions and a decreased ability to cope.

When we take our own desires and turn them into demands and aim these *musts* and *shoulds* and *have to* statements at our self, we create a dangerous situation where, if we do not live up to our own self-demands, we will denigrate ourselves and feel unworthy, unloved, incapable, and even fraudulent. Part of maintaining a positive sense of self-worth is to adopt the mantra, *"I am a worthy individual, no matter what."* Failing something does not make us a failure. Behaving poorly or making mistakes does not make us a mistake, only human. These are very basic concepts that are simply not well taught.

Dr. Chapunoff: That is so true! In addition, it applies particularly to the reaction we have when a relationship, marital or of any other nature, becomes disrupted. Not being a psychologist, but trying to help some of those affected who were close to me, I told them, *"You didn't fail, the relationship did."* I noticed that some felt more comforted and relieved.

Dr. Paul: What people get from success and achievement would best be a sense of accomplishment, pride, admiration from others, and many other positive outcomes. Even if we have a perfect day and accomplish at a high level, we are no better a person than at the beginning of the day.

Many of us are fortunate enough to have led relatively successful lives, so that we are not constantly confronted with the dread of inadequacy and the remarkable degree of anxiety that it can cause. If we still carry unrealistic internal demands, and we have been lucky enough to satisfy or come close to satisfying self-demands, we will dodge the, *I'm no good* bullet. However, if we carry these internal demands, and almost everyone does, we will only be fortunate as long as we are successful, and we will be one failure away from feeling inadequate and less worthy.

The fear of being inadequate is universal. It exists on a continuum with some people being less affected and others having many struggles that are more significant. As I have said before, having a poor self-image is not separate from what is normal. People feeling they have insufficient self-esteem is the norm, while people feeling good about themselves is unfortunately rarer.

Ed, you ask how parents can be aware that the self-esteem of their children is reduced and if they can be taught to recognize and reverse what they might be doing to cause or worsen this problem.

Firstly, it would be wise for parents to understand that their discipline style may be a fundamental reason for their child's poor self-esteem. Remember, if anger is involved in exchanges with our children, we are telling them that they are inadequate. Using a nonanger-based management style can really help.

As to recognizing low self-esteem in our children, it actually is not hard to recognize. There is a classic study, where children given a basic task are asked to take a beanbag and throw it into a wastebasket. The children were not told how far away to stand. Prior to this study, the children had their self-esteem measured by one of the standardized tests that are available to do this. The findings were quite interesting in that those children with good self-esteem turned this task into an enjoyable challenge. They stood at some distance from the wastebasket so that there was some challenge. They knew that they would not be able to toss the bag easily into the basket. Those children with a poor self-image did one of two things: they either walked right up to the basket and dropped the beanbag straight into it or they stood so far away that, realistically, there was no chance they would ever be able to hit the target.

Dr. Chapunoff: Howard, what do you make out of the relationship between self-esteem and the desire to win?

Dr. Paul: Children with poor self-esteem believe they must always either win or think they can never win. They have turned winning into proof that they are adequate and are caught up in the trap that if you must prove adequacy, you will never have it.

Children with poor self-esteem will often be dependent in their social relationships and will sometimes be very clinging to their parents. They are at increased risk for anxiety and social fears. When such children play, they either are followers or tend to be very bossy and directive. Children who engage in a good deal of name-calling, teasing, and even sibling rivalry when it is extreme are dealing with self-image issues.

Dr. Chapunoff: What can you expect from these children as they grow and become adolescents?

Dr. Paul: When children become adolescents, self-image issues are often at the base of eating disorders and other disorders where there are distortions of body image and chronic dissatisfaction with either behaviors or features of the self. In some severe cases, children grow up to see themselves as unlovable. They can behave in very destructive ways when they try to seek caring, recognition, validation, and nurturance.

Self-mutilation is a strangely increasing phenomenon, which is becoming more and more socially acceptable with tattooing and piercing becoming more and more commonplace. Whether piercing and tattooing is destructive really depends upon the individual and the particular motivations behind these behaviors. I would like to make it clear that I am not saying that anyone with a piercing or tattoo is emotionally challenged. Many people do these things for aesthetic and other healthy reasons, but not everyone does.

Dr. Chapunoff: How does the connection between emotional control and self-esteem work? Let me give you an example: If someone offends me, is it my fault if I feel offended? In addition, if that's the case, does it mean I have poor self-esteem?

Dr. Paul: Ed, we personally are in charge of our feelings. When people say that someone else makes them feel bad, they are giving the power and control of their emotions over to that other person. Part of having good self-esteem comes from the awareness that other people can and often will do things that we do not wish, but it is up to us to determine how we wish to respond emotionally. When people have a sense that they are more in control of their emotions, their feelings of self-efficacy and self-worth increase, and it is easier to maintain contact with the idea that they do not have to prove their worth by their actions.

This is such a key concept, yet it is one that few people have given much thought. Parents tend not to behave in ways that maximize the odds that their children will have a sense of constant and undiminished value. We are too hung up on perfection, and we set up far too many systems that focus on perfectionism and high achievement, as the only ways to gain self-esteem and a sense of personal value. Many people fall into such a huge trap. When we were born, we were bequeathed with all of the worth that we will need and can ever have. It is so important that we all do a better job making sure we don't give our worth away by adopting beliefs that are so counterproductive to maintaining personal comfort. As I said earlier, working hard to achieve is to be commended. I am in favor of high achievement, just not linking it to our sense of value.

Some people are fearful that if they do not *have* to achieve, then why bother. Too many are fearful that dropping demand will lead to a lack of motivation and a worsening sense of self. People with these concerns are unaware that inner-directed motivation, based on personal value and a sense of what is best, leads to much better emotional health, less blocking and resistance, and increased probability of success. Teaching children to work hard because it is laudable and important, rather than because they *have to*, would decrease the number of individuals sitting across from me.

Let's go back to school, and let me give you another example. Let's look at two second-grade classrooms, with two very different teachers trying to teach their students math. In one classroom, there is a very stern teacher, who every time a student makes a mistake, loudly hits that student's desk with her ruler. She makes it very clear that she expects the seven-year-olds to carefully inspect their work and make sure they never make a mistake. By contrast, in the classroom across the hall, this teacher works diligently to teach her students that mistake making is both expected and a part of the learning process. When students make mistakes, rather than denying the mistake or avoiding working on the problem, they get stars for finding the mistake and turning it into a learning process. At the end of the year, when these teachers say, *"It's time for math,"* very different reactions will occur in these different classrooms. In the first, all but the brightest children will probably become anxious, and even some of the very bright ones will too, if they are already on the road to being perfectionists. They may be afraid to moan and groan, but most will surely say that they do not like math, and when they do math, they do not have a good sense of their own capacity to succeed. In the second classroom when math is presented, it will probably be accepted positively, with very little anxiety. Most of those students will feel good about their own ability to succeed.

Ed, as you can see, self-acceptance, self-worth, and self-esteem are all created by adopting a base of acceptance, by not using demand, and by having people tolerate not only success, but also error making. It also rests on separating worth from achievement. When people confuse their worth with their achievement, achieving is often disrupted by anxiety. People with self-confidence and an internal sense of value, tend to do better and have far less anxiety interfere with their challenges, making it easier for them to be successful. Individuals with a poor sense of self-esteem often avoid challenges. People who have been well taught that even if they mess up they are still valuable, seek out challenge. This often leads them to maximize their ability to be successful.

18

NARCISSIM: ME, ME, AND ME

Dr. Chapunoff: Arthur was a 42-year-old man, who was referred to me by his primary care physician for an evaluation of his chest pains. His wife was present during our interview. She projected a gracious character and intelligence. From the outset, it was obvious that she wanted to talk about their marital relationship and *some problems in his character.* I refrained from telling her that she was in the wrong medical office to talk about this issue. I did, however, spend time listening to both of them. He appeared pleasant to me and more reserved than she was. She thought her husband had a *strange personality.*

One of her main concerns was her husband's lack of tenderness and emotional sensitivity during intimacy. He could have sex many times a week if he wanted to, and he was proud of it. His wife confirmed this. However, she felt he was always *distant, detached, and kind of insensitive, and unable or unwilling to express sweetness or tenderness.*

He said, *"I don't know why my wife is not happy, she can have all the sex she wants."* Then, as our conversation unfolded, he talked about how good he was as a bank executive, and when asked what he felt about his work he said, *"I'm a superb executive, the best there is."*

His wife also mentioned that during social gatherings, he would always talk about himself. The rest of the world, or the people who surrounded him, seemed to have very little relevance to him. When he played tennis, he thought he was a great player, but his best friends disagreed. When he went fishing, he didn't want to return home until he got the biggest fish.

As our interview was coming to an end, I suggested he and his wife consider an evaluation by a psychotherapist because of his wife's unhappiness during intimacy. While he was getting dressed, I asked his wife to give me a phone call to discuss the results of his cardiac evaluation and to discuss briefly other important issues. She did that, and I told her, *"Janet, we'll see how the cardiac tests come out, but as far as Arthur's character, although I'm not a psychologist, it seems to me that he has narcissistic features in his personality. I can't help you more in that sense but I think a psychotherapist will be helpful in making both of you understand what's going on and what might be done about it."*

Howard, how does this kind of personality disorder originate? Is there a genetic factor, the wrong upbringing by parents, other childhood traumas, or other noxious influences? It is very difficult to deal with a person who feels that he is the center of the universe, and deep in his soul, nothing really matters but himself.

Dr. Paul: Ed, narcissism is considered a personality disorder and is one of a number of personality disorders listed in the *Diagnostic and Statistical Manual* of the American Psychiatric Association. Narcissism was first described at the turn of the 19th century, then later picked up by Freud and further addressed. The name narcissism came from the mythological character Narcissus who was lured to a pond, where he saw his own reflection and fell deeply in love with it; he could never leave it, and therefore perished there. While some people may be familiar with the story of Narcissus, far fewer will remember that the name of the mythological figure that lured Narcissus there was Nemesis. It is from this story that the word nemesis, meaning a rival who is out to get you, emerged.

As you can gather from the above story, narcissists are people who are in love with themselves. Befitting any tragedy, this usually results in their demise or at least their being unhappy. Narcissism as a problem has been given a great deal of attention and thought, by both psychodynamic and social learning theorists. Dynamically, some people see narcissism as the other side of jealousy. Jealous individuals are always worrying about how others might be better than they are, while narcissists try to prove that they are better than everyone is.

Dr. Chapunoff: The narcissistic individual loves him or herself very much, indeed! Do jealous people love themselves as much as narcissists do?

Dr. Paul: That is an interesting question. Jealousy equals self-love plus self-pity, while narcissism is seen as self-love plus vanity.

Dr. Chapunoff: Isn't it true that narcissists think they're larger than life and above everyone else?

Dr. Paul: Yes, they do. Narcissists frequently believe they are also above the law and are above social obligation and morality. Perhaps Bernie Madoff fits in here. Such individuals have an exaggerated sense of their own importance and tend to brag about their successes and accomplishments, while at the same time downplaying or being uninterested in positive occurrences happening to anyone else.

Dr. Chapunoff: Would it be accurate, Howard, to consider the narcissistic expression as an obvious display of arrogance of the first order?

Dr. Paul: You are right, Ed. Narcissists are often arrogant and come off as snobs, in part because they define themselves by the people they are either able to influence, buy, or associate with. Such individuals are often exploitive and have an exaggerated sense of entitlement.

Dr. Chapunoff: Do narcissists suffer from anxiety?

Dr. Paul: They do. They need to stay self-absorbed in order to mask the anxiety, which exists beneath.

Dr. Chapunoff: I'm intrigued by the possible causes that lead to this disorder. Are genes very important here, or do other upbringing factors greatly contribute to the narcissistic character? Is poor parenting the culprit?

Dr. Paul: Ed, there is little evidence that there is a large genetic component to narcissism. There is a small genetic component to any personality distortion you can think of, but this one seems to stem mostly from an overindulged childhood and associated faulty strategies of handling anxiety.

In trying to understand narcissism, I again refer to my basic strategy of keeping things simple. I often joke that if I were ever to write a book, it would probably only have 20 pages in it, as after I had said whatever needed to be said, everything else would simply be repetition. Well, I must say, I am somewhat surprised that I have exceeded my 20-page expectation. With the basics that I have laid out, we can understand most difficulties, including narcissism.

I have said on a number of occasions that it is the responsibility of all adults ultimately to outgrow their childhood. It is not that far a stretch to realize that with narcissism, individuals continue to look like very young children, believing that in order to be satisfactory, they must be the best! This belief is typically hidden from their consciousness. The core of most personality pathology is the same, with just little twists and turns manifesting in different labels or diagnoses, as the case may be.

Narcissism is simply too much *me first-ism*.

In one of our conversations, I mentioned that there are many children in kindergarten who believe that if they are standing in the front of the line, everyone else behind them is less worthy and they, by virtue of being in front, are the best around. Narcissists never outgrow this childish notion.

Dr. Chapunoff: In other words, narcissists are grown children.

Dr. Paul: That is right. There bodies have grown; however, their emotional maturity has not. We all start as children and all go through periods, where we are significantly indulged and showered with a great deal of love. Sometimes the message learned is that we are, indeed, better than everyone and are entitled to have adoration continue forever.

I have stressed in our previous conversations, the need for parents to teach equality, not superiority and to make it clear that equality is based on simply being human; not on achievement, status, the amount of toys we own, or how thick our wallet happens to be.

Dr. Chapunoff: Many individuals with apparently normal behavior feel superior to others, don't consider themselves equal to other people, and feel important when they touch a thick wallet. Am I too impertinent if I ask you if many people, including you and me, have narcissistic components in their personality without anybody, including themselves, being aware of it?

Dr. Paul: Ed, you just put your finger on the truth. All of us, at one point or another behaved selfishly, have had ideas of grandeur and thought of only our self with little regard for others. The elements of narcissism are both common and inside all of us. It is yet another example of how there is a continuum of challenge on almost any pathological variable we choose. Narcissism represents the extreme, but it is not separate from what is normal and what everybody at one point or another does. I have said many times that we must come to know our internal, silent beliefs to be able to understand why we behave as we do.

Dr. Chapunoff: Typical narcissists try to convince the rest of the world that they are superior to the rest of us. However, in the depths of their soul, do they truly believe that or disguise themselves with a camouflage of fear and insecurity?

Dr. Paul: Narcissists believe they must be first or best. They often do not hear that they have made this a demand. Very few are aware of the catastrophic fears they would have, if they were unable to behave and act as if they are better than everyone is. As I have said before, narcissism is simply another example of people failing to grow up.

Dr. Chapunoff: A child is born. You don't want that child to become a narcissist. At what point or at what age do you want to make sure you provide that child with some kind of specific training that will minimize the chances that he or she will grow into a narcissistic nightmare.

Dr. Paul: I cannot tell you how crucial it is to start at about age two and try to teach children the basics of having a healthy psychological mind. It is best for children to learn they cannot always have it the way they wish. There are innumerable variations to this theme which include, we cannot always be first, we cannot always win, we cannot always be the best, things do not always have to work out our way, people can and will do unpleasant things to us, others can behave in ways we do not wish, and in all of these instances, it is important to believe that it isn't terrible. It may be frustrating, aggravating, annoying, and disappointing, but it's not terrible. Lastly, it is very important we teach children that they have the capacity to cope.

It is easy to see the notion that they must be first and best persists with a narcissistic personality. Such individuals say to themselves that if they are not the best, it is catastrophic and they cannot handle it.

Dr. Chapunoff: Considering that the narcissist feels he or she must be the best, would it be appropriate to define this personality as a perfectionist?

Dr. Paul: Because narcissists always equate being the best with being just satisfactory, it can also be seen as a twisted form of perfectionism, which only fuels internal anxiety. Individuals with narcissistic personality disorder are typically very insecure, even though they work very hard not to appear like that, and as you might guess, they have low self-esteem.

Dr. Chapunoff: That is a very interesting and dramatic twist! This insecurity and low self-esteem you just mentioned raises another question: How do narcissists, who by definition need the adulation of others, behave when that adulation is missing?

Dr. Paul: Without the continual attention and admiration of others, narcissists often become anxious and can have significant difficulty coping. Narcissists are especially distressed when they receive any kind of criticism. Even minor criticism can sometimes lead to rage and attack or it's opposite, social withdrawal. While narcissists tend not to handle criticism well, they handle failure even worse. People with narcissism will go to great lengths to avoid situations where failure might be possible.

Dr. Chapunoff: What role does envy play in the life of the narcissist?

Dr. Paul: While some see narcissism as the antithesis of jealousy, envy is shared. With jealousy, envy is of others. With narcissism, there is often the hope that others are envious of the narcissist, who would incorrectly believe that this elevates their status.

Dr. Chapunoff: The narcissistic patient I introduced to you at the beginning of our conversation was described as insensitive during intimacy by his wife. I presume that he would display a similar attitude toward other people.

Dr. Paul: Socially, narcissists tend to have little empathy and little interest in the lives of other people, expecting people to be devoted to them with no need for reciprocity. *"What have you done for me lately,"* would be the narcissists' mantra. Ed, your last question revolves around how much of a challenge it is to deal with someone who believes that the world revolves around them. I often quip that the hardest person to treat is one who is not there. Since narcissists have a great deal of difficulty tolerating criticism or the sense that they may have failed, few present themselves for treatment unless they have had some painful epiphany that served to open their eyes. Often, narcissists will come to therapy because someone else, often a child or spouse, is not providing them with something they believe they are entitled to, like love, obedience, caring, or respect. As a rule, personality disorders are a great challenge. When there are other psychiatric issues, such as anxiety, OCD, depression, or any other personality disorder, it makes successful treatment much more difficult. Unless people are motivated to examine their own beliefs and work to alter their internalized patterns, the outlook is frustrating and sometimes somewhat bleak.

I mentioned previously that often a crisis is needed in order to make a difference. With narcissists, this may very well be the case, as it may take a crisis to provide the motivation to look at their own beliefs and habits.

As with anything else, when you have an interested, motivated, and dedicated patient, rather miraculous gains can take place. Absent those things, the outlook is less positive.

19

SUICIDE, THE FINAL ESCAPE

Dr. Chapunoff: Ana was a 70-year-old woman of poor socioeconomic status, who suffered from numerous medical illnesses, including heart disease and diabetes. She also had chronic depression and anxiety. A psychiatrist treated her with an antidepressant and medicated her with the tranquilizer lorazepam. She attempted suicide three times. The first time I had to deal with her overdosed, comatose state, she survived. I warned all the doctors treating her that she should not be medicated with any tranquilizers, as she was a candidate to try to kill herself again. Somehow, she got the sedatives, and there I was again in the emergency room, pumping her stomach out, and doing my best to revive her. She survived the ordeal once more. I asked her, *"Ana, why have you tried to kill yourself two times?"* She answered, *"I have no money, I'm alone, I have nobody to talk to, and I keep on getting bills and more bills I can't afford to pay! This is no life. I really want to die!"*

Her third attempt was successful. She got her wish. She didn't have tranquilizers, but took a full bottle of an oral antidiabetic. That sure did it!

- * -

Bob and Helen were married for 35 years. Both were deaf-mutes and had worked for decades for a New York newspaper in the maintenance department. They were both sweet and very pleasant. He always kept a big smile and had an excellent sense of humor. Unexpectedly, he acutely got very depressed and refused to eat or drink. I immediately admitted him to the hospital. We tried intravenous feeding, and he pulled out the lines. We tried a nasogastric tube, and he did the same thing. I called the chief of psychiatry and asked him for help. I'll never forget the words in his written consultation. They read as follows, *"If this man wants to die as badly as he indicates he does, he will!"* Two days later, he had a cardiac arrest. That was the end.

- * -

A bipolar 46-year-old physician neglected to follow up his treatment with his psychiatrist. As usual, he went to his office and made his rounds in the hospital. Occasionally, he lost his temper and was heard screaming at the nurses. One morning he shot himself in the head.

- * -

It seems that at times those who want to commit suicide cannot be saved, despite appropriate counseling and therapy. However, there are cases of severe depression that, with early and proper diagnosis, may have a far better outlook.

Howard, can you share with us your experience in the prevention and management of these difficult cases?

Dr. Paul: Ed, I remember quite vividly in 1971, in my very first session with the first adult I saw in my doctoral training, her telling me that she was contemplating suicide and wished to jump in front of a train. Since she took the train to New Brunswick, New Jersey, to have our session, and I knew she had to take the train back home, this certainly got my attention! It was imprudent to allow her to travel. Our conversation quickly focused on hospitalization and safety. Through good management, she improved, survived, and ultimately thrived. Not everyone is as fortunate.

Ed, you have brought up an extraordinarily important topic. Suicide is correlated with depression. It is also highly correlated with schizophrenia, as well as bipolar disorder and substance abuse. In fact, these latter three may well be more lethal conditions than depression, in that the prevalence rate of suicide for these disorders sometimes exceeds the suicide rate of people who are depressed. When all these factors are taken into account, there are many people who are at risk. In the United States at any given time, 20 to 30 million people may be suffering from depression alone. Depression is often undertreated and frequently underdiagnosed. Of those with depression, over the course of a depressed person's lifetime, only about half seek treatment. Epidemiological studies indicate that only about 20 percent of individuals who are depressed are in treatment. One fact that is of great concern is that the age of onset of depression has steadily decreased over the last 50 years.

When it comes to suicide and taking a global view, the numbers are staggering. The World Health Organization has estimated that somewhere in the world someone kills themself every 40 seconds. In a year's time, nearly 1 million people will successfully commit suicide. For the same time period, that represents more people who were murdered or killed in war! When suicide is attempted, men are four times more successful at killing themselves than women are. Women make more suicide attempts. Suicide is affected by the geographic region, with different parts of the world having dramatically high suicide rates. Interestingly, Asian and Latin countries have relatively fewer suicide attempts. Whites are about two and a half times more likely to attempt suicide than either African-Americans or Hispanics.

As you can see Ed, this is a compelling and genuine problem. As I said previously, many people link suicide only with depression; however, there are many other psychiatric disorders that are either comorbid - exist along with - or are primary diagnoses (eg, schizophrenia, substance abuse, bipolar disorder) that are associated with the desire to kill oneself.

Dr. Chapunoff: I've seen a couple of people who tried to commit suicide when their depression was on what seemed to be a definite course of improvement. They caught everybody by surprise. That seemed to me to be a paradoxical phenomenon.

Dr. Paul: Clinical wisdom tends to suggest that when people are very depressed, the incidence of suicide is low. The time to worry, the time when people become increasingly lethal, is actually, when they begin to improve!

Dr. Chapunoff: That's amazing! Can you tell me why that happens?

Dr. Paul: When people are very depressed, they often have the desire but not the energy to kill them selves. When they begin to improve, their energy level increases, but their level of depression has not remitted sufficiently, rendering them at highest risk.

Dr. Chapunoff: Could the improvement seen with the use of antidepressants have something to do with this tragic outcome?

Dr. Paul: It would not surprise me if this were one of the mechanisms behind the concern about antidepressant medication and suicide. People may very well be at higher risk for committing suicide on antidepressant medication, just as they are when they start psychotherapy, because it works. Just as with psychotherapy, antidepressants will begin to improve mood and increase energy, while there is still sufficient depression to make people more vulnerable to their depressed thoughts. While it may be true in some cases that antidepressant medication instigates suicidal ideation, it would certainly seem possible that what happens with psychotherapy would likewise happen with antidepressant pharmacotherapy, that is, people get more dangerous when they begin to improve, and then the risk subsides as further improvement takes place. Thank heavens they have not put a black box warning on psychotherapy!

Dr. Chapunoff: What about suicide in persons who are not depressed?

Dr. Paul: There are some people who are not depressed and who, through their own thought processing, come to believe that suicide is the only escape from their circumstance or their pain. These people are the hardest to detect because not all the signs and symptoms of depression are there. These people can surprise you the most.

I mentioned in another conversation that psychologists, just like anyone else, could be fooled. It is hard to hide depression, but it is easy to lie about whether or not you really plan to kill yourself. No amount of training makes a psychologist a mind reader. So once again, there are people who can surprise you with their behavior.

Dr. Chapunoff: You are following a depressed patient at your office. What would motivate you to hospitalize that person immediately in a psychiatric unit?

Dr. Paul: Typically, when people present themselves with both the desire to kill themselves and a plan to do it, it is time to think about putting them in the hospital. Most people are afraid to ask a depressed person if they plan to kill themselves. There is no substitute for being direct, and if I suspect that someone might be suicidal, I will simply ask if that is the case. More often than not, and especially if I have had an opportunity to create a good working relationship with them, they will be honest and tell me their intent.

I took a break in order to see my afternoon patients. My first patient was a teenager coming to see me for an initial consultation. She recently began to self-mutilate and cut her wrists. In my interview with her, she explained how her feelings of depression simply descend upon her, even when she is enjoying herself or doing activities she likes. I explained to her that there are two forms of depression, endogenous and exogenous. We are not talking here about the various diagnoses of depression because from a diagnostic standpoint there are many depressive forms. When depression is endogenous, it has a high biological-genetic component and can be unrelated to what is going on in people's lives. Exogenous depression, or reactive depression, is directly related to negative events that are occurring in our life space. That is, it comes from coping poorly with current problems.

For exogenous depressions, where we are simply bummed out by life events that we do not like, the best management is psychotherapy. When there is a clear endogenous component, psychotherapy or psychotherapy and medication is indicated.

Of the many studies that have been done comparing medication with psychotherapy, the outcome tends to be a draw. Each is potent, and each can be effective. Where pharmacotherapy is used, there is a tendency to remove people from their psychoactive drug too quickly and to lower the dose quickly when improvement is seen. Studies seem to indicate that it is wise to remain on antidepressant medication for about a year after symptoms have remitted in order to decrease the likelihood of relapse.

But, back to my afternoon and my second patient, one of the few patients I have seen for an extended period. She has a very clear biologically based severe depression. She has made multiple attempts at suicide over the course of her life and has had many hospitalizations. Fortunately, while seeing me, her suicidal attempts have been remarkably reduced, and hospitalizations have been much fewer and more for safety than because she made a suicide attempt. Unfortunately, she is very refractory to psychiatric medication and has tried almost everything there is to try. Medications often provide a brief respite of relief followed by a return to a more depressed state. We have not worked to eliminate her depression, as that would probably be impossible. Here we are dealing with her depression as if it represented a chronic condition, just like chronic pain.

Chronic pain has several similarities with chronic depression. When pain is acute, the common wisdom is to not use the affected, painful part and take pain-relieving medications until the pain is gone. Some pain, such as with arthritis, can be quite severe and can often become chronic. Management for acute pain and for chronic pain needs to be different. When pain becomes chronic, the agenda to eliminate the pain needs to be given careful thought. Often, this leads people to jump from doctor to doctor looking for the one person finally to get rid of their pain. People become vulnerable to treatments based on snake oil, and what is far worse, often give up important reinforcing elements in their life until their world becomes smaller and smaller. With chronic pain, I teach people to adopt a mindset of acceptance and management, rather than elimination of pain. With chronic depression, this same mindset is required. Medication can reduce, but infrequently eliminate chronic pain or chronic depression.

It became very clear to me that medicines would not relieve this second patient's depression. We have been focusing on coping with, not eliminating her pain, even if it is psychic. Now, this individual is the most well-adjusted, depressed person I know! We have been able to help her achieve a more active life, be less angry, and therefore more accepting of her mood disorder, and she is working on *having a life* rather than getting rid of depression.

My next patient was involved in a motor vehicle accident and now does not wish to get back into a car, even though it is needed to get to work and earn a living.

My last patient this afternoon suffers from depression that reached a point where she could no longer drag herself to work, and she began hoarding pills just in case. She lost the desire to live and truly began to believe that dying was better than living. Her first trial on antidepressant medication was a failure; however, with a new doctor and a second attempt with a new drug, she found relief and was able to resume a much more normalized life.

I mention this afternoon's group of individuals to try to impart how much of a problem depression is. This is a random sample. It just happened to coincide with my answering your questions on depression. Two of this afternoon's three depressed people had suicidal ideation with one having multiple attempts. The third, a teenager, while not suicidal, began to utilize self-mutilation, often described as a parasuicidal behavior, as a strategy to cope.

Dr. Chapunoff: Psychologically speaking, what does self-mutilation mean? Why would a depressed person do such a thing?

Dr. Paul: Cutting and other self-mutilations are attempts to *cope* with bad feelings, while suicide is an attempt to *end* them.

Dr. Chapunoff: Howard, it seems that you see more suicidal patients than a number of other mental disorders.

Dr. Paul: Ed, dealing with depression and suicide is often a frequent part of my day.

Dr. Chapunoff: What makes people more vulnerable to suicide?

Dr. Paul: There are a number of factors, both dispositional and psychological, that make people more vulnerable to depression and therefore to suicide. Suicide is most highly correlated with feelings of helplessness and hopelessness. What often brings people to this precipice are vulnerabilities of impulsivity, aggression, poor problem-solving skills coupled with limited ability to generate effective solutions, difficulty with putting solutions into operation, cognitive distortions which alter the accuracy of beliefs, perfectionism, and negatively selective memory, to name but a few. When depressed, people develop a selective attention and tend to see only the downside of both the situation and the self.

Dr. Chapunoff: How can parents recognize depression in their child?

Dr. Paul: There are many warning signs parents can use to determine if their child is depressed. The same warning signs apply to adults.

Depressed individuals have increased thoughts that they are nobody and a failure. Their mood can vary from extreme sadness to intense anger or heightened worry. In adolescence, depressed individuals often turn to alcohol or substance abuse and tend to isolate themselves, or they only involve themselves with individuals who are in the same emotional place and who embrace the same negative and destructive thoughts and behaviors. People may complain of having racing thoughts or flashbacks, and people may cry with increasing frequency and ease.

Dr. Chapunoff: What is the best approach for parents to adopt?

Dr. Paul: The best thing parents can do is to have an understanding of what depression is and how it is formed and then utilize positive, proactive, childrearing strategies, including good cognitive coaching and good modeling.

I would like to take a minute here, Ed, and review some of the fundamentals that we discussed in previous conversations.

Firstly, it is important for individuals to recognize that sorrow and disappointment are normal and unavoidable. When things do not work out the way we wish, being disappointed is a natural human reaction. Our disappointment can be amplified by *awfulizing*. If we add anger to disappointment, then we produce emotions that can be destructive. If you recall the conversation where I detailed the concepts I use to understand people and their problems, I tried to explain carefully that if I were angry with you, I would think badly of you. Even if I never say the words, you will hear *you are no good* in my message. By the same token, if I have unrealistic self-demands, and I become angry at myself because I have not succeeded in reaching my *have to*, I will be angry at myself, and I will think that I am a mistake, worthless, inadequate, or just a bad person. This is the essence of depression. I noted that if I were angry with you, I would know that I am angry. If I am angry with myself, I will not know that I am angry, but I will be aware of my own sense of despair and worthlessness. A second way to make myself depressed comes if I am angry with you, but for whatever reason, I either choose not to or cannot confront you. Once I am angry, that angry energy needs to go somewhere, and if I cannot give it to you, I will internalize and *eat it* myself. Depression is one of the likely outcomes when this is the case. *Shoulds* create anger, and anger creates depression. It makes sense that it would be helpful for parents to recognize that a childrearing style, which involves being over-demanding, makes their children vulnerable to both anxiety and depression. Too many parents tell me that the only time their child listens is when they yell. They have inadvertently taught their child not to listen when they speak normally. Often, parents are fearful if they take away the demands, their children will lose motivation and not be manageable. This is clearly not the case. Teaching collaboration, teaching good coping and problem solving skills, reducing demands, increasing positive reinforcement, focusing on work habits and not on outcomes are all strategies that decrease children's vulnerabilities to depression. Even when depression has a biological basis, the impact of that predisposition can be somewhat mitigated by a sound psychological capacity and good coping skills.

20

STUBBORNNESS
The Dark Side of Self-Imposed Fixed Ideas

Dr. Chapunoff: Howard, stubbornness has been defined in different ways. Stubborn persons refuse to change their mind about an idea or a course of action, even when the change of decision would clearly benefit them.

Stubbornness has also been called obstinacy, *dogged insistence*, and intransigence. It is an entrenched resistance to change.

I have observed the behavior of stubborn individuals for many years. None of them ever had any kind of psychological counseling. Their character dysfunction persisted for life, unchanged and unimproved. In fact, of all the stubborn people I have met in my life, I do not remember anyone who ever became flexible. I had the impression that their brain cells were stuck together with cement.

I'll present to you two cases of stubbornness. The first one is described in my book, *Answering Your Questions About Heart Disease and Sex* (Hatherleigh, Pages 106-107).

David was a 68-year-old man who collapsed in a restaurant, was revived by the rescue squad, and treated in the hospital's intensive care unit. He had a massive acute myocardial infarction. That was the first time I treated him, although Sarah, his wife, had been my patient for many years. He had heart failure and dangerous cardiac arrhythmias, but these responded to treatment and he was progressing well. After a few days of intensive treatment, he decided to leave the hospital against medical advice. Why? Specifically, he wanted to have sex with a girl in her early 20s. He did not believe he had sustained a heart attack, much less a very serious one. He had not had any chest pain. In his own mind, that meant he had not had a myocardial infarction. I explained to him that sometimes heart attacks present without chest pain and that leaving the hospital could be fatal. In addition, if he was going to have sex with a woman in her 20s, I was ready to sign his death certificate in advance. I couldn't change his mind. His wife Sarah came to my office a while later to ask me for advice. She said, *"My husband has always been the most stubborn individual I've seen in my life, with a very difficult character and a fondness for young girls."*

I straightforwardly told her that I expected her husband to die that afternoon, while having sex with the young girl. I thought the man had no chance of surviving his critical heart damage, combined with the strain of intercourse with a woman 45 years his junior. A while later, the police found him dead in a motel room. A young girl was seen running away in the parking lot. He still had on his wrist the hospital's bracelet with his name and mine.

- * -

The second case occurred quite a few years ago. Since stubbornness has existed on this planet for as long as humans have, the story remains useful.

When I was a child in the late 1940s, one of my mother's friends, Maria, a beautiful 20-year-old teacher, married a man who was 25 years older. In those days, premarital sex was nearly unthinkable. It was clear that these two people were not made for each other. My mother advised her not to marry the man, since she thought they had nothing in common. Maria was as stubborn as she was beautiful. She was aware that the relationship was a mistake, but she decided to go through with the marriage, because he had *"touched"* her *"too much"* and *"nobody can do that to me." "Now, he'll have to marry me!"*

This way of thinking is seen as ridiculous nowadays, and I'm sure it was ridiculous 60 years ago. However, in the old days, many women with an ultraconservative sex education thought like that. Maria got her wish. She married him. The result was disastrous. They lived miserably for the rest of their lives.

Howard, now I'd like to learn from you more about stubbornness. Let's begin by asking you to give us a definition.

Dr. Paul: Ed, by this point in our conversations, I have a feeling that you know what I am about to say. Stubbornness is a combination of arrogance and insecurity, with arrogance trying to mask the insecurity. If it is used against you, it will be seen as bad. If it helps you, it may be seen more positivity as determination. In many of our discussions, I have carefully tried to make the point that one needs to understand the internal scripts people use in order to have insight into their behavior.

It seems clear to me that stubbornness is another disastrous consequence of *absolutism*. Somewhere along the way, people learn and strengthen irrational internal statements that then control them emotionally. Statements such as, *"I must always be correct,"* or corollaries such as, *"people must always agree with me,"* or *"no one is allowed to have an idea that is contrary to mine,"* or any variant of absolute thinking will create emotional pathology.

Dr. Chapunoff: A reasonable, emotionally balanced person doesn't like being wrong. In reality, nobody does! However, if a person has a fixed idea of his/ or her self-attributed rightfulness, and proves to be unequivocally wrong, how do such people confront this personal dilemma?

Dr. Paul: Once people get the disastrous idea in their head that if they were wrong it would be catastrophic, it often does become an emotional catastrophe. Some people come to incorrectly believe that if you do not agree with them, they are somehow diminished. They truly believe that everyone must both admire and agree with them. Disagreement is seen as an insult. Some people come to believe that their ideas are not given the appropriate amount of respect and attention by others, and they become stubborn, just to make the point that their opinions are to be reckoned with, even when they know that they are wrong!

Dr. Chapunoff: Many times I've seen stubborn persons using a verbal barrage as a camouflage to hide their wrong ideas, while they are fully aware that their points are clearly mistaken.

Dr. Paul: You are so right, Ed! Stubborn people will even argue a point that they know is wrong, so no one perceives them as weak or makes them feel disregarded. Sometimes, and this is especially so with children, they may become stubborn because of anxiety. These children are typically shy and anxious, and their anxiety causes them to lock onto a position or idea and defend it as a way of reducing anxiety.

Dr. Chapunoff: Adults do more or less the same thing, don't they?

Dr. Paul: Yes, Ed, sometimes they definitely do. The reality is that even in adults, who are often just big children, there is an anxiety component behind stubbornness. What is fascinating is that if you suggest to a stubborn person that there is an anxiety-base to their being stubborn, they may laugh at you and absolutely deny it in an attempt to reduce their anxiety!

Dr. Chapunoff: I'm certainly not a psychologist, but stubborn individuals have given me the impression that their denials are as frequent as their wrong conclusions.

Dr. Paul: That is quite accurate, Ed. Stubbornness comes from being insecure and insecurities present as anxieties. As I mentioned above, the display of hubris and arrogance are meant to mask the anxiety stemming from insecurity. The more insecure, the more stubborn! Stubborn people may argue that they are not stubborn, even when they know that they are. Facing the fact that they have a flaw might be too much for them to deal with.

Dr. Chapunoff: In the course of our lives, we all have to face challenging situations. I presume that the stubborn person, with a base of insecurity and anxiety, will have a rough time every time something unexpected happens.

Dr. Paul: That is true, Ed. Since stubbornness is related to an underlying anxiety base, it would be easy to see why people might fear new or different situations. With insecure people, new or different situations are threatening, and it is this increased threat that fuels more stubbornness. Change becomes an enemy.

Dr. Chapunoff: Defining an individual we know fairly well as stubborn may not be very difficult. I'd like you to help me to recognize a stubborn person, when I am not that familiar with him or her.

Dr. Paul: Spotting a stubborn person is easy. They tend to be argumentative, controlling, intolerant and, as I have mentioned, often arrogant. It might take a little bit of time to be with somebody to understand that their argumentativeness and their fixed position taking is characteristic of their style, but identifying stubbornness is a bit of a no-brainer, unless they happen to be on your team, and then they are stalwart and single-minded of purpose!

Dr. Chapunoff: I once interviewed a man because of heart disease. His wife accompanied him. I knew the couple socially, and I was aware that their marriage was on the rocks. They had been together for 25 years. This woman had a monumental degree of stubbornness. Our dialogue led to a discussion about their relationship, and she immediately began to attack him mercilessly. At one point, our dialogue went like this:

Dr. C: *"Janet, would you accept the fact that in your marriage of 25 years, you made some mistakes?"*

Janet: *"No, I wouldn't accept that!"*

Dr. C: *"Why, may I ask you?"*

Janet: *"Because I never made any mistakes in my marriage."*

Dr. C: *"Never...never?"*

Janet: *"NEVER! ...Didn't you hear that...?"*

To me, that answer was almost surreal. That day, I really understood what stubbornness truly is.

Dr. Paul: This woman's typifies stubbornness at its best or as its worst.

Superior people, in the mind of a stubborn person, do not lose. If you are stubborn, accepting defeat, just like agreeing that you have erred, would be unacceptable. Defeat, or even being wrong, becomes tantamount to having the world know that you are inadequate.

When I previously explained the cognitive basis of anxiety, I mentioned that anxiety metaphorically comes from fearing that we are about to be eaten by a tiger. I also said that the biggest tiger people face is the fear that their inadequacy will be discovered. Stubbornness is simply one way to try to keep insecurity under control by never admitting any vulnerability or weakness. By being correct, stubborn people try to preserve their own sense of control and adequacy. Since any attempt at perfectionism is bound to fail and stubbornness is clearly one variant of perfectionism, as an adjustment it can never work. This continually fuels the internal dread of inadequacy, which continually produces the need to maintain stubbornness.

Dr. Chapunoff: We all like to enjoy happiness and peace of mind. I always compare happiness with champagne and peace of mind with water. You can live without happiness, as you can live without champagne. However, drinking water, which I equate to having peace of mind, is a basic, essential need. You just cannot do without it! How can a stubborn person be happy and have real peace of mind?

Dr. Paul: Stubborn people are not happy people, and they do not have peace of mind either. They are often full of unrecognized self-loathing, which they are too frightened to admit or allow to surface. While stubborn people will never admit it, they are often plagued with shame, guilt, and hatefulness directed both inwardly and outwardly and an irrational need to control everyone and every thing. They camouflage their anxieties with pride and arrogance, which pushes people away from them, leading to more unhappiness and a constant undercurrent of fear, which they must deny. They often overreact by trying to convince people how magnanimous, charitable, and pleasant they are. The only people they succeed in fooling are themselves, and this actually really does not work either.

Dr. Chapunoff: Howard, the victim of a stubborn individual consults you and asks you what would be the best way of dealing with that person. Not seeing that person any more would be great, indeed, but that isn't always an easy option. The stubborn person could be a mother, a father, a spouse, a son, etc. What's the best way to manage such a difficult task?

Dr. Paul: Dealing with someone who is stubborn is learning the art of not being sucked into his or her pathology. One of my favorite phrases is, *"Don't keep sticking your finger into an electric pencil sharpener!"* You deal with stubborn people by giving them permission to be stubborn. Do not argue with them, and do not expect them to be anything other than stubborn. Like a stone, only expect a stubborn person to act like a stone, that is, be stubborn. Stones do not fly. Do not ask them to fly.

You will only be disappointed. You will be angry if you turn your wish into a demand.

Once you understand that stubbornness is based on a significant underlying personality problem fueled by anxiety and inadequacy, the humbling revelation that no amount of your love or understanding will fix this may come to you.

Dr. Chapunoff: I hope that readers who are closely involved with stubborn individuals will remember what you just said. It is very revealing and intensely therapeutic.

Dr. Paul: It really does not matter how reasonable a point of view you may take, it may not be able to dent the stubbornness that people put up as armor, which in some people is very thick. Stubborn people fear that if they let their armor down, they will fall apart!

Dr. Chapunoff: I've seen stubborn individuals strenuously defending their points of view and defining their position not as stubbornness but as assertiveness. What do you make out of that comparison?

Dr. Paul: Stubborn people will often simply say that they are standing up for themselves. There is a huge difference between being assertive, standing for your rights, and being stubborn - one is rational, the other is irrational.

Dr. Chapunoff: Rational here means reasonable, right?

Dr. Paul: That is correct, Ed. Rationality implies being flexible, reasonable, and being able to consider other people's positions. Stubbornness is irrational, inflexible, and unreasonable.

Clearly, the art of dealing with this kind of person in psychotherapy is not in knowing what to do but in knowing when to do it. This is one of those cases, where if you move too quickly, you may cause damage to the person because they are not ready to have their shield be eliminated.

Standing up for yourself is one thing, but having a stubborn personality is quite another thing. Many people find dealing with stubborn people very draining.

Dr. Chapunoff: One would like to ask stubborn persons why it is so difficult for them to admit being wrong? Do they feel inferior doing that? I would argue that failing to admit your own mistakes is a sign of weakness, and their admission is a reflection of a logical and mature mind. In dealing with stubborn individuals, it took me time to realize that no amount of reasoning would ever be sufficient to change their stony opinions, and as you said, *"Stones don't fly."* Any expectations of minimal flexibility by them were simply nonexistent.

If I had known in the past what to expect from a stubborn individual the way I know now, thanks to your very clear and effective explanations, I wouldn't have wasted my time trying to extract crude oil from a can of 7-Up.

21

THE PERILS OF PORNOGRAPHY

Dr. Chapunoff: Bob and Sarah had been married for 18 years. They had a son of 14 and a daughter of 16. The couple had problems with their relationship. They had different ideas about sex, as well as different ways of expressing it. Bob was raised by religious, orthodox parents, who believed that sex should only have the purpose of procreation and never recreation. He was a handsome, gentle man in his 40s. Professionally, he was a successful chemical engineer. His wife was very attractive and five years younger.

Sarah's ideas about sex were in stark contradiction with those of her husband. She was obsessive about having plenty of sex. When she got together socially with her female friends and spoke candidly, she openly discussed her personal problems, stating that during intimacy her husband *"was extremely boring"* and that *"he didn't know how to stimulate"* her or make love to her *"the proper way."* He *"never, absolutely never"* used anything other than the missionary position. His premature ejaculations didn't help either.

Sarah openly spoke to her daughter about her sexual frustrations and encouraged her to satisfy her fantasies and sexual needs *"no matter what."* One day at noon, the girl and her boyfriend had unrestricted sex inside a car parked in an open downtown area. Many people saw how the teenagers had sex, very oblivious to the presence of several strangers, who had been attracted to the show.

Bob learned that his wife was visiting the Internet regularly to watch porno movies. He correctly sensed that his wife wasn't satisfied with his sexual performance but was unable, unknowledgeable, timid, or too afraid to correct the problem. He became even more disturbed when his daughter confessed to him that she was *addicted* to pornographic material and had no intention of giving it up.

Howard, imagine that Bob and his wife consult you about their intimate disagreements, and Bob tells you that the frequent viewing of pornographic movies by his wife makes him feel diminished and very inadequate.

Understandably, he is upset and distressed about the fact that their teenage daughter adopted her mother's habits, with no intention of changing them.

How do you deal with this marital and family difficult situation?

Dr. Paul: Ed, the questions you raise and the title, "The Perils of Pornography," might be more aptly changed given the vignette presented, to the perils of being puritanical and too up tight! It is very clear that 22 years ago, this couple did not do any premarital counseling. They certainly would have benefitted from going through the questionnaire you offered in our earlier conversation on marriage. I wonder if this couple ever speaks to each other about their concerns. Did Sarah ever try to teach Bob how to satisfy her, or did they treat sex like the elephant in the room that they both chose to ignore? Did they ever try to resolve the issues caused by their very different upbringing? Did Sarah realize she was acting out, and did she understand that her encouragement of her daughter to be free might have come from her being angry with Bob? Did she not realize that her daughter might not yet have the discretion to use her sexually unrepressed attitude in a wise and legal way? There would be many background questions I would want to ask.

As I have explained, therapy often starts with psychoeducation. With pornography, and the circumstances you outline about Bob and Sarah, education and providing some basic facts would be a good place to start.

Pornography is difficult to tackle because, at least in the United States, we are dealing with generally repressive attitudes towards sex. Many see pornography as a threat to maintaining positive sexual boundaries and keeping the status quo of seeing sex as dirty. Bob would certainly agree with this fear. People who grow up in an environment where being

200

sexual is repressed or where views on sexuality are negatively distorted, have difficulty with pornography.

Dr. Chapunoff: What's the reaction toward pornography by persons who were raised in a tolerant and more open-minded environment of sex education?

Dr. Paul: People who were blessed with a positive self-concept, whose parents were not reluctant to discuss issues about sex and who were not subjected to repressive political/religious views about sex and sexuality, tend to have few problems and have less interest in pornography.

To some, increased acceptance of sexuality, and especially pornography, is troublesome on moral and ethical grounds, fearing that people will become more accepting of deviance if they watch porn. Remember that exposure to anything, even pornography, reduces anxiety.

Dr. Chapunoff: Reduction in anxiety that results from repeated exposure to anything, in this case, pornography, has a desensitizing effect, correct?

Dr. Paul: You are correct, Ed. There are a number of studies suggesting that prolonged exposure to sexually explicit material desensitizes people, at least for a short amount of time, and they become more open and tolerant to sexual behavior in all of its various presentations. For those who believe that much of sexuality is inappropriate or sinful, this desensitization factor is of great concern. Interestingly, some sex therapists use this very same desensitization as a part of their treatment of sexual disorders.

Dr. Chapunoff: I remember I read in a psychology book years ago, the case of a woman who suffered from an aversion to the penis. The psychotherapist desensitized her by showing her an artificial model of male genitals that he placed at a distance. During the next visits, this model would be closer and closer to her. At one point, the artificial penis was placed just in front of her, and she touched it without any kind of adverse reaction. That's a typical case of the desensitization process you just referred to, right?

Dr. Paul: That is right, Ed. That's a good example of how to apply the desensitization technique to some sexual dysfunctions. But, back to the topic of porn. Pornography is difficult to address, as there is an extraordinarily wide range of pornography that, on one end, shows mature consenting adults engaging in appropriate and caring lovemaking, while on the other extreme children are being sexually abused. There is no lack of variety of pornographic material from group sex, sex with animals, sex with same-sex partners, female-centric sex, and the list goes on.

Another factor that makes commenting on pornography challenging is that some of the research done on sexuality and on pornography has been biased. One must be careful when reading the literature to make sure it is not backed by either religious or other groups, who have essentially paid to have their ideas made legitimate.

Dr. Chapunoff: People who like to see pornographic movies will deal with this issue in widely different ways. Some may adopt a casual approach and see sex videos occasionally for some stimulation and entertainment, whereas others will become obsessive and will not rest until they have saturated their minds and genitals with porno stuff.

Dr. Paul: As with many other social temptations, it is how much people are bound up in something that determines whether it can be a positive or negative factor in their life. Drinking is not a problem. Drinking and drinking is a problem. This same formula can be true for pornography. Many of the things we have discussed are temptations, and any of these can be turned into addictions.

Dr. Chapunoff: At the beginning of our conversation, you suggested that an appropriate name for this chapter would be "The Perils of Being Puritanical."

You have a good point, and I don't disagree with you. Nevertheless, I do believe that pornography has its own share of perils that are disturbingly real. I'd like to know if you agree with that concept.

Dr. Paul: Ed, since your title is on the perils of pornography, I guess a good place to start would be to see if any peril exists. The answer would have to be a clear yes. The risks of pornography are many.

Overconsumption of pornography, or even a naïve vulnerability to what is depicted, can negatively affect some peoples' attitudes about sex and about relationships. Some men can become dissatisfied with their partner because the women in pornographic films seem completely uninhibited and hungry for sex, which is often quite different from what they encounter with their wife or girlfriend, who may be more inhibited. Similarly, both the men and women in pornographic films seem to be more beautiful, better endowed, and for many middle-aged men are more agile, active, and younger than their current sexual partner.

Dr. Chapunoff: Which will most likely lead to marital conflict!

Dr. Paul: Right! For many, this can put a strain on the marital relationship by eroding libido and the desire for sex with their partner. I mentioned that, on one end of the spectrum, pornography depicts consenting adults in a caring and mutual exchange of sex and affection. This is too often not the case. More often than not, caring is not what porn films are about. Too frequently, women are depicted as sexual objects, which many see as degrading. For many reasons, sex films often end with the male ejaculating on the face and body of the female.

Dr. Chapunoff: Yeah! Sometimes these ejaculations appear to have the size and force of a tsunami wave!

Dr. Paul: To many, this is disgusting and simply presents a very warped picture of the grand finale of lovemaking. Sex films are obsessed with orgasm and make sure that you see it. Sex would best not be about orgasm, but about a sensual and shared loving experience.

Dr. Chapunoff: The way I see it, pornography has the strange ability of combining reality and fantasy. Reality is what happens in the couple's bedroom. Fantasy is what people see in the video. I call this fantasy because in real life the couple who watched the video may not be able to reproduce what they saw on film.

Dr. Paul: Some are concerned that pornography makes it difficult for people to separate fantasy from reality and, as I said, creates a distorted view of the normal female body. Sex films may be good for the silicone industry, but may not be so good for the average woman.

Dr. Chapunoff: How do men who are frequent viewers of porno movies think about their daughters? They may enjoy the show, but I doubt they would be as elated if their daughter was the performing star.

Dr. Paul: Some studies have shown that men who watch a great deal of pornography are less likely to want daughters. Notions of equality between men and women also typically threaten them. Their view of what is normal is often distorted, leading them to have an exaggerated estimate of the frequency of group sex and bestiality.

Dr. Chapunoff: Many who view porno movies do this alone and they get their sexual satisfaction alone. This solitary sexual activity is a definite incentive for masturbation.

Dr. Paul: One real concern is that pornography, and the masturbation typically associated with it, is an asocial activity. There is no social exchange, except with a fantasized figure. Viewing porn is typically done behind closed doors, actually enhancing rigid and repressive attitudes about sex. In case anyone is wondering, this is not an endorsement of masturbating in public!

Dr. Chapunoff: Do you see in pornography any kind of social redemption?

Dr. Paul: Pornography certainly does not enhance social skills.

Dr. Chapunoff: Persons who desire a high level of sexual stimulation see porno movies with the hope and expectation that their volcanic desires will be pleased. However, is the same intense sexual stimulation that resulted from the porno movie reproduced during normal sexual activity?

Dr. Paul: Some individuals crave higher than normal amounts of stimulation. For some, exposure to material that produces strong sexual excitement makes it more difficult for these individuals to respond to normal sexual stimuli and normal sexual activity. In our other discussions, I noted that some people are more prone to addictions than others are. Smoking, drugs, alcohol, gambling, shopping, overeating, use of computer games, and many more can all become addictions, as well as pornography. Anything that stimulates the morphine receptors in our brain is subject to being addicting.

Dr. Chapunoff: Howard, do you have an idea about the number of people who are watching pornography at this moment?

Dr. Paul: As I am having this chat with you, some estimate that about 30,000 people are watching pornography right now as we speak. When large polls are done, 4 million people admit to being addicted to pornography.

Dr. Chapunoff: Are you referring to the United States alone?

Dr. Paul: Yes, Ed, I am. The results are typical when other western cultures are studied. The concerns I mention above seem to have a legitimate base, and there is support for concern being valid.

Because this is such an emotionally laden area, there have been many concerns put forth that when scrutinized, do not hold water. The Internet has proven to be a dramatic gateway to acquiring and viewing pornography.

Dr. Chapunoff: Does pornography increase the risk of sex crimes?

Dr. Paul: Many have concerns that the ease with which pornography can now be obtained increases the risk for sex crimes. Studies seem to suggest just the opposite. Since the Internet, there has actually been a decrease in the reported frequency of rape. It may seem that there is an increased frequency of rape, and it is easy to see why people might think that there is a link between pornography and rape, but this does not appear to have merit when it is studied.

By recent estimates, there are well over three billion pages of information on the Internet and almost 10 percent of that is made up of pornography. It is very hard not to stumble upon pornography, even by accident. Sometimes it just shows up in e-mail without it even being requested. Since it is so prevalent, it has to have some impact. You can predict that for some, the outcome will be fine, and for some it will not be.

Divorce attorneys at one of their national meetings believed that Internet porn did play a significant role in divorce. There is little doubt that Internet-based hook-ups abound, and it is easier for lonely people to meet other lonely people because of the Internet. I think it is more probable that the Internet, not pornography, has put many marriages at risk. The Internet is an escape, and when things are not going well, too many people use escape instead of problem solving.

At about the same time of the attorney poll, a survey of over 7000 adults found that almost 5000 stated that they regularly visited porn sites. That is about 70 percent of people admitting that they viewed pornography! I am sure that some would say that the other 30 percent were lying. George Carlin, a wildly funny and irreverent comedian, whose keen wit is sorely missed, did a skit on pornography. His premise was that the Supreme Court would not ban pornography because it was too much fun! In addition, making it illegal would make the judges themselves all criminals. Of the 5000 who admitted to viewing porn, most did not believe it significantly affected their relationships. I am not sure that if this same survey were given to only women these same findings would emerge.

Some link the free availability of pornography on the Internet to sex crimes targeting children. While the Internet does put children in new peril, recent studies show that children are being more harmed by peer cyber-bullying than by online sexual predators. This fact certainly does not get a lot of press, unless there is a suicide related to it. Some reports seem to suggest that the regular stream of TV reports highlighting the dangers of sexual predators exceeds what the real crime frequency would warrant. Many feel that these stories are given headlines because of the attention-grabbing nature of these crimes. The motto around the newsroom is *"if it bleeds, it leads!"* This also holds true for crimes involving sex, especially where rape or child sexual abuse is involved. The media also presents a somewhat distorted view of what is known about sexual predators and abusers. People have the wrong assumption that most Internet-based molesters pretend to be peers. In reality, less than one in 10 do so. People have the notion that contact between molesters and children is brief, and that these problems spring up quickly on an unsuspecting individual. The reality seems to be that most abusers correspond with their victims for at least four weeks or more, and many have telephone conversations or meetings before any molestation occurs. People also have the notion that sex is never mentioned by the abuser and that underage children are frequently coerced. While this is sadly sometimes true, only about one out of eight children are forced into having sex. Here, I am not talking about very young children, but adolescents. When it comes to adolescents, most have discussed sex with their molester and have agreed to it. I fear that many will now be outraged with these statements and believe that I am somehow condoning this behavior. What I am trying to do is simply report what has emerged from the little study that has been done in this area.

From what we now know, exposure to pornography seems not to directly contribute to rape or other sex crimes, and there even is some evidence that it actually reduces these crimes. Preexisting biases aside, there is little evidence that, for most, viewing pornography is damaging.

If pornography is not bad for many, does it do any good at all? Some researchers are detecting a change in attitude toward pornography, with many young people saying that it is simply a part of the online world. For many youngsters growing up online, pornography holds less interest for them than it does for many adults who grew up in a much more sexually repressed time. There seems to be a greater sophistication in pornography viewers. They seem to understand better that the people, as well as the situations they are looking at, are not typical or real. A lot more young people understand that the scenes depicted exceed the boundaries of normal and common sexual predispositions. One real problem of most pornographic films is that they tend not to depict safe sex. The prevalence of pornography has also put pressure on sex education to do more than simply *just say no*. Pornography is forcing a more honest and open discussion of human sexuality in all its ramifications and dimensions. The *just say no* strategy has not worked, and has left many individuals at higher risk for pregnancy and sexually transmitted diseases.

In a relatively recent and much commented on article in *Psychology Today*, a Danish psychologist reported that he found many men and women who believed that hardcore pornography was a positive influence on their lives, sexual knowledge, their attitude towards the opposite sex, and even their quality of life. They must have been looking at very high-quality porn.

Ed, as with many of the discussions we completed, the effects of pornography typically depends on how well put together the person is who is watching the porn. For relatively well-adjusted individuals, there is no harm. For those at risk, there is the inevitable higher probability that it will create more difficulties.

Ed, you ask how I would deal with this situation if this couple presented themselves to me. As with any therapy, we would start with psychoeducation. I would try to gain an understanding of their background and try to understand more fully, what they believed and what they were taught by their family of origin. It is very clear that this couple would have greatly benefited from your questionnaire because it might have gotten them into treatment many years earlier and averted much of their distress. Since it did not, we would try to inform them of current thinking about the use of pornography and correct beliefs that seem to be blatantly untrue, especially on Bob's part. What would happen next would depend upon their commitment to stay married and Bob's willingness to engage in sexual therapy. He appears to have very moralistic beliefs, and he would have to determine if he was willing to look at his ideas and alter them. My not agreeing with his way of looking at things would give me no right to change the way he viewed things, unless he was willing to do so and found my information and arguments compelling. Dealing with this couple would involve both marital therapy and sex therapy. Staying true to all that I have said in our discussions thus far, I would try to help Bob understand that viewing pornography could not make him feel diminished. Only he could do that by the meaning he attributes to his wife's behavior. There is a good chance that he does harbor feelings of inadequacy, and this too would need to be addressed. The different attitudes they each bring to their children would need to be discussed and some common ground forged. Even the wife might come to see that her lack of supplying sufficient boundaries to her daughter could be dangerous. Having uninhibited sex can be fantastic. Having sex in public can get you arrested.

22

CODEPENDENCY
A defective attachment that holds like a magnet

Dr. Chapunoff: Alice was 45 and married to Frank for 22 years. She was extremely subdued when dealing with her husband. His temperament was hot and strong, and he had a marked tendency to give orders to her, as well as their two teenage girls.

"What are we going to have for dinner tonight?" he'd ask, and she'd answer,

"Anything you want..."

Next day he'd say, *"We'll go to the movies this weekend."*

Her response, *"Yes, darling. Can we see a comedy?"*

His response, *"No, I want to see an action movie, if possible, a horror movie."*

Her response, *"That's okay. Anything you want, Frank."*

It was obvious that the focus in her life was her husband. She gave the impression that she never thought about herself or her needs and desires. All that mattered was pleasing her tyrannical spouse.

Another typical exchange:

"I love my dress, do you?"

"No, I don't! Change it!"

In addition, she'd always comply with his wishes, his demands, or his orders. Moreover, when she didn't focus on her husband, which she did

95 percent of the time, she'd focus on her daughters. The focus on her was no higher than 0 percent.

On numerous occasions, I have seen husbands treat their wives with utter disregard for their dignity. Some of them were educated professionals.

The wife was always wrong, the despotic husband was always right. She kept apologizing, and he kept on throwing poisonous darts at the woman's unprotected, unshielded soul. In addition, these individuals did the same thing with their children: *"You've got an A in just 90 percent of the exams at school? Why didn't you get the best grades 100 percent of the time? Are you stupid, lazy, or what?"*

Here comes my question:

Where does codependency come from? Where did this woman's weak character, as soft as melted butter in summer time, designed to please and satisfy another person's taste and needs, while depriving her of everything imaginable including, of course, her self-respect, originate? Why does this victim endure her spouse's attacks and abuses?

Dr. Paul: Ed, your questions throughout our many conversations have led me to do a great deal of thinking about what situations I find very challenging. Your question about codependency has crystallized what are some of the sadder situations that I come across and represents those that can be of great challenge.

Just a few weeks ago, I started seeing a woman who was in a very controlling and psychologically degrading relationship, even worse than the one you described. She had been in this relationship for many years and, for lack of a better way of putting it, had gotten used to being psychologically abused. She was involved in a few previous relationships, all of which failed, and she was not of the mind to leave this one. As I am having this conversation with you, she is in a psychiatric hospital, where she hopefully will get the support needed to work on her severe codependent issues.

Another sad case that I am working with regards a man, an ex-firefighter, who was injured and now suffers from chronic pain that is the result of losing use of one of his arms and his hand. He recently lost both his mother and father, and now he and his brother are taking care of their grandmother, who has an advanced neurological disease. He feels duty bound to support his brother and his grandmother. His brother is obsessed with keeping the grandmother at home and taking care of her without assistance. He refuses to bring support care into the house. My patient has become codependent to his brother, has lost a significant amount of weight, has exacerbated his chronic pain and, for his many reasons, is increasingly unable to take care of himself, sacrificing himself for his brother and grandmother.

Dr. Chapunoff: Howard, would you be kind enough to define codependency and explain to us how it originates and develops so pervasively in so many people?

Dr. Paul: Yes, Ed, I will be glad to. Codependency is rampant. This word is a general term that covers a number of different behaviors and symptoms. Simply put, the main characteristic of the codependent person is that he or she devotes excessive energy, time, and focus on others, typically on one other person. This other person is usually a spouse or loved one, but it can be a lover, boyfriend, or girlfriend.

Codependent individuals have lost the balance between taking care of themselves and taking care of others. They devote inordinate amounts of time and energy taking care of everybody else and put themselves last.

The term codependency was originally used in research involving alcoholism and focused on the spouses and children of alcoholics. It has been expanded to involve individuals who are also taking care of chronically ill people and has then been further expanded to describe any relationship in which there is an overfocus on the other partner.

Codependent individuals have difficulty being assertive and are overly compliant, even with demands that are either preposterous or degrading. When asked the question, *"What is it that you wish to do or want for yourself?"* codependent individuals often have difficulty coming up with an answer because their thought process revolves around what other people want, to the exclusion of what they themselves would like.

When codependent people are in long-term relationships, they run the risk of actually forgetting what they personally like, instead assuming the likes and dislikes of the person to whom they are codependent.

Dr. Chapunoff: Are codependent persons victims of a defective upbringing and dysfunctional families?

Dr. Paul: Codependent individuals often come from dysfunctional families, where the process of individuation to become a unique and independent person is never completed. Some codependent people are actively taught that they must suppress their own desires in order to take care of others, that they are worthless, and that they need to stay with someone who will take care of them, even if the relationship is abusive.

Often, because they did not receive good nurturing as a child, individuals turn this around and work to be the most caring people that they can be. Psychodynamically, this is an example of what is called a reaction formation.

Dr. Chapunoff: Isn't it a fact that codependents tend to try to please persons who don't appreciate their efforts and devotion at all?

Dr. Paul: Yes, that is unfortunately true. Codependents often pick an emotionally unavailable, unfeeling, insensitive person to care for. No matter how much caring they give, the relationship will never be satisfying or successful.

Dr. Chapunoff: Do they recognize how futile their efforts are?

Dr. Paul: Rather than recognize the futility of their behavior, people do that uniquely human thing, which is to simply to try doing what does not work longer and harder. It is almost as if codependent individuals become addicted to pain, which maintains them in unhealthy relationships. They tend to live in a fantasy world of how things could be, rather than in the real world of how things are. Codependent individuals often have romantic fantasies, which can become obsessions. They often idealize the people to whom they are codependent, believing that maintaining a relationship with that person is somehow fulfilling and makes them complete.

Dr. Chapunoff: Now, I'm curious to know what possible reaction a codependent person might have if he or she was advised to separate from the dominant individual who treats him or her so abusively.

Dr. Paul: Speaking to such people about leaving the codependent relationship will often create intense anxiety. Individuals are often quite terrified of abandonment and have truly come to see themselves as unable to cope without the support of the other individual, even if the other person is abusive. Codependent individuals are willing to take far more than 50 percent of the responsibility in any circumstance and are the type of individuals who, if someone else bumps into them, they will be the one who says, *"I'm sorry."*

Dr. Chapunoff: From what you're saying, it appears that codependents get a slap in the face and thank the offender for the gesture.

Dr. Paul: Yes, that is often the way it is. Codependents frequently blame themselves for their partner's abusiveness. I, unfortunately, too often hear something that goes like this, *"...if I had only done a better job, then he would not have hit me."*

Dr. Chapunoff: In a loving relationship, giving is certainly more important than receiving. Howard, do codependents fall into the trap of giving too much and to a person who does not appreciate at all that kind of generosity?

Dr. Paul: That is right. As with most psychological pathologies, these tendencies exist on a continuum. In order for a marriage to be successful and sustainable, there will be many times where one or the other member of the dyad would best suppress his or her own desires and work to please the other person. Wishing to take care of others, not always putting yourself first and thinking of others are all parts of being a mature adult in a committed relationship, as well as contributing to the community. It is only when these positive attributes are taken to extremes that they become pathological and are labeled codependency. As I said in our discussion on pornography, drinking is not a problem. Drinking and drinking is a problem. Giving is not a problem. Giving and giving and giving is

Interestingly, codependency is, in fact, one form of being controlling. Typically, the codependent individual complains about how controlling their partner is without really understanding that their attempts to always help, please, and assist the other person are, in and of themselves, control strategies.

Dr. Chapunoff: Does that mean that in codependent relationships, both the person who is under siege and the individual who is the recipient of the codependent efforts to please him or her are trying to be the controllers in their own peculiar and different ways?

Dr. Paul: Ed, you have it right. Most people easily see the abuser as being controlling and side with the person being abused. Where there is severe codependent pathology, this too is a control strategy. For example, you cannot have sadism without masochism. They are a pair and often inseparable. Therefore, the problem is also between the partners in a codependent relationship. One reason for having the codependent person see it this way is to help them realize that they play a role in their own bad situation. Since they contribute to it, they can also extricate themselves from it. This conceptualization is not meant to blame the codependent person, but instead, to empower them and help them see that they can steer this problem in some other way.

Dr. Chapunoff: A codependent relationship, from what I gather, appears to have more problems and conflicts than pleasure. Is there any room for true love in the context of such a messy and pathological process? In addition, does the codependent person look for a certain kind of personality to get involved with in a relationship?

Dr. Paul: Ed, codependent individuals become accustomed to having no love in their relationship. They substitute security for love, while at the same time trying to obtain the unobtainable with compliance and subjugation. Some theorists believe that codependent individuals are drawn to people with problems that they believe need to be fixed.

Dr. Chapunoff: Yeah! Some people are drawn to tornados so they can get very close to them to get a nice picture!

Dr. Paul: That is right, and this typically enmeshes them in situations that are unstable and often chaotic. By maintaining some level of anger at the person they are enmeshed with, they create a false sense of being correct, which, as you may recall, comes from being angry. They also try to hide from themselves their own sense of low self-esteem, as well as their fear of abandonment and rejection.

Dr. Chapunoff: Codependents, though, like all of us, I'm sure would love to love!

Dr. Paul: Absolutely, they do! However, while they desperately seek love, there is a frequent ambivalence that they do not deserve love and that they can never be happy. It is truly a difficult situation.

Dr. Chapunoff: Gee, that's really very sad!

Dr. Paul: Yes, Ed, it is, and because this is such a no-win situation, depression and anxiety are often the features that bring such codependent individuals into therapy.

Dr. Chapunoff: Howard, how do codependent individuals react when they are told that their codependency will only give them unhappiness and it will surely end in an Olympic failure?

Dr. Paul: Ed, such individuals often respond with anger, denial, guilt, or anxiety. Codependent individuals, as with many individuals with low self-esteem, are often overly concerned with the opinions of others. This is not to say that we should not be mindful of others' opinions; however, it is important not to lose our own opinions in the process. Receiving feedback from others is part of the learning process, but it is always best to weigh others' opinions against our own sense of what is real, coupled with the understanding that other people's opinions are not superior to or more important than our own.

Dr. Chapunoff: You've been dissecting the problems of codependency in a very clear manner, and everything thing you said about this disorder invites us to think that the codependent is hooked on the dominance of another person, as other individuals are pathologically linked to cocaine, alcohol, or gambling. Does this situation evoke an addictive kind of behavior? In other words, is codependency an addiction, besides being many other unpleasant things?

Dr. Paul: I am glad you brought up that point, Ed. In fact, codependency emerged from addiction literature because it can be a serious and sometimes fatal addiction. Codependency is sometimes called relationship addiction.

The good news is that serious codependency can be managed with good treatment. It does take time, patience, and a good deal of commitment and motivation on the part of the individual, but it can be done.

Dr. Chapunoff: This is very good news for codependent persons, and I hope they are taking notice right now and learn about the anatomy of codependency, as explained in this conversation. I truly hope that people reading this, who suffer from codependency, will manage to get proper treatment, modify their thoughts and behavior, and achieve happiness.

Dr. Paul: I second what you just said, Ed.

Codependency can exist in lesser forms, such as individuals who are such people pleasers that they cannot say no to anyone for any reason.

These individuals often do not have enough time in the day to satisfy the time requirements of all the things they have agreed to do for everyone else. Such people often believe that if they do not say yes or help everyone they can, that they are being irresponsible, disloyal to their friends, and essentially not a good person.

I am sure that you can hear the perfectionism that rings through these kinds of emotional-guidance statements these individuals possess.

Let me be clear, codependent individuals often have good and proper motivations, as well as a genuine desire to be helpful. That is a good thing. What is wrong is the exaggeration of this good tendency and the inclination to take it to the pathological extreme.

Dr. Chapunoff: True! Too much of a good thing often ends being a bad thing!

Howard, can you tell us something about therapy of codependency? How can people with this condition be helped?

Dr. Paul: Codependency has a largely learned element to it and is often passed on from one generation to another generation. Since it is learned, better alternatives can also be learned. Just as there are support groups for alcoholics, there are support groups for the spouses of addicted individuals, typically focusing on codependency. Such groups often use a variant of the 12-step program used in Alcoholics Anonymous.

From my standpoint, when I work with someone who has significant codependency issues, I try to help them discover their underlying belief issues and the impact that their family of origin may have had on their learned behaviors. Helping them discover their own personal strengths and helping them see themselves as more competent and capable individuals, becomes part of the process. Helping individuals deal with their anger, loneliness, and depleted sense of worth becomes the core of any treatment. I work to empower individuals to understand that they can make a difference. Their choices keep them entrapped, not the circumstances that they describe.

23

BULLYING
The vicious, never-ending attacks

Dr. Chapunoff: A woman of 58, married three times, divorced all her husbands or her husbands divorced her. Even as a child, she displayed an arrogant and pushy behavior toward her siblings, mother, and other people.

Her mother is now 95 and still alert but weakened, due to the debilitating characteristic of her advanced age. Her bully daughter continues to mistreat her, abusing her verbally and emotionally. She always thinks she is correct, and everyone else is wrong. She is *always right*. When she does something wrong, and that happens daily, she always justifies her actions by blaming others.

I just presented to you a case of bullying. Bullying is the abusive use of force or coercion to affect others. A repeated aggressive behavior done to intentionally hurt another person.

Bullying is widespread. It happens in many families, as well as in churches, homes, schools, workplaces, neighborhoods, and in every country in the world.

Historians noted that WWI and WWII happened because countries started bullying each other. Some child victims of bullying at school are so emotionally damaged that they have committed suicide.

Bullying even happens to doctors in training. I personally suffered a number of bullying episodes during my medical training. I wasn't the only one.

Bullying in teaching institutions is a common thing. I remember, at one point during my postgraduate training, I badly wanted to have an accident, like a fractured femur, to have a justification not to attend the rigorous medical training to which I was being subjected. The same occurred to me during my military service.

I don't know if these experiences modified my character for better or worse, but after enduring them, I was never the same person.

Those who practice bullying do it to intimidate or victimize others.

I witnessed incidents of bullying caused by people who did not appear curable or even treatable. They were manipulative, cynical, and had an undeniable touch of cruelty.

I'd like to know if teaching a person to manage the attacks of bullying is preferable to teaching a bullying person to behave correctly. The bullying perpetrators I met in my life did not seem to have any kind of disposition to change their attitude or be amenable to any kind of treatment that would soften or sweeten their character and toxic disposition toward others.

I'd like to know how wrong or right I am about bullying. One thing you can be sure of: I intended no bull…if you know what I mean.

Dr. Paul: Ed, it is noble (no bull intended) of you to ask these questions, especially since you shared some of your own personal experiences. Bullying is a function of insecurity, just as is stubbornness and many of the other problems that we have discussed. Bullying occurs when we try to make ourselves feel aggrandized, bigger, stronger, or better than the other person does by making them feel worse than we feel.

You could ask the simple question, what kind of person makes themself feel better by making someone else feel worse? The answer, quite plainly, would be someone who doesn't really feel that positive or strong about themself to begin with.

Dr. Chapunoff: You just said that people who bully are insecure individuals. Do you see bullying coming from secure, assertive persons?

Dr. Paul: Ed, secure people simply do not bully. Bullies are typically those who are not in the achieving group, or if they are in the top group, feel that their position in it is tenuous and needs to be strengthened. They try to fool themselves into believing that they are strong and powerful by intimidating others.

This is not the unique purview of children, as I am sure that many people are aware of bosses who do the same thing. You mentioned that this happened during your medical training, so it is clear that insecurity exists, even in settings where people are achieving. The dynamics remain true, no matter how old the person doing it happens to be.

Dr. Chapunoff: Bullying appears to be even more common than the common cold. If you observe peoples' attitudes in different cultures, different races, and different countries, this despicable behavior is present.

Dr. Paul: That is right, Ed. Bullying is universal. It is impossible to have been in school and not, at one time or another, been bullied. For most who are bullied, it represents unpleasant memories while for others it can be devastating and lead to catastrophic results, even suicide.

Interestingly, 30 to 40 years ago bullying was seldom discussed in school and received very little attention from behavioral scientists. There has been a slow change in attitude over the last 20 years, not only in the United States, but also throughout the world and a spate of books have been published within the last number of years dealing with bullying suggesting numerous ways that it can be addressed.

Dr. Chapunoff: What countries have worked harder and done more research on bullying?

Dr. Paul: The leading researchers are from Australia, Great Britain, and the United States. Programs aiming to reduce peer victimization are been studied, and there are now strategies that are shown to have a positive effect. When people try to figure out how many students actually have been bullied, at least one third of all children report occasional bullying or victimization. One out of 10 reports that it is severe and chronic. These numbers may be low because in recent polls, half of all school principals reported that bullying is a severe problem in their school. Half of all elementary students also report that bullying is a severe problem. This problem peaks in middle school where 75 percent of all children see this as a big problem, which then drops down again to about half of all students reporting it as a problem in high school.

Dr. Chapunoff: These numbers are impressive and disgracefully high. You send your child to school, and sometimes you ignore that he or she is bullied mercilessly. I learned about the case of a high school student who was bullied by two juvenile delinquents, who demanded a regular payment of several dollars every week. The request included a knife pressing on the victim's abdomen. He elected not to report these incidents for fear of reprisals. He told the story to his parents when he became an adult. He managed to survive by dutifully paying the ransom, as demanded. The bullying and the payments ended when he graduated from high school and no longer saw his attackers.

Dr. Paul: In this modern day and age, bullying has surpassed the simple face-to-face harassment it used to be. Bullying now can occur with electronic media. So-called cyber bullying can include text messaging, e-mails, and the use of social media, such as Facebook. Some groups have often been more prone to being bullied, especially those with gender identity or homosexual proclivities. Unfortunately, being called gay is one of the more standard bullying epithets.

Once again, especially with emerging adolescence, gender identity elicits anxiety, anxiety elicits insecurity, and bullying is a way too many people try to cope with their own insecurities. Those insecure individuals who use bullying to make themselves feel bigger or more powerful, typically target individuals who are of lesser social status or whose appearance does not quite fit in. If people have a tic, stutter, are shy or are somewhat withdrawn, or as mentioned above might be gay or lesbian, they become high candidates for being targets for bullying.

Dr. Chapunoff: Howard, now that you are describing how people who have lesser social status may be especially prone to be victims of bullying, you remind me of a homeless US Army veteran I treated years ago who, as expected, owned nothing and never carried any money. He had multiple bruises on his body, resulting from regular beatings from different street gangs. They regularly made fun of him, bullied, and hit him.

I asked him, *"Why would they do that?"*

He told me, *"I asked them the same question."*

"And what did they say?"

"You're so f….poor and disgraced that you deserve to be punished!"

Dr. Paul: That is indeed, a very sad story. One compelling factor, which determines whether bullying will continue, is how people react to it. Behavior increases when it is reinforced, therefore, if the bullied person reacts in ways that are pleasing to the bully, more teasing and bullying will probably ensue.

When teasing is verbal, it is far easier to teach people to respond in ways that are more appropriate. However, teasing is often physical, at which point it would be wiser not to call it bullying but to call it what it really is, assault. Boys have a much higher frequency of using physical intimidation with girls tending to stick to verbal bullying, but one sign of these more modern times is that girls are catching up to the boys and are being more physical.

Dr. Chapunoff: It doesn't take a genius to figure out that a person who is homeless and has no more satisfaction in this life than the joy of breathing will be emotionally and psychologically vulnerable and affected by who knows how many different mental dysfunctions.

Dr. Paul: That is the point, Ed. People really understand that individuals who are chronic targets of bullying are at risk for significant mental health issues. They are subject to low self-esteem, increased stress, as well as depression and anxiety. Suicidal thoughts are much more prevalent and, as I noted above, the risk of suicide for those severely affected is real.

Dr. Chapunoff: It is easy to think that the mental status of bullies themselves is not particularly healthy.

Dr. Paul: That is right. In fact, a higher risk for mental illness also exists for those who bully. Bullying is a form of violence, and bullies are at greater risk for violent behavior when they grow up. One out of four elementary school bullies will have a criminal record by the time they reach adulthood! By the time bullies are in high school they often find themselves rejected by the bulk of the student population, have difficulty maintaining friendships, and find themselves lonely and increasingly threatened with anxiety and depression. Bullies also tend to have a higher proportion of school failure and dropout. It is a real issue on both sides of the coin. Most people have little sympathy for bullies, but recognizing the underlying pathology that may create the problem and the devastating cost that it can incur to society makes it important to address the issue and deal with not only those who are bullied but also with bullies themselves.

Dr. Chapunoff: Many years ago, one of my sons was bullied badly at high school by a juvenile delinquent. He wanted to force my son to take drugs. I complained to the principal, who told me that he couldn't do anything about the situation. He said to me, "We have to live with these criminal guys in the school system."

Therefore, I personally went to the local police station and spoke to the officer in charge. He listened attentively to my description of the bullying against my son. When I finished explaining my concern, he took the aggressor's photos from a file, showed them to me, and said, *"Dr. Chapunoff, we cannot help your son. The bad person who constantly bothers him has been arrested many times. We keep him in jail for two to three days, and then he is released and goes back to business as usual. The way I see it, you'll only be able to solve this problem by moving your son to another school. And make sure that that school is located as far as possible from the school your son is attending now."* And that's what I had to do!

Dr. Paul: I am sure this was a very aggravating experience for you and your son. As with most pathologies, identifying bullies when they are young is much better than trying to change this type behavior when it has been solidified and practiced for a number of years.

Bullying can be relentless. It is common for children to develop psychosomatic reactions to bullying. It is much easier for some children to complain about a stomachache, instead of the fact that they are bullied. Stomachaches, irritable bowel syndrome, headaches, and other legitimate medical complaints are often psychosomatic reactions to being bullied.

Dr. Chapunoff: Howard, should these complaints become a warning for parents that the child is having problems at school and that bullying could be one of them?

Dr. Paul: Yes, indeed! When children frequently complain of not wishing to go to school and have frequent and consistent medical complaints, savvy parents would best begin to question whether or not their children are being bullied or ask if there might be other issues creating anxiety and stress in school needing to be unearthed and addressed. Not only can being bullied manifest itself in illness, it can also be the cause of poor school performance and increased social isolation.

If a child comes home from school, seems to be very hungry, and tells you he was not hungry during lunchtime, find out if lunchtime has become an unpleasant experience because of bullying. Lunch could be regularly stolen or extorted.

Dr. Chapunoff: I hope that parents will never forget what you just said!

Howard, there are different forms and degrees of bullying. All of them are bad, but some are worse than others are. When teachers or parents consult you about a bullying episode of a child, how do you respond?

Dr. Paul: When I deal with children who are the targets of bullying, the first order of business is to determine if it is limited to name-calling and verbal harassment or if it involves being hit, kicked, shoved, or involves other forms of physical intimidation.

I said earlier that I believe when bullying is significantly physical, it is an assault. Assaults are best handled by the police. If it occurs in a close neighborhood, it is often wise for parents to speak to the parents of the offending child and give a stern but polite warning that action will be taken if this behavior persists. Where that fails, involving the juvenile section of the police department seems appropriate.

In my practice, most of what I deal with is name-calling and verbal taunting. As I said earlier, the way we respond tends to determine how much we will continue to be targeted. I use this little device to teach a lesson. I ask the child who is the target of bullying what would happen if they would hit me and, in response, I gave them a dollar! Most children are able to realize that if this really happened, when they were done spending the money, they would come back and hit me again. If at that point I gave them another dollar, we would be well on the way to have this be a chronic problem. I then try to explain that while bullies may not be out for real money as a payoff (although sometimes they may be, then it is extortion, not just bullying), they are more out for emotional money. The bully is out for an emotional payoff. That payoff is the distress of the bullied child. If children can be taught not to give emotional payoffs, their target value decreases, they become much less fun to bully, and typically, the bully will move on and find a better target. Children are frequently told that if they simply ignore the bully, they will go away. What children are not taught is that responding has to do with much more than what they say. We speak with much more than our mouth. If my mouth is silent but my body is still screaming, I am still going to be seen as responding to the bully and paying him or her off. Ignoring only works when it is a whole body reaction.

It is also at this point that I introduce what I call the soda machine phenomenon. I tell a little story of an individual whom every day on their way home from work or school, stops at a little store or bodega to buy a soda from the soda machine. Like clockwork, they put the money in and the soda machine delivers the soda. One day, this individual stops into this store, puts in the money, and no soda is dispensed. What do most people do then? They bang on or kick the machine! The real lesson here is that if you are used to delivering emotional currency to the bully, you are the soda machine in my little story. When you no longer give the person what they want, it will initially result in their behavior escalating and worsening. If you are the soda machine, which really means if you are the person being teased, you are used to giving the bully what they want, and you stop delivering, they will kick the machine, meaning that it will get worse before it gets better.

Dr. Chapunoff: About 20 years ago, I used to work with a nurse who had a 12-year-old son who happened to be a juvenile karate champion. Two big, muscular, heavy people constantly harassed a girl at his school. When the young karate boy saw the girl being touched and in danger of being subjected to more physical aggression, he asked the giants to stop their attack on the girl. They saw the little, slim boy warning them and laughed at him. The attack on the girl continued. In less than a minute, he incapacitated both attackers and an ambulance was called because they had been hurt so badly they couldn't stand on their feet. One of them had suffered a neck fracture.

Dr. Paul: Ed, that was indeed, an interesting experience. It is the classic David versus Goliath fantasy.

Dr. Chapunoff: It sure is! The school authorities congratulated the boy for his courage and ability. The principal knew that these people were dangerous, but had been unable to deal with them and also feared them badly.

Dr. Paul: Ed, times have changed. Today, the karate hero would be suspended due to the zero tolerance programs many schools utilize. In addition, violence, while sometimes effective and appropriate, can escalate to larger violence and is not a sure cure for teasing. When bullies are intimidated, they sometimes gang up and make the odds far worse when the next attack occurs. One way to control bullying, as your story notes, is to outfight them. Sadly, most bullied children will never be karate champions. They are less physical than their tormentors and cannot be taught effectively to be aggressive. As such, I more frequently endorse other control strategies.

I like to explain further the notion of control to children and their parents. If I tease you and you get upset, I am controlling you. If I tease you and you do not get upset, and instead I get upset because you are not reacting to my bullying, now, you are controlling me. If I can get children to understand this concept, then when they begin to ignore the verbal taunts of their bully, and the bully increases the severity of their verbal onslaught, and the child understands that now they are in control of the bully, it can be a very potent and liberating understanding, as the controlled now becomes the controller!

Dr. Chapunoff: How do you teach a child to master the control of the bully?

Dr. Paul: In order to do good ignoring, it is imperative the children deliver a positive self-control message to themselves, which they have had time to practice. Being bullied produces a negative emotional response.

Going back to what we have previously discussed, emotional responses are best understood if they are broken down into three parts:

1) What happened

2) What did I say to myself about what happened

3) How did I feel and react

Children know that they are bullied. Children know that they feel bad inside. What they don't know is what they are saying to themselves to produce that bad reaction. Children are usually saying to themselves that it is awful, terrible, and horrible to be teased. They are often saying that the other person must be fair, that they must not behave the way they are behaving, or they may have self-directed demands that they must retaliate but are too fearful to do so.

When I work with groups of children, I have them play a game called, "Insult Your Neighbor!" We break up into teams, and each team tries to figure out ways to get whoever is it on the opposing team upset. The children take turns and switch back and forth between being the bully and being the teased person. If you are on the team with the bully, you try to help the person elected to be the bully come up with some juicy verbal comment that will push the button of the teased person. If you are on the team of the bullied person, your job is to help that person talk sense to themselves and figure out a positive, proactive, self-control statement that would enable them to ignore the bully's negative comments, while maintaining good self-composure.

In order to do this, I try to explain to individuals, especially if they are children, that teasing is nothing more than a request. It is a request to feel bad. I start out by saying, *"What would happen if someone walked up to you and said, I'm really feeling crummy inside, and it would make me feel wonderful if you felt rotten for me."* I ask the child if someone gave you that request, what would you do? Some children actually tell me that they would feel bad for the other person, just because they asked. Most kids, when you phrase the question as I have above, understand that the best answer is to say, *"No thank you, I really don't wish to feel bad just because you would like me to."*

At this time, I try to point out that teasing or bullying is not about the words. It always boils down to a request; please feel bad for me so I can feel big and strong. When we play the Insult Your Neighbor game, we use it as an opportunity for the children to rehearse some variant of the self-statement, *I don't have to feel bad just because you want me to.* I send the children home to do teasing practice with their parents or siblings, especially when there is sibling rivalry coupled with teasing. It actually takes a few weeks of rehearsal before children are able competently to use this cognitive skill to combat being teased or bullied.

When children come to understand the teasing is not about the words, bullies are simply out to feel good at their expense, and they do not have to comply, they feel quite proud of being able to demonstrate this increase in self-control and emotional control.

The same holds true when it comes to adults in any situation in which someone is trying to get you. If you respond emotionally, you are paying off the other person and increasing the likelihood, that bullying will continue. Too many people try to think of the best thing to say to the other person. Actually, the most important person to speak to first is yourself. Remind yourself that feeling bad is optional. The words the other person is saying are only tools to try to get you upset. You do not have to feel bad because someone else wants you to!

24

ADHD: ATTENTION DEFICIT AND HYPERACTIVE DISORDER
Is it getting the ATTENTION it deserves?

Dr. Chapunoff: Howard, just a few days ago, I saw a 35-year-old woman at the office for hypertension refractory to treatment. She had severe chronic stress. She was married and had three children, ages 16, 14, and 8. The youngest is a boy who, for several months displayed inattentiveness at home and at school, had been making too many mistakes doing his homework, acted silly many times, and when his parents and brothers tried to tell him something, he looked like he ignored everybody. He was also very disruptive.

His mother explained, *"At the dinner table, he interrupts conversations and unexpectedly jumps from his seat and starts running looking for who-knows-what."* His parents recently took him to a pediatrician who diagnosed ADHD and advised an evaluation by a child psychotherapist.

Howard, will you please tell us about your experience with this disturbing condition? Would you first elaborate on symptoms that are related to inattentiveness, hyperactivity, impulsivity, or any of the above in combination? How does a psychotherapist confirm the diagnosis and make sure that the patient is suffering from ADHD and not another disorder, such as depression, sleep deprivation, a learning disability, a tic disorder, or behavior problems?

Dr. Paul: Ed, this is a topic that is near and dear to my heart and one that I have been studying for the last 40 years. Locally, I am considered an expert in ADHD. Many of the area physicians and pediatricians refer people to me for proper diagnosis of this condition. Currently, the distinction between attention deficit disorder (ADD) and attention deficit hyperactive disorder (ADHD) has been eliminated, and all individuals are diagnosed with ADHD. It is specified as inattentive type, hyperactive type, or combined type. The primary symptoms are, as the name implies, inattention and excessive activity.

The diagnostic criteria for ADHD are simple and straightforward. For the inattentive type, individuals have difficulty sustaining attention to tasks or even play. They are easily distracted. Individuals with inattentive ADHD have difficulty finishing tasks and following instructions. They have difficulty organizing tasks and frequently lose things.

The criteria for those that are hyperactive and impulsive reflect that they typically run around, climb on things, cannot sit still and are always fidgeting. They often act impulsively and without thought of what consequences might be. Such individuals also have difficulty waiting their turn. When you speak to some parents of ADHD children, they often say their child seems to daydream a lot or loves singular fantasy play.

ADHD children typically require more redirection than most other children do. These kids are often yelled at more because they have difficulty working without supervision and have difficulty finishing jobs.

Children with ADHD have trouble with vigilance or the ability to maintain effort and sustained attention, especially when the task is not of real interest to them.

Put a youngster with ADHD in front of a computer or exciting video game, and they will sit rapt for hours. Put them in a math class, and they may not last five minutes. What appears to be distractibility seems more realistically to be a constant seeking of attention and a search for more exciting material.

Impulsivity, just like inattention, has many aspects, including being able to wait, being able to listen, and being able to do good planning. This has been termed executive control.

Hyperactivity is easy to spot, as the person who is demonstrating hyperactivity looks like they just had a caffeinated coffee on steroids, and they simply cannot sit still.

Diagnostically, symptoms must be in existence for at least six months and have started in childhood. While sleep deprivation can cause inattention and many of the subsymptoms of ADHD, it does not meet the criteria of starting in childhood, and symptoms go away after a good night's sleep.

Anxiety can cause many of the symptoms of ADHD. I do see many individuals who look like they have ADHD but when you treat their anxiety, many of their symptoms to go away. Depression also can cause inattention. Unless someone has bipolar disorder and is in a manic state, depression usually causes people to slow down, not become hyperactive.

As you correctly point out, some learning disabilities, especially nonverbal learning disabilities (NLD), masquerade as ADHD. It does take a skilled diagnostician to be able to make these discriminations.

Too many physicians and too many schools simply use the various checklists that are available to diagnose children with ADHD, rather than referring the child or adult for a more careful diagnosis. It is better to refer people to a neuropsychologist or developmental clinical psychologist, who can combine checklist information with a thorough behavioral sampling, derived from psychometric and neuropsychological testing to increase the accuracy of the diagnosis.

Dr. Chapunoff: Howard, I know you are a clinical psychologist. Are you also a neuropsychologist as well?

Dr. Paul: Yes Ed, I have been a member of the National Academy of Neuropsychologists for about 20 years.

Dr. Chapunoff: You mentioned checklists used to diagnose ADHD. What are these checklists, and are some of them better than others are? Are there any other tests available, other than a comprehensive neuropsychological battery, to diagnose accurately ADHD?

Dr. Paul: Ed, there are a number of checklists currently being used to diagnose ADHD. There is no superiority of one over the other, in that they all ask the same questions.

Dr. Chapunoff: If they all ask the same questions, where do these questions come from, and which ones are most commonly used? Are there any tests used which are not simple checklists?

Dr. Paul: These questions all come from the *Diagnostic and Statistical Manual* of the American Psychiatric Association, where the criteria for ADHD are spelled out. The three most commonly used checklists are the Connors checklists, the Barkley checklists, and the Vanderbilt Assessment Scale, which is the one often used by pediatricians. The differences in these scales are not so much in the questions they ask, but how many they ask, with the Connors and the Vanderbilt checklists asking the most, and the Barkley Scale asking the least.

One other frequently used diagnostic instrument is the Continuous Performance Test (CPT), which is a computer delivered vigilance task and not a checklist. I do not use this measure because of the relatively high number of false positives that can come from it. Because it is a test that relies on eye-hand coordination, as well as brain processing, children with poor motor control or visual perceptual limitations are often falsely diagnosed with ADHD. Interestingly, when the government studied all the diagnostic instruments used today, including checklists and the CPT test, they determined that *none* met the criteria needed for an instrument to be supported by the government. With the tools that we have, there are frequent misdiagnoses.

Dr. Chapunoff: Were you ever involved in a case that was diagnosed by another professional as ADHD but in due time, you discovered that the previous diagnosis was wrong, and the child, or adult, suffered from something else and not ADHD?

Dr. Paul: Ed, I have done well over 5000 evaluations during the course of my career, and I currently do about 100 assessments every year. Actually, I stopped counting at 5000, and don't know what the real total is! A good many of these assessments were concerned with ruling in or ruling out the diagnosis of ADHD. In most cases the individual was suspected of having ADHD or another professional had diagnosed it. Quite frequently, somewhere between 25 to 40 percent of the time, I find other more compelling reasons for the person's difficulty with attention and disagree with the diagnosis of ADHD.

Dr. Chapunoff: I suspect that an inattentive child is more difficult to diagnose than a disruptive hyperactive child, who makes his behavioral issues loud and clear. Am I correct on this?

Dr. Paul: The hardest child to diagnose is the youngster who is having trouble, but is creating no behavior problem in the classroom. It takes longer for them to ever be seen. You are quite correct that if the youngster is simply inattentive, but not making noise in the classroom, it will usually take longer, if ever, for them to be spotted and referred for assessment. Once referred, it is actually not that much more challenging to diagnose ADHD with only inattention. ADHD with hyperactivity is a no-brainer because after a certain amount of time, the child is unable to sit in the seat and is on the floor, zipping around the room and displaying other clear signs of hyperactivity. By sitting next to a child for a few hours and taking them through a variety of mental and physical tasks, inattentiveness is also identifiable.

Dr. Chapunoff: In cases of suspected ADHD, when the diagnosis is presumed but not entirely certain, do some neurological tests help to establish the diagnosis, or is the diagnosis of ADHD always a clinical one?

Dr. Paul: As we speak, there is no agreed-upon medical test to confirm ADHD. ADHD is a clinical diagnosis. I do believe that, with what we know now about the neurobiology of ADHD, this situation may change as further research steers us in a clearer direction.

At this point, I am going to take the risk of boring you by providing you my notions about ADHD. This is a little technical, but I think it is important enough to spell out. I am going to do this by providing some insight into the studies that I think are most important.

Dr. Chapunoff: Howard, I get the sense that you are about to hit me with some technical information, which might put some of out readers to sleep.

Dr. Paul: Ed, as usual, you are very perceptive and are correct. Since the ideas that I am about to explain have not been generally disseminated, I think it is worth the risk of explaining them. I am sure that some will find them very interesting.

HOWARD PAUL, PhD, ABPP, FAClinP and EDUARDO CHAPUNOFF, MD, FACP, FACC

Most everyone has heard about the Russian psychologist, Pavlov, and his dogs. He would ring a bell when he presented food to his animals after which they would salivate. After a while, just by ringing the bell alone, he was able to have the animals salivate. What most people do not know is that this training did not work with all of his animals! The part of his research that most people are unaware of is most important to me. Further neurological research coming from his laboratory led to concepts that were termed *strong* and *weak* nervous systems. Animals were said to have weak nervous systems if they were easily conditioned and learned rapidly. Animals were felt to have strong nervous systems if they either were slow to learn or did not learn the conditioned response at all. Strong and weak does refer to the tendency of the nervous system to guard itself against incoming stimulation, and therefore, learning.

Strong nervous systems were said to be difficult to arouse, while weak nervous systems responded quite readily to even small stimuli.

In the 70s, I rediscovered these concepts using college students as my study subjects and electroencephalographic (EEG) studies. Rather than making people salivate, I tried to produce what is termed an alpha blocking response. When people were making alpha waves, waves that our brain makes between eight and 12 cycles per second (cps), they are said to be in an alpha state. When my study subjects were in such an alpha state, I would stimulate them with light, called photic stimulation, which is bright flashing light. This light burst would then end the production of alpha waves arousing the brain, which would then make beta waves.

Photic stimulation was paired with a tone in a standard classical conditioning paradigm.

Chapunoff: Would you please explain what *a tone in a standard classical conditioning paradigm* means?

Dr. Paul: The tone is simply any sound. It could be a bell ringing, a buzzer sounding, or anything that can be heard. It actually does not have to be a tone; any stimulus would do, such as a touch, a smell, or anything that is paired with something that causes a repeated normally unconscious reaction.

When I analyzed my data, I found that those whose alpha frequencies tended toward the higher range within alpha of 11 or 12 cps conditioned rapidly and produced a stable learned-conditioned response. Those whose alpha waves were closer to 8 or 9 cps either never learned the conditioned response or learned it slowly, and it went away rapidly. People with Pavlov's weak nervous system were those who had higher frequency alpha waves, and individuals with Pavlov's strong nervous system had alpha waves on the slower end.

These two groups had no overlap and represented very different ways of learning and behaving. Those with slower waves tended towards inattention and over activity, while those with higher frequency waves tended to be more anxious and were, as a rule, much more compliant.

I'm sure you can see where this is going: ADHD is most likely a syndrome produced by increases in slower brainwave activity. The frequency of our brainwaves determines the degree to which our brain becomes resistant to stimulation. Since brains like to be stimulated, those with higher resistance to incoming stimulation, try to find stimulation by either increasing activity or looking for things that have high excitement value. Unfortunately, such things are often immoral, illegal, or fattening! Having your parents yell at you also fits in here. This can be emotionally damaging, but unfortunately, for those with ADHD, yelling and parental anger makes some parts of their brain happy.

To bolster my ideas about brainwave frequency being one probable diagnostic candidate for ADHD, I would like to introduce and explain some of the data on postconcussive syndrome (PCS). In PCS, the primary medical complaints will be headache, occasional dizziness, and occasional hypersensitivity to sound and noise. Psychologically, the symptoms are varied and can include increased irritability, mood instability, increases in anxiety, increases in aggression, and the ones that are important to what were talking about now, increased impulsivity, distractibility, memory problems, poor problem-solving ability, decreases in good judgment, restlessness, and hyperactivity. What is diagnostic and confirming of PCS using an EEG (electroencephalogram) is increases in slower wave activity.

It seems clear to me that ADHD symptoms, just like in PCS, are highly correlated with slower brainwave activity, which is related to increases in the brain's resistance to incoming stimuli. ADHD is duplicated when people are concussed, and their brainwave activity slows down. With ADHD, there is no concussion, but the brain acts as if it is chronically concussed!

Modern computers have enabled us to look at brainwave activity by doing what is called a fast Fourier transform (FFT). With this, we can create a three-dimensional picture of brainwave activity over time. When you do a study on individuals with ADHD, it looks like someone has taken the frequency distribution of the EEG and pushed it toward the slow end of the spectrum. There is apparently a compelling relationship between increases of slower wave activity and ADHD.

Neurobiologically, this makes sense. When we sleep, our brain makes delta waves, which are big slow 1 to 3 cps waves. When we are making these waves, we are in deep sleep. People in deep sleep are hard to arouse and difficult to have a conversation with! The slower our brainwaves, the higher the barrier to incoming stimulation is raised in our brain.

When we are in lighter sleep, we are making theta waves, which are 4 to 7 cps. Above that is alpha and above alpha are beta waves, which are from about 12 to 33 cps. As our brainwave frequency increases, alertness, awareness, and the ease with which we are aroused and can be stimulated increases.

It would appear that the gate or barrier that stops external stimuli from reaching people's brains, never is fully lowered if they have ADHD. This is why stimulant medication works. It was thought that peoples' response to stimulants was paradoxical or backwards, in that, giving overactive persons stimulants would calm them down. Biologically it makes good sense that, if you wake the brain up and the gate finally comes down all the way, the person no longer needs to seek stimulation because it finally has enough input making it to the brain, making their brain happy.

Dr. Chapunoff: The explanation you just provided about the way overactive individuals improve when they receive treatment with stimulants, clarifies a concept that would appear senseless otherwise.

I understand that 3 to 5 percent of children in the United States suffer from ADHD, and there is a similar estimate on the incidence of this disorder in adults. I also learned that it is like this throughout the world, not just in the United States.

Most clinicians never received much training on this disease. Therefore, the awareness factor that exists in the professional medical population, to put it mildly, is very low. When primary care physicians deal with depressed or highly irritable individuals, they may think they are dealing with a typical depressive or bipolar disorder. It takes a careful interrogation, enough time for the patient's examination, and above all, expertise, to figure out what the real diagnosis is.

General practitioners, family physicians, internists, and medical subspecialties, such as cardiology, endocrinology, pulmonary diseases, etc, do not have either the time or the knowledge to diagnose or seriously suspect that a patient is suffering from ADHD. I include myself in that list.

I think that some cases of ADHD in childhood are not recognized, and when this condition extends into adulthood, patients remain improperly diagnosed and inadequately managed. Do you agree with this?

Dr. Paul: Ed, I do believe that in adults there is a significant underdiagnosis of ADHD. This may be because the hyperactive component of ADHD tends to soften and mature out during adolescence. As for kids, we live in a time where an excuse is often needed every time a child does not do wonderfully in school. It may be that ADHD is overdiagnosed in trying to explain why some children are not doing well.

ADHD, when it is real, has a significant negative impact on individuals with this problem. As a rule, individuals with ADHD underachieve in school, have more car accidents, have more failed marriages, and are at higher risk for drug abuse and alcoholism - all of which are associated with an increased incidence of depression and anxiety. Individuals with ADHD tend to be risk takers and often injure themselves at a higher frequency than others without this problem. When any physician takes a history and discovers underachievement, either at work or in school, frequent job changes, or failure and frequent relationship challenges, a referral for assessment may be wise.

Dr. Chapunoff: When children, adolescents, and adults who were never properly diagnosed, suffer from ADHD, what coping mechanisms do they use to survive and adapt to society?

Dr. Paul: Some individuals with ADHD, whether properly diagnosed or not, are able to ultimately cope because they create a life space which supports their higher need for stimulation or difficulty with sustaining attention to mundane activities. Such individuals tend to find work that is not behind a desk. This would be work that keeps them active and interested. Under these circumstances, the effects of ADHD can become minimized, at least vocationally.

Dr. Chapunoff: What limitations in various jobs or occupations do patients with ADHD have? When the disease is diagnosed at age six or older and the patient suffers from florid ADHD and the child's parents ask you what studies or professions that child should never pursue, what do you tell them?

Dr. Paul: At age six or seven, I would not tell any parent what professions their child should or should not pursue, and to be precise, as you know from our previous conversations, I would steer away from the use of *shoulds*! Realistically, if a child responds well to a stimulant or other proven and FDA-approved alternative medication for ADHD, they may be able to do quite well in whatever profession they ultimately find themselves. For better or for worse, since ADHD is a neurobiological syndrome, just like with insulin-dependent diabetes, there is no substitute for good pharmacological management. The gold standard for ADHD is stimulant medication in all of its varied forms, coupled with good behavioral management when needed.

As children get older and arousal problems and hyperactivity tend to diminish, what most people are left with are problems of impulsivity, problem solving, judgment and self-control. If a proper pharmacological regimen can be put together and people work with a good neuropsychologist or clinical psychologist familiar with ADHD to deal with the behavioral and emotional issues that ADHD can create, then the individual may be fortunate enough to have few limitations at all.

If undiagnosed, or if medication is not used, jobs that are not tedious and keep the individual active and involved become much more necessary. All of the other risks of ADHD remain.

Dr. Chapunoff: Smoking and drinking during pregnancy and exposure to lead have been linked to ADHD.

Dr. Paul: That is right Ed. Nicotine leads to the fetus's brain having hypoxia (low oxygen), and since ADHD also shows a very strong genetic predisposition, women who suffer from ADHD and smoke or drink alcohol, have a higher risk of having children with this disorder because they too may be affected by it and have not overcome their own heightened risk to addictive substances.

Any traumatic injury to the brain, whether it be mechanical or induced through toxins, can cause a permanent postconcussive syndrome or traumatic brain injury, part of which will produce the symptoms of ADHD.

Dr. Chapunoff: Many parents are very much against using drugs on their children. There is a great deal of misinformation on the Web regarding the evil effects of stimulants. Many people seem to cling to the notion that allergies to certain foods cause ADHD symptoms.

Dr. Paul: I understand why parents would not wish to medicate their children. I join them in this sentiment. The services I provide are based upon nonpharmacological interventions. Since ADHD is such a clear neurobiological problem and is caused by a brain that simply hasn't quite woken up, there is no effective nonmedical treatment for ADHD. Work is being done on neurofeedback, as a possible intervention.

Dr. Chapunoff: Howard, would you please explain to us what is neurofeedback?

Dr. Paul: Neurofeedback is accomplished by putting superficial scalp electrodes on a child or adult's head and measuring particular EEG frequencies. The short version is that a computer detects both slow waves, which may be at the root of ADHD and certain specific faster waves, which are thought to improve attention. The person is then taught to make more fast waves and less slow waves. In some cases, this can make a big difference. I provided neurofeedback in the 70s and had some remarkably positive results. Unfortunately, I was only able to produce dramatic positive change in about 25 percent of the children I saw. For 25 percent of the children, the procedure seemed to make no difference, and for the balance, while some improvement was seen, it did not seem to warrant the expense and time of the treatment, especially since many insurance companies would not pay for this type of treatment. Some improvements in technology have been made, but neurofeedback for ADHD is still in its experimental stage.

As for those who think ADHD may be related to food sensitivity or an allergy, in some very limited circumstance this could be true. Food coloring has been soundly disproven to be a cause of ADHD in every scientific realm, but not yet on the popular Internet!

Sugar, likewise, cannot and does not cause ADHD. Sugar, like any simple carbohydrate, actually causes drowsiness. For many children, their worst time behaviorally is when they are drowsy. This actually makes good sense if we go back to our discussion of brainwave activity as, when drowsy, children's brainwaves slow down, which does produce a temporary ADHD state.

When parents come to me and are sure that a particular food makes their children hyperactive, I suggest the following experiment: I have the parents develop a behavior rating scale that measures attention, compliance, and energy level. When the parents are at a point where they believe their scale is accurate and reliable, I then have one parent continue the rating and keep it secret from their partner while the other parent, over a 14-day period and unbeknownst to their partner, spikes the child's food with the forbidden substance. At the end of this two-week period, we sit down and see if there is any overlap and agreement between those days when the child received the forbidden substance and increases in activity level or decreases in attention and compliance.

In the 45 years that I have been doing this, I have yet to have the parents' belief proven to be true. I have read one study, and only one study published in a trusted Journal, where such a link was substantiated. Quite interestingly, when I do this with a single-parent family, where the person doing the rating is the same person who spikes the youngster's diet with this suspected food, it comes back with 100 percent proof of the relationship. In my experience, when done blind, as in the first example, it has never come back showing any relationship.

240

Dr. Chapunoff: How do you treat patients with ADHD and those with ADD? What can you tell us about the psychological effects on families of those with ADHD? Are these patients candidates to follow up treatment with a psychotherapist for many years, a lifetime, or for shorter periods?

Dr. Paul: Ed, as I explained earlier, ADD is no longer used as a proper diagnostic term with everything now in the ADHD basket. Even though I think that the old ADD and ADHD distinction was valid and sensible, I now stick with the official nomenclature.

Whether or not individuals need a therapist depends upon the emotional damage caused by their condition, secondary to the failures and disappointments ADHD can produce. If managed properly, both medically and psychologically, being an annuity for a psychotherapist is certainly not necessary. Occasional tune-ups when people find that they are in trouble are always a good idea.

As I mentioned earlier, ADHD symptomatology changes as individuals grow and becomes harder to recognize. By adolescence, much of the hyperactivity is often gone, leaving distractibility and disorganization. This can often follow people forever.

About 25 percent of individuals with ADHD are fortunate enough to have most of their symptoms disappear by the time they reach teen age. These individuals typically no longer need medication and do satisfactorily. Twenty-five percent of individuals need medication for their entire life. For the 50 percent that are left, most choose not to take medication. That decision causes a range of problems for those who are in this middle group. Understandably, parents as well as teens and adults with this problem, are very concerned about the side effects of ADHD medication. What they often lose sight of is that the side effects of not taking the medication are often far worse than the side effects of taking the medication. For some, medication produces miracles, and children become normalized and are able to function quite well. Some are unable to take the medicine because of changes in mood and in some rare cases, suppression of personality. Stimulants are diet pills and youngsters on stimulants sometimes lose weight. This is another concern and possible reason for their discontinuation. This would really only need to be the case when it affects growth, which is quite rare. In some cases, stimulants can cause cardiac complications because they can cause some arrhythmias and can cause an elevation of heart rate. Development of motor tics is another possibility. The real effects of ADHD are, as compared to the side effects of ADHD medication, that ADHD tends to produce an impaired self-image, due to frequent failures and interpersonal difficulties created by the disorder. Within families, it often creates chaos as youngsters tend to have difficulty listening, can frequently be oppositional and defiant, leading to a good deal of anger, yelling, screaming, and increased use of spanking and other physical means of discipline, all of which can be damaging to the child and often, to a lesser extent to the parents. One finding of recent brain imaging studies is that the brains of individuals with ADHD do not respond well to punishment. They seem impervious to it. Taking things away, grounding, yelling, and hitting seldom work in the end. They may cause some short-term improvement; however, this is a parent trap, as there is little long-term carryover. Individuals with ADHD crave excitement. Parents must learn to use precision management if they have a child suspected of having ADHD. Standard parenting simply may not work with most kids who have ADHD. While psychologists cannot alter the neurobiological base of ADHD, it is the secondary emotional challenges to ADHD that requires a well-trained psychologist.

Dr. Chapunoff: Howard, I deeply thank you for the way you explained ADHD, a condition that is frequently ignored, poorly understood, insufficiently diagnosed, and inadequately treated.

The consequence of this defective awareness by the general public and health care practitioners carries the potential of serious consequences for those affected, their parents, siblings, and society.

Only parents who have to cope with a child suffering from ADHD and the disruption this disorder causes in their lives, will fully understand what we are speaking about.

During our conversation, you described scientific data and the research you did on this disorder. When I reviewed your technical explanations, I was afraid that our readers would find several pages containing them difficult to digest. I was wrong for this reason: Parents who have a child with ADHD or adults who suffer from this condition should find your technical explanations of great value. I recommend they read those technical pages, as many times as necessary to assimilate them properly.

It is not through the vacuum of ignorance, but through the benefits of knowledge, that we best approach problems, including, of course, problems of this caliber.

You did original research on ADHD, you are a recognized expert on ADHD, and have had many years of dedication to this condition. We are all very fortunate to be the recipients of that knowledge and experience.

25

DOMESTIC VIOLENCE
What is the Victim Supposed to Do?

Dr. Chapunoff: She was 40 years of age and brought to my office in a wheelchair. Jane was having pains all over her body from her husband's beating, and she was unable to stand on her feet. I hospitalized her, and she proved to have several fractured ribs, huge hematomas on her arms, legs, and abdomen. Her face was unrecognizable. All you could see was hematomas around her eyes and nose; she was spitting up blood, and several teeth were missing.

Her husband went to prison, but he wasn't going to stay there for too long. She was afraid that during the next beating, he might kill her.

I got involved with the hospital's Social Service Department, and sisters in a convent in Italy mercifully gave her a job as an assistant in the kitchen. Two years later, she came back and told me that she had had a great time, and above all, a peaceful time, without the regular beatings by her husband. I told her that she should have remained in Italy. Her husband was a dangerous man and he would probably look for her to have another round of violence. That was the last time I saw her. I never heard from her again.

- * -

Vicky was a beautiful 35-year-old alcoholic female, who regularly appeared at the hospital emergency room to be treated for the extensive bruises and multiple injuries her 6'4" husband, all muscle and brute force, inflicted on her.

Many parts of her body were red and blue due to hematomas. Her face looked like someone who fought Muhammad Ali when he was at his prime.

What was remarkable here was that every time I arrived at the ER, I saw her husband holding her hand and kissing her with impressive, and suprising, tenderness.

He was an alcoholic too. He was handsomely dressed, and he spoke to me like a gentleman. His breath had so much alcohol odor that if I had decided to light a match close to his face, I would have blown up the entire building.

During her different visits to the emergency room, always due to her husband's beatings, he always displayed the same affectionate attitude toward her. Her parents and parents-in-law, were invariably inebriated, all refined and extremely well dressed and polite.

Vicky's father once told me, *"Dr. Chapunoff, this is disgraceful; we are a family of alcoholics. All of us are alcoholics. We were advised by Alcoholic Anonymous and other specialized professionals, but we never strictly followed the directives of any program, so here we are."*

Howard, ideally, ordinary people should be able to identify individuals who are perpetrators of domestic violence and learn about their personality traits. How could a woman know that she started a relationship with a man who will victimize her in the future?

In addition, when a woman becomes a real victim, how can she extricate herself from this dangerous situation and solve her drama on a permanent basis.

Now, I'm going to make an observation that has nothing to do with placing any kind of blame on the victims of domestic violence: Some of the victims, who become free from the first offender, start relationships with other violent men.

Does this behavior have anything to do with a woman's psychological or emotional dysfunction that makes her act that way, or is the new choice of another victimizer just pure coincidence?

Dr. Paul: Ed, you have brought up yet another topic that has devastating consequences for those individuals involved in abusive relationships and your questions are realistic and observant.

Firstly, I do have to say that the best predictor of future violence is:

- A history of previous violence; if you know that your current partner has a history of previous battering

- When they speak about their previous failed relationships, they tend to overly find fault and exclusively blame their partner; there is a risk that their abusive tendencies will spill over into your current relationship

- If your partner, when angry, tends to threaten, throw things, or break things, your risk is raised

- If, when your partner argues with you, they tend to be rough and use any force at all, even if it means holding you against your will, you are at higher risk for abuse

- Also, if you are in a disagreement and you wish to end it or leave and your partner makes you stay so that you must listen to whatever they say, the risk for abuse is raised

You ask about the personality characteristics of those who abuse and whether or not there are warning signs that women or men can use to increase the odds that they will not be in an abusive relationship.

Typically, when we think of an abusive relationship, we think of a man battering a woman. While it is this way most of the time, there are, depending upon whom you speak to, an increasing number of situations where it is the other way around. What I'm about to explain, in terms of things to think about, works for whoever is on the wrong end of such a relationship.

For better or for worse, and it often is for worse, individuals who land in abusive relationships, tend to have a relatively short courtship and only know their abuser for six months or less before they are either living together, engaged, or married.

Dr. Chapunoff: Is there anything during the relatively short courtship that the abuser shrewdly deploys to manipulate the feelings of the sexual partner that encourages the future victim to fall into the trap and continue the relationship?

Dr. Paul: Often, because of the possessive nature of abusers, courtships are a bit of a whirlwind. I am not so sure that this is done out of craft or shrewdness. It probably occurs more due to the personality dynamics of the abuser and may often be done unconsciously. The abuser may be saying many kind and endearing things, such as *"You are the only one,"* or *"I've never felt love like this for anyone,"* which serves to sweep the other person off their feet and pressure them into an early commitment.

Dr. Chapunoff: Are there any other signs or expressions by the abuser that suggest additional manipulative or sinister intentions?

Dr. Paul: Even if it is on a subconscious level, abusers are not above pressuring the other person to feel guilty and have them believe that they would be letting this person, the potential abuser, down if they leave the relationship or delay commitment to it.

Dr. Chapunoff: There you go! I'm glad I asked you that question!

How does the abuser behave with respect to the social aspects, such as friends of the person they care for?

Dr. Paul: Right from the get-go, abusers tend to isolate the person they care for, splitting them off from their friends and wishing to spend most together time alone. For people who become initially enamored, this does not seem unusual; however, jealousies will begin to emerge. Friends, or even conversations about friends, may begin to elicit negative evaluation from the abusing partner, as well as anger that the person might wish to spend time with them, be away from, and therefore out of the control of the abuser.

Dr. Chapunoff: That behavior seems to define perfectly a controlling person. Am I correct?

Dr. Paul: Yes, Ed, you are. Controlling behaviors may be seen at this point with the abuser either actively or passively punishing their partner for wanting to continue involvement with past friends. Isolation not only can happen with friends but with attending school or maintaining contact with social and religious activities. If your partner begins to refer to your friends in demeaning ways or puts down activities that you found enjoyable, be very cautious.

Don't be surprised if you hear the abusing person say to you that they are doing what they are doing, such as being controlling and restricting your activity, simply because they care for you and wish you to be safe. If you come home late, even by a few minutes, and your partner becomes angry and grills you about where you may have been, this is not about caring or love, it is about control and subjugation. Control can extend to the point where the person being abused has no decision-making power, cannot choose clothing or food or what religious organization or activities to attend. If you find that you must ask permission to leave the house, make phone calls, or even speak to your friends, you are in a dangerous situation.

Dr. Chapunoff: The abusing individual appears not only to be a controlling person, but probably has another serious flaw in his or her personality, commonly seen in individuals who want to control other people's lives and that is jealousy. Does my assumption make sense?

Dr. Paul: Yes, Ed, it sure does! There is a high probability that jealousies will surface early on in an abusive relationship. You and I have already had a conversation on jealousy, as well as on codependence, so much of what I mention here may sound familiar. If your partner begins to describe his jealous behavior as part of his way of loving, be very suspect.

Dr. Chapunoff: I don't remember exactly when you said this to me, but I can't forget it, *Jealousy has nothing to do with love, but with other personality problems.*

Dr. Paul: Jealousy is not about love, it is about fear and control, as well as lack of trust. If your partner begins to accuse you of showing interest in other people that he or she finds threatening, there is most likely jealousy behind it.

Dr. Chapunoff: A jealous person is an insecure person. One could logically assume that this additional feature makes a bad situation worse.

Dr. Paul: It certainly does. Since jealousy is, to some extent based upon insecurity, it is not surprising that this insecurity is also related to expectations about relationships that are faulty, that will lead to anger and controlling behavior. Abusive people, as a rule, have an unrealistic expectation that the job of the other person is to make them happy, to meet all their needs, and to do whatever they wish. They wish their partner would take care of them totally, from an emotional standpoint, and when this does not occur, anger and attempts at control then emerge. Since their expectations are unrealistic, no matter how hard a partner may try, they will never succeed.

Dr. Chapunoff: That is so true! With some people, no matter how good you are to them and how much logical reasoning you deploy to them, you are never able to satisfy them.

Dr. Paul: Ed, Abuse is about anger, and anger is about irrational demands. Sometimes people get angry in order to cover up depression. Depression is about feeling that everybody else is better than you and that you are no good. As soon as we get angry, we feel that we are superior to the person with whom we are angry. By the same token, if individuals are insecure and cannot tolerate the notion of being incorrect because of their own internal and probably silent irrational demands that they be always right, always be taken care of, and always bowed down to, getting angry is also a way to stave off the anxiety that is generated when these demands cannot be met. As soon as I am angry, then I am right and you are wrong, no matter what! This mechanism is inherent in being angry, in that anger provides us a way to believe that we are always correct. The flipside of always having to be correct would naturally be that the person cannot tolerate being wrong. One way to spot this is when people speak as if anything and everything is everybody else's fault.

Dr. Chapunoff: These ideas of blaming everyone else for the angry person's conflicts invite me to suspect a certain component of paranoid ideation.

Dr. Paul: Yes, Ed. In fact, people may develop paranoid ideation and believe that others are out to get them. Some people think that if they have made a mistake, it is because they have been set up to fail. An abusive person typically cannot tolerate that they may have erred, so they will typically blame others, especially their partner for whatever is wrong. This blame game not only applies to behavior but also to feelings. If the abuser is feeling badly, they actually believe that the occurrence of these feelings must be the fault of their partner. Anyone involved in a relationship in which it feels like they are being given all of the responsibility for everything that goes wrong would best be aware that there is a good chance there is an abusive undertone and higher than acceptable risk, even if no active abuse is currently occurring.

Dr. Chapunoff: The physical abuse is just part of the story. The abuser has enough imagination to machine-gun victims in other ways.

Dr. Paul: They surely do! I think it's important for people to understand that when we are speaking about abuse, most people think about physical abuse. Verbal and emotional abuse can be just as devastating and just as painful as physical abuse, as the self-worth of the abused person is always denigrated and castigated. Also, keep in mind that even if the words, *you are no good*, are not being said, where there is chronic anger, the message that you are no good is always being sent and, unfortunately, too often believed.

Individuals would best be sensitive to other factors when trying to stay out of abusive relationships. Since abusive people tend to have a base of insecurity, they can often be hypersensitive and have feelings that are easily hurt. As I said above, hurt feelings often lead to anger as a way of dealing with unwanted feelings, and anger can then lead to abuse.

Dr. Chapunoff: Do you find that the abusing individual has a stronger tendency to abuse certain people or the abuse shows no specific predilection for the abuser's parents, spouse, children, or others?

Dr. Paul: Abusers tend not to discriminate between their partner and their children. The abusers' relationship with their children is often contaminated with the same negativity, criticism, and control issues coupled with, if not physical, then verbal putdowns and derision.

Since abusers are egocentric and selfish and tend to think mostly of their own needs, their need for control often spills over and contaminates their need for sex and closeness.

Dr. Chapunoff: How is the abuser's typical sexual behavior pattern, if such a thing exists?

Dr. Paul: Rough sex has a much higher probability of occurring within an abusive relationship. Men often see intimacy as a time simply to act out their fantasies, whether or not the woman wishes this kind of sexual exchange.

Speaking only about men in abusive relationships, they tend to have fixed notions about gender roles and have a rather chauvinistic view of what men do and what women do within relationships. They see women as inferior, lacking equality, and only good for sex and menial tasks. While they may see women as only good for sex, there is a good chance that the woman will be criticized that their sexual responses were not good enough. Equality, be it sexual, spiritual, philosophical, or emotional is simply too anxiety provoking to be considered. Abusers do not want a partner to cherish; they want a partner to control.

Dr. Chapunoff: It looks like enjoying life with an abuser is as difficult as expecting not to have pain when an impacted tooth is removed without anesthesia.

Dr. Paul: Just about, Ed! While abusers may tell you that what they are doing is for your own good or because they care about you or because they are concerned about you, this is not love, this is over control. Abusers will use any tool, including guilt, shame, and intimidation in order to get you to do what they wish. They may threaten you, hurt you, or even threaten or hurt those you care for in order to have you comply with their desires.

Dr. Chapunoff: Is the abuser's personality more commonly observed in heterosexual or homosexual couples or some socioeconomic groups?

Dr. Paul: Abuse is not the purview of only heterosexual married couples. It happens between gay and lesbian couples and affects people of all backgrounds and socioeconomic levels. As I noted, men are not the only abusers; women have also joined in. Importantly, abuse is often aimed at children and teenagers; it does not draw the line with only adults. If you are abusive, you will tend to abuse whoever is near you and doesn't do exactly what you wish. Men tend to use violence that is more physical, while women use more verbally directed and emotionally based abuse.

Dr. Chapunoff: Evidently, abusers can be manipulative. Do abusers often disguise their true pervasive tendencies and pretend to be something they are not?

Dr. Paul: While I have given a number of characteristics and tendencies of abusers, it would be wise for people to be aware of the fact that there is no standard abuser. When not angry, abusers can be very loving and say all the right things.

Dr. Chapunoff: Can you produce a list of warning signs that would alert people to suspect that they are dealing with an abuser? What are the tips that might be helpful?

Dr. Paul: Ed, you are at a high risk of facing an abuser if:

1) You are in a relationship and occasionally feel afraid of your partner and you recognize that you must avoid certain topics.

2) You feel that no matter what you do, it is never good enough, and you can never satisfy your partner.

3) You believe that if you only did things better, you would not be abused.

4) Your partner humiliates you, criticizes you, or embarrasses you in front of your friends and blames you for whatever is wrong.

5) Your partner has a bad and unpredictable temper and when angry, threatens to harm you or kill you.

6) Your partner destroys things out of revenge or rage.

7) You are forced to have sex against your will.

8) Your partner threatens to commit suicide if you leave him or her.

9) Your partner acts excessively jealous, controls what you are able to do, and keeps you from seeing your friends or family.

10) Your partner limits your access to a car or money.

11) Your partner is constantly checking up on you.

12) When you read this above list you say yes to more than three items, you are in need of help.

Dr. Chapunoff: What makes people reluctant to abandon the stressful, traumatic, and dangerous life that is shared with a difficult and often obnoxious person?

Dr. Paul: Leaving is often seen as just too frightening. People's self-images are so shattered that they have come to believe that they are inadequate and cannot cope without the protection of their abuser. There are support groups, shelters, and people out there who can help. Many people stay in abusive relationships because they think it simply would be better or more secure than anything else that is unknown. Many women, especially if they have children, believe they must stay in an abusive relationship in order to support their children. It takes a great deal of courage and fortitude to leave.

Dr. Chapunoff: On several occasions, I asked women who had been victims of domestic abuse, why they had not made a decision to separate from the abuser sooner. Some mentioned the desire to protect their kids, but the most consistent explanation was the fear that their husbands would kill them if they did. The separation from an abuser in domestic violence is, undoubtedly, a very risky business.

Dr. Paul: Your own peace of mind and your safety, and potentially the safety of your children may be well worth the risk.

Dr. Chapunoff: You're right! Nevertheless, I believe that that is easier said that done. In such situations, the fear for your life and the life of your children is unspeakable. Knowing that you have somebody carrying a gun and who is playing Russian roulette with you, is nothing less than terrifying.

At times, when I actively tried to help a desperate woman separate from her abuser, and the social worker and the police became involved, I was afraid that a rejected, violent husband would come to my office with a semiautomatic weapon to make a few holes in my belly.

When we talk about domestic violence, we immediately tend to relate it to physical aggression. However, other forms of abuse don't produce bruises and fractured ribs but do certainly cause emotional and psychological damage.

Dr. Paul: Sadly, this is very true. Some people believe that if they are not being hit, their relationship is satisfactory and don't see their partner's behavior as abuse. If what your partner does erodes your feeling of self-worth and independence, you are, in fact, in an abusive relationship. Yelling, name-calling, shaming, and threats are all part of abuse. Verbal and emotional abuse leaves scars that are just as deep and long lasting as physical abuse. Verbal abuse is often minimized or overlooked, even by the person who is receiving it.

Dr. Chapunoff: Can you explain to me the psychological mechanisms that make the tolerance, if not the total acceptance of the victim, an option to tolerate what other people, like you or me, would consider unacceptable and intolerable?

Dr. Paul: Ed, this interesting question has an interesting answer. The very same psychological mechanisms that enable individuals to be abusive and live with themselves, are the very same ones that individuals use if they are abused and can lead them to stay in the relationship. There are factors that not only enable the abusers and the abused to continue with their highly dysfunctional coexistence that also increase the likelihood that people reseek abusive relationships.

Dr. Chapunoff: Before you explain the psychological mechanisms that have a similar base for both abuser and abused, I'd like to ask you a question about a bad marriage. In a bad marriage, where abuse of some kind is commonplace, do children assimilate the dynamics of disruption and chaos that they see and are they involuntarily trained to become heavy-duty, aggressive, neurotic, and violent individuals?

Dr. Paul: Ed, history repeats itself. Domestic violence is one real factor that puts a child at risk of becoming an abuser if he or she observes that kind of behavior between their mother and father. This is very sad and very true.

Dr. Chapunoff: And now, I'm very curious to hear your explanation about the psychological mechanisms that, as you suggested, are shared by the abuser and the abused. How can that possibly be?

Dr. Paul: I will tell you, Ed, when things happen that we do not like, and we see them as an unsatisfactory part of our self, we resort to escape mechanisms, with denial being the most frequently used. When you and I had the discussion on anger, I noted that denial is often used as an adolescent way to numb the pain of believing that we, ourselves, are inadequate because we have failed our own or others' expectations. Denial can also be used to minimize and underplay the fact that abuse exists. It is also used to shield people from their own self-loathing that they are maintaining themselves in an abusive relationship.

In one of our previous conversations, I introduce the concept of awfulization, which is essentially the magnification of feelings. For example, instead of saying, *"I don't like it,"* we would say, *"I hate it!"* Instead of saying, *"It's hard,"* we say, *"It's impossible."* Instead of saying, *"It's bad,"* we say, *"It's terrible!"* Interestingly, the opposite can also get us into trouble when we actively choose not to see something very bad as very bad. Abusers will often believe, after severely injuring their partner, that *"I didn't hurt them, I just pushed them."*

Abusers are quite good at rationalizing and working to make what they have done seem acceptable. People on both sides of the abuse coin lie, but make their lies sound positive and rational. I have mentioned before that people can be taught or convince themselves of just about anything. When used as a defense mechanism, it can prolong very negative situations.

Throughout our discussions, I have mentioned that the emotional age of anger is two. People grow up, but their emotional control systems, once they become habit based, go underground and operate stealthily in the background with people being unaware of their presence and therefore their impact.

At age two there are three key things that we try to teach our children. First, it is important to teach children that:

A) They do not always have to be correct, they cannot always have what they wish, and things do not always have to be their way.

B) If things do not go the way we wish, it is not terrible or awful or horrible; something that may be sad, frustrating, irritating, aggravating, or painful, does not have to be considered awful.

C) If things do not go their way, they can handle it.

In all anger problems and especially with abuse, these key elements of growing up and having good mental health and coping mechanisms have either been forgotten or never learned.

26

ANOREXIA NERVOSA
A condition more serious than many believe

Dr. Chapunoff: Myriam was 16 and beautiful. Her family didn't notice that she had a serious eating disorder. It was one of her concerned friends at high school, another teenage girl, who contacted the parents by phone and said, *"I want to tell you this: I think Myriam is anorexic."*

She sure was! She was losing a lot of weight fast and ate very little. She had no desire to eat. For some time she hid the fact that she had been taking laxatives and diet pills. One evening, she went out with her parents, ate a pizza slice and ran to the restroom as fast as she could to vomit. She showed signs of depression. The family brought her to a psychiatrist who prescribed an antidepressant. A couple of days later, she swallowed the full bottle of these pills and was taken to an emergency room in a comatose state. She never woke up. A week later, she was dead.

Howard, will you please share with us your experience with this serious disorder?

Dr. Paul: Ed, imagine if you can, someone who wakes up every day and deeply feels that they are ugly, bloated, and distended. They feel that, because of their misperceived overweight, they are loathsome and unlovable. Their convictions are so deep that they can become unaware of their own distress and are blind to the pain and concern of those that care for them. They are so focused on control of their weight that they are insensitive to their own pain, both psychic and that caused by starvation. The situation is unrelenting, intense, and all consuming. As the pain mounts, the need for control grows, creating a lethal circumstance, where one out of 20 individuals with anorexia nervosa ultimately take their life, through either suicide or the medical complications caused by this disorder.

This potentially crippling disorder alters the sufferers' ability to see themselves accurately, distorting their relationship with their body, food, and most importantly their family. Such individuals are essentially held hostage by this disorder, becoming slaves to their idealized, yet wildly distorted sense of weight and shape.

One big problem is that anorexia anesthetizes the person who has it. They become insensitive, not only to the pain within but to the pain without borne by loved ones. Anorexia takes away any accurate perception of shape and alters ones sense of proper weight.

From my little introduction to anorexia, I am sure that you may be able to see that at the core of anorexia is a damaged self-image and a remarkable level of insecurity.

Dr. Chapunoff: Is it true that the anorexic person is, characteristically, a perfectionist individual?

Dr. Paul: Yes, Ed, perfectionism, that ultimately destructive demand, is at the core of anorexia. Perfectionism is simply another way to characterize demand that has gotten out of control. Demand, as I have noted so frequently in our conversations, leads to anger, and in anorexia's case, anger at the self.

Self-loathing is simply how one feels when anger leads to self-denigration and hatred, which becomes internally focused. Demand, as you now know, creates opposition and resistance. In order to overcome our own internal resistance to demand, we become obsessive and overfocused. I do believe that this is one clear pathway involved in the rigid and absolute obsessive control of weight anorexics use to manage their own anxiety, stemming from their perfectionistic demands. Being thin takes on such proportion, that accurate self-perception ceases to exist. To be perfect, you can always be a little bit thinner. Whenever anorexics look at themselves, they can never be satisfied, interpreting what they see as not good enough.

Dr. Chapunoff: What is one of the biggest difficulties a psychotherapist faces when dealing with the anorexic patient?

Dr. Paul: Ed, an anorexic's negative body image is simply a metaphor for their never being satisfied with themselves, but because of their obsession with weight, helping them to have this insight is a challenge.

Dr. Chapunoff: An anorexic patient is an angry patient. An angry person, by definition, always thinks he or she is right. It must be excruciatingly difficult to convince an anorexic that he or she is on the wrong side of the equation.

Dr. Paul: Ed, you have noticed the fact that one troublesome consequence of being angry is that it always makes us believe we are correct. The anorexic is convinced that their view of themselves is accurate and that what they are being told by their friends, family, and even their therapist cannot be believed.

Anorexia is a perfect example highlighting how, if you wish to understand the mysteries of the mind, it pays to think in terms of the basics. Keep it simple. With anorexia, the idea that being thin becomes the demand that thin is necessary. We falsely think that this will make us feel valued and worthy as a person. We then up the anti believing that to be worthy, we must be thinner or even thinnest, just to be okay. To do this, anorectics become obsessed.

Dr. Chapunoff: But this obsession leads to nowhere; it's an exercise in futility!

Dr. Paul: Correct. Since they can never succeed, they remain angry with themselves, worsening their sense of inadequacy, and driving the demand for thinness to higher and higher extremes.

Dr. Chapunoff: One would think that occupations or professions where physical thinness is an unavoidable requirement could be a breeding ground for anorexia.

Dr. Paul: That is true, Ed. Professions that have a high demand on thinness, especially for women, place vulnerable people at greater risk. Actors, singers, gymnasts, and models lead the list of famous people who have died from this disease.

Dr. Chapunoff: Howard, in the case I presented, the young girl not only starved herself, she also purged. Is this part of the problem?

Dr. Paul: Yes, Ed, it is. Anorexia can exist with simple food restriction or it can be coupled with binge eating and purging, which is a very polite way of saying overeating followed self-induced vomiting. Some do not even overeat, but when they feel full, they are so afraid of gaining weight, that they will induce vomiting.

Since this frequently brings up stomach acid, the medical consequence, in addition to not taking in enough calories, is the erosion of enamel and the destruction of teeth.

Dr. Chapunoff: There are many additional medical complications of anorexia, including bradycardia, which is an abnormally slow heart rate coupled with very low blood pressure. There is an increased risk of heart failure with anorexia. Not only do anorexics often not eat, but also they often do not take enough fluids leading to dehydration, which can result in kidney failure. The lack of fluid intake can also cause electrolyte imbalances, which can lead to irregular heartbeats and even death. Lack of good fluid balance also results in cosmetic changes, such as dry hair, dry skin, and hair loss. Because of the lack of intake of calcium, osteoporosis can ensue, leading to dry and brittle bones. There can also be muscle loss and weakness. Because patients with anorexia are so thin, they often grow a downy layer of hair, which is their body's way of trying to keep them warm.

You are correct when you mentioned dental complications due to purging; however, there is more. People have been known to literally bust their gut or rupture their stomach during episodes of binging. The acid that you mentioned being brought up into the mouth could also cause esophageal inflammation and the severe retching, a possible rupture. Peptic ulcers and pancreatitis are known complications. I am sure that you are probably about to mention this, but people who suffer from anorexia also abuse laxatives, which can cause significant abdominal and bowel distress.

Dr. Paul: Ed, you have pretty much gone through the list and rightly noted that some complications can be deadly. When I see a patient with anorexia, my intake interview is not only concerned with the psychological issues but with these possible medical issues. You did leave out one complication, which is heavy exercise. Frequently, people with anorexia grossly overdue their exercise.

I will often work along with physicians, and depending upon the severity of the anorexia, will consult with their physician on their having an EKG, bone density scan, and blood testing to confirm proper electrolyte balance. Often, early on in treatment, vitamin supplements, as well as potassium and calcium supplementation, may be necessary.

Dr. Chapunoff: Proper body weight is not a capriciously derived issue. There are measures and standards that are applied to determine what is satisfactory.

Dr. Paul: So right again. The body mass index, or BMI as it is typically referred to, is the standard used by both physicians and psychologists alike who deal with eating disorders. A healthy body weight involves a BMI that ranges between 20 and 24.9. Overweight begins at 25, while low weight exists between 19.0 and 19.9. Underweight is from 17.6 to 18.9, and below 17.5 is significantly underweight. For some examples, a 6-foot tall individual who weighs 180 pounds would be considered at the upper range of just right, 145 pounds would be low weight, and anything under about 130 pounds would be underweight. A 5'4" person would be considered to have ideal weight between 110 and 145 pounds. Anything below 110 pounds would be considered underweight, and below 100 pounds would be significantly underweight.

Dr. Chapunoff: What about the therapeutic outcome of anorexia? It strikes me that these could be challenging patients to treat.

Dr. Paul: Ed, you are quite right about anorexic patients being a challenge, primarily because initially, many believe they do not really have a problem. When individuals with anorexia can be engaged in treatment, two out of three individuals do make excellent recoveries.

The leading evidence-based treatments for eating disorders involve a cognitive behavioral base enhanced with specific components tailored for people with eating disorders. Treatment for teens also involves the inclusion of family members and a good deal of social structure and support. When people start treatment, if they are significantly underweight, the first order of business is medical stabilization and refeeding. Only after people have been stabilized medically, can the psychological work safely begin.

Dr. Chapunoff: I am sure that there are other issues that also interfere with the initiation of treatment. I wonder if you could point out a few.

Dr. Paul: Right you are again, Ed. Along with compromised health, if someone is suicidal or is suffering severe depression, it must be addressed before the treatment of anorexia can be tackled. If someone is involved with persistent substance abuse that would also have to be first taken care of. Sometimes, people are involved with major life crises, which would interfere with their ability to simply attend, pay attention, or follow through with any treatment program. A generally stable period, where stressors are not at an interfering level, increases the likelihood of success by quite a bit. In treatment, issues such as the person's overvaluation of shape and weight, as well as their overvaluation of control of overeating are significant topics to discuss.

I help people look at events or mood triggers that tend to signal changes in eating. We try to establish a normal, healthy eating pattern, including three planned major meals a day plus at least two planned snacks. If purging is a part of the problem, that too needs to be addressed.

People are encouraged to plan, in terms of what they wish to eat and to make sure that there rarely is more than a four-hour interval between a meal and snack. I make it clear that feelings of hunger or fullness, or the lack of them, are to be distrusted. I look at what people think they will gain socially by being thin and challenge them to achieve these goals by means other than food restriction. I help them confront the notion that being thin makes them more acceptable to others and especially to themself.

Since this whole mess is typically related to a poor self-image, a good deal of time is spent on trying to look at issues of self-worth. By dealing with self-worth, I would also be dealing with anxiety and depression, which often come from having a damaged sense of worth. The prognosis for anorexia goes up when it is caught and dealt with earlier, rather than later, so if you know someone that has become obsessed with thinness or is throwing up to keep off weight, try to get them to a qualified and experienced therapist who deals with eating disorders as quickly as you can.

27

TEACH YOUR CHILDREN WELL

Dr. Chapunoff: Howard, in all of our conversations, one recurrent theme revolves around the idea that how people do in life has a lot to do with early positive attachments to their parents and to the style with which they were parented. As you said, children seem to be mirrors, reflecting back to their parents the exact things that parents do not wish to see. You mentioned that angry parents raise children who are prone to anger. Destructive and abusive parents raise children who are at much higher risk for repeating the same behaviors.

Up until now, all of our conversations have been about unraveling the mysteries of the mind. I wonder if you would feel comfortable taking some time to provide parents with some tips and suggestions that seem never to be included with the mythical owner's manual we are supposed to receive when we have or adopt children.

Our conversations have been about understanding, so that informed readers might then reach out locally for those who might be of assistance to them. In this particular case, a little bit of advice might go a long way improving the mental health of parents and their children, as well as increasing the odds that expertise might be sought, when needed.

Dr. Paul: Ed, there are a number of good books on the market regarding child rearing, such as *Parents are Teachers: A Child Management Program* and *SOS: Help for Parents,* so my response to your question, as it typically is, will be brief and focused.

There are a number of things that are important for parents to keep in mind and use as guidelines on how they behave and interrelate with their children.

Dr. Chapunoff: I remember you mentioned in one of our conversations that in dealing with children, it is much better to teach them to work hard than demanding the best grades at school.

Dr. Paul: Oh so true! We have discussed one key to mental health is to have a strong and secure self-image that is not based on achievement or competition. This is something that most parents do not take the time to actively teach, in part, because they have not been taught it themselves, and they think like the rest of the world that to feel okay about yourself, you have to be good at something.

One thing I might suggest is for parents to go back and reread our discussion on self-image and self-worth.

Dr. Chapunoff: It concerns me that good parenting might be the exception and not the rule. This, I suspect, may be the result of parents' own upbringing, lack of knowledge and education about raising children, and problems, sometimes of gigantic proportions, in their personal life.

Dr. Paul: That is true, Ed. Standard parenting is the rule and, for many, this works well enough to keep people out of significant trouble. While it is true that good parenting helps in raising good children, it is also true that good children make good parenting a whole lot easier.

Some tips for parents are that it would be helpful to think about what their children do and what their children believe. Think in terms of the behavioral and the cognitive. We are in an age where emotions and feelings are almost worshipped and held as sacred. It is what we believe that gives expression to how we feel, so looking at beliefs can at times actually be more important than looking at feelings. I am not saying that feelings should be ignored, but their place in the scheme of things would best be well understood.

When it comes to behavior, it is helpful for parents to break behavior down into two big categories:

- Behavior that you would like to have more of

- Behavior you would like to have less of

When it comes to behavior you would like to have more of, there is no substitute for using reinforcement. This can be verbal praise, a positive social activity, food, money, or anything else that has the likelihood of increasing behavior.

Dr. Chapunoff: When you use the terms *increasing behavior*, in lay terms, do you mean improving behavior?

Dr. Paul: Hopefully, if we get more behavior, it would be good if it were improved!

Dr. Chapunoff: I presume that not all reinforcements yield positive results. I wonder about giving money or providing other material stimulants.

Dr. Paul: Reinforcers, by definition, always increase behavior. Reinforcement is defined by its outcome. If we are getting more of something, it is being reinforced. Not all reinforcers are the same, and just because it might be reinforcing, does not mean it would be wise to use it. For example, using money or anything that comes from a store as reinforcement is to be avoided. Verbal praise is where we start and, as we have discussed, praise is ultimately more effective when it is targeted on work habits, rather than work outcome. To make that more understandable, reinforce working hard, rather than getting A's.

This is so important that I will say it again. Anything that gives you more behavior is a reinforcer. If your child's negative behavior leads you to yell, and the negative behavior does not reduce, there is a good chance that your yelling is either of no value, or worse yet may be serving as a positive reinforcement, even though emotionally, it is negative.

Dr. Chapunoff: I guess that judging the results of reinforcement is easy. If we are getting more of any behavior, it is being reinforced; however, we need to think about the selection of reinforcements and whether or not they are the best we could have used.

Dr. Paul: That's a good point, Ed. We know that we are reinforcing behavior when we get more of it. If we are not getting more and hopefully improved behavior, whatever we think we are doing that we believe is a reinforcement, isn't. It is never true that reinforcement does not work.

It is sometimes true that we selected and chose to use an ineffective reinforcement.

There are times where properly focused verbal praise will not give us more of what we want. Sometimes giving children special bonuses, such as an extra bedtime story, helping make dessert, or slightly extended time playing, can be useful reinforcers.

I often suggest that reinforcers that focus on a little extra parental attention are the ones to pull out of the bag when verbal praise is not sufficient: helping plan a meal, playing a game with a parent, and many more interactive activities that foster positive family interactions can motivate children to improve their behavior.

Dr. Chapunoff: There are different types of reinforcements, but I'm sure their selection varies according to the child's intelligence, personality, and age.

Dr. Paul: That is correct, Ed. There clearly is a developmental factor that one might keep in mind; what you do with a four-year-old might not be appropriate with an eight-year-old and would most likely not be appropriate for a 12-year-old and would not be fitting for a 16-year-old.

Some common sense, even if *common sense is not very common*, needs to be applied to figure out what reinforcers to use. It is important for parents to keep in mind that once you use more than verbal reinforcement, it will ultimately take longer to undo the program.

Dr. Chapunoff: Howard, why would that be?

Dr. Paul: Any reinforcement program needs to start as a teaching program. This needs to be altered so that it ultimately becomes a maintaining program.

Dr. Chapunoff: What is the difference between the two?

Dr. Paul: With a teaching program, the use of reinforcement works best when it is immediate, frequent, and strong enough to work. If verbal praise does not work, using something more potent becomes necessary.

Dr. Chapunoff: Do you find parents who resist reinforcement methods? In other words, do some parents feel that their children should be subjected to more discipline instead of more reinforcement?

Dr. Paul: Parents often tell me that they should not have to pay off their child in order to obtain desired behaviors.

Dr. Chapunoff: But that's not the way it works, right?

Dr. Paul: It sure does not! If you do not use appropriate reinforcement, you will simply never get what you wish. *When parents say they should not have to reinforce their child, they are unfortunately dealing with an unrealistic demand and have an unfortunate lack of understanding of the laws of learning.*

Dr. Chapunoff: Parents should read what you just said several times and never forget it!

Dr. Paul: The laws of learning are always operating. Either you use them to your advantage, or your own children will use them against you, often!

Getting behavior started requires frequent reinforcement. The problem with a teaching schedule is that whatever behavior is created, based on frequent reinforcement, will be unstable and highly subject to extinction, which simply means that the desired behavior you created may go away quickly. This is one reason why token economies and *star charts* are initially effective, but the gains often go away. In order to make behavior more permanent, the frequency of reinforcement needs to be reduced on purpose until we come to a maintaining schedule, where reinforcement is infrequent and intermittent. It is only then that behavior becomes stable. Most parents do not give a thought to this purposeful transition; however, it can make all the difference in the world, as to whether plans work or not.

Dr. Chapunoff: How do you handle reinforcement techniques when you deal with kids who are anxious or kids that don't seem to listen or learn well?

Dr. Paul: If you are fortunate enough to have a child who is prone to being anxious, standard parenting, which involves yelling, screaming, and spanking will work very well for you, but not necessarily for your child who will, sadly, typically have worsening anxiety and, potentially, depression. Anxious children also need more precise parenting. For many children, especially those with the *strong nervous system* we spoke of previously, punishment seems not to be very effective. This fact is corroborated by scientific investigation of youngsters with this type of brain. If parents cannot yell and scream, what could they possibly do instead? The answer is quite a bit. A positive approach often gives the most beneficial outcome and makes for a more adjusted child.

Dr. Chapunoff: For a parent to know what to do with a child and to struggle between choosing punishment versus reinforcement, sometimes it must be quite a challenge.

Dr. Paul: It is important for parents to decide whether they wish to be teachers or punishers. If you have too much of some behavior that you do not like, it also means you have not enough of the behavior that you would like.

The best way to have less of what you don't like is to work to create more of what you do like.

Many parents are concerned that if they do not have firm boundaries and stiff punishments, their children will have no discipline.

Dr. Chapunoff: Discipline is necessary, I'm sure, but how far do you want to go?

Dr. Paul: Parents are correct that firm boundaries are a requirement for mentally healthy children, but stiff punishments are not. If I can take you back to the old-time teacher's classroom, where when you walk in the children are all sitting upright, and you could hear a pin drop, you might presume that these children have wonderful self-control. What typically happens, however, when the teacher is called outside of the class in order to speak to someone for a moment or two? Chaos typically erupts in the classroom. The so-called good control is not within the children but sits in the ruler nearby the teacher's desk.

Dr. Chapunoff: Children can be controlled by rigid, demanding methods or by teaching them to behave properly. During my childhood at school,

I was subjected to the strict method. I was lucky to have parents who provided me discipline but also love and common sense.

Dr. Paul: There is a huge difference between self-control and externally maintained control. Externally maintained control requires fear and the presence of a feared and controlling person. With self-control, that certainly is not the case. Most parents try to be that old strict teacher, failing to understand that when they step outside, all hell could break loose.

The strategies that I suggest are those that are meant to create internally based control, and while they are slightly harder to administer, they certainly work better in the end.

Dr. Chapunoff: Parents need to be taught how to behave with their children when they run out of patience. When yelling and screaming replace well-balanced parental behavior, that means there's a need for improved parental education in child management, don't you think?

Dr. Paul: Yes, Ed. Children do need firm boundaries, parents need to have realistic, definable, easily applied consequences that are swift, sure, and consistent to produce desired results. Yelling does not qualify.

When you have too much negative behavior and you have started a reinforcement program to increase the kind of behavior you do want, there still is a need to punish the negative behavior. Just as the definition of a reinforcer is anything that will increase behavior, the definition of punishment is anything that will reduce behavior. I like to use the term consequence, as it is less emotionally laden than punishment, and punishment carries the overtone that you need to be angry. Typically, parents will yell or hit or use takeaways when they run out of alternatives and become angry because they are blue in the face, due to their repeating things over and over again. By using consequences that focus on restitution, positive practice and overcorrection, much better and more permanent results are often obtained.

Dr. Chapunoff: Will you please explain these ideas?

Dr. Paul: Overcorrection is about practicing the correct way to do something, and then practicing it repeatedly, until it is automatic.

Dr. Chapunoff: Howard, by restitution, do you mean making an effort to return things to normality?

Dr. Paul: Correct! If you break it, fix it. If you mess it up, clean it up. If you take something, put it back. If children take away the comfort of their sibling, they would best do a nicety to their brother or sister. Not only things can be cleaned up, but emotional messes too.

Positive practice, as the name implies, is the regularly scheduled rehearsal of behavior that you want to continue. *The best consequence for doing something wrong is to practice doing it right.*

Dr. Chapunoff: Howard, we've been talking about behavior. You mentioned that we need to think about cognitions, which means how children think. How do you deal with what you'd call straight and crooked thinking?

Dr. Paul: The strategies I am talking about not only apply to behavior but to beliefs. Sometimes children need to practice what it is you would like them to think. When children are doing crooked thinking, a helpful consequence is to have them do positive practice by rehearsing what the straight thinking might be.

Dr. Chapunoff: Do you mean to tell me that the rehearsal of straight thinking should be done right after the child displayed crooked thinking?

Dr. Paul: Not really, Ed. In fact, I mean exactly the opposite. These practices would best not occur right after the faulty behavior, but are best practiced on a regular basis, when nothing wrong precedes it.

Dr. Chapunoff: I find that observation very interesting and a little surprising for a person like me, who is not a psychologist.

When you talk about overcorrection, what happens if anger is utilized for overcorrection? Is it true that overcorrection may result from the parent's loss of control or loss of patience?

Dr. Paul: That is correct, Ed. Overcorrection at that point becomes a more traditional punishment. When we are angry, our real goal is to hurt, not to teach. Overcorrection is the hardest strategy because we have to make sure that we are not angry.

Dr. Chapunoff: When we are angry, we impair our capacity to make the right decisions. What's the best advice you can provide to parents who try to correct their children when they are very upset?

Dr. Paul: If parents are aware that they are angry, it is best to do nothing in the short term until the parent is back under good emotional control and can go back to the role of being a teacher to their children.

Dr. Chapunoff: Do you have any other strategies, especially simple ones?

Dr. Paul: Yes Ed, here is another very important strategy. When children are young, up to early adolescence, simply ignoring can work very well. If you tend to overfocus on negative behavior, there is every chance that negative behavior will grow by your attending to it. Attention is a tool that needs to be wielded like a scalpel. Similarly, differential ignoring is a tool that needs to be carefully managed and can be remarkably effective. There are times where it is very hard to ignore your child. This is when Time Out comes into play.

Dr. Chapunoff: What is Time Out?

Dr. Paul: The whole name for Time Out is Time Out from positive reinforcement, which means that the way we reacted to the behavior we did not like was probably serving as reinforcement for it.

Dr. Chapunoff: Let me make sure I understand the Time Out concept correctly. In other words, Time Out means that you, as a parent, in trying to correct your child's behavior, realized that your reaction to your child's problematic behavior was ineffective and instead of influencing that behavior in a positive way, you reinforced the child's erroneous behavior. Then you decide to use Time Out, which means giving yourself a break by avoiding the original parental behavior that did not work adequately.

Dr. Paul: You got it! When this is true, we need to do a better job.

Dr. Chapunoff: How do you do that?

Dr. Paul: Ignoring. Here is how to do it correctly. I counsel parents that whenever they need to speak to their children, especially when they are young, they need to go up to them and stand three feet away or less and wait for eye contact.

Parents are instructed not to ask for eye contact. If you walk up to your child and he or she does not look at you, they are already not listening! When you make your request, *only ask once.* Do not repeat, do not warn, do not threaten, do not make deals, just ask once. If your child does not do what you request, or if he or she does not give you eye contact, calmly say, *"Because you are having trouble listening, you have to go to your room."* If your child is compliant, and you are sure they will not tantrum or pester you, there is no need to put a wall or door between you. Sitting on the *thinking chair* or sitting on the stairs will work just fine if your child does not put up a fuss.

If they do fuss, there actually does need to be a physical barrier, otherwise it will be truly impossible for you to ignore their behavior. Children need to be separated for two minutes. The two minutes begins when quiet starts. If your child throws a three-hour tantrum, they will be in their room for three hours and two minutes. There is a popular myth that as children grow older you need to add more time to Time Out. This just is not true. Two minutes is all you need.

Let's go back to the Time Out directions. There are four reasons why you may go into the room once your child is placed there. First, you have two minutes of quiet. You may go into the room if you smell smoke, if you hear the sound of breaking glass, or if blood is coming out from under the door! Under no other circumstance should you respond to anything your child says or does, unless it is one of the above. Clearly, this is said tongue in cheek. If you suspect danger, go in, but not for any other reason. This also includes your child telling you that they have to go to the bathroom!

As soon as you say the words, *"Because you have trouble listening, you are to be in your room,"* it is important that you withdraw your own eye contact, put on a poker face, and no matter what your child says or does, do not respond. For the same reason, if you must go into the room, do not look at your child, do not respond to what they are saying or doing, make them and the room safe, leave the room, and wait for two minutes of quiet.

Kids can throw great tantrums. They may tell you that they hate you, that you are mean, and they may curse and say hateful things. IGNORE IT ALL.

Many parents worry that their child will develop a fear or aversion to their room if this procedure is used. Not to worry, this just does not happen. Remember, this is not done angrily and is not meant to be a traditional punishment, just precise, controlled ignoring. This method will work much better that yelling.

We all would best be taught to cope with the many negative things that often happen. There are big deals, medium deals, and small deals. When children are old enough, I suggest that parents put three envelopes up on the refrigerator. On one, the word *big* is written, on the second, the word *medium,* and on the third, the word *small.* As the day goes on and children respond to their own particular vicissitudes of life, ask them, "Is this a big deal, medium deal, or small deal?" Write down what the problem is and have them put it in the envelope that they believe well characterizes the problem. Keeping in mind that these guidelines are only suggestions, you may wish to teach your children with ideas such as these:

1) If someone we love dies or has a maiming crippling disease from which there is no cure, that is a big deal. Big deals are about irreversible human loss.

2) If I have cancer and get cured, or if I have an accident and fracture my hip and need an operation to fix it and several months of physical therapy to recover, that is a medium deal. If I move out of town and will not see my friends again, but I can make new friends in the near future, that is also a medium deal because it is a reversible human loss.

Most of the things that worry people every day of their lives are temporary upsetments, such as aggravations, monetary losses, or having a job you do not like. Consider each of these a small deal.

Parents have the key role of teaching their children that it is not awful when things do not work out the way they wish. The kindest thing we can ever do for our children is to provide them with an ongoing sense

273

of value and worth and help them understand that they can manage adversity. Do not teach when they are upset. Wait until they are calm and there is no pressing challenge.

Love your children and, more importantly, be loving toward them.

Be their teacher and teach them good coping and good cognitive skills.

Be mindful that you avoid the perfectionist trap. If you can do these things, you will be giving them a great gift.

The world does not do a good job of helping people adjust well. Demands are everywhere, and the world, in general, provides little support for your children to think in ways that promote good mental health. Make your family a place where they can strengthen their coping skills and maintain their positive view of themselves.

28

THE FUTURE OF OUR MENTAL HEALTH

Dr. Chapunoff: Howard, as you well know, even as the science of psychology has evolved, there are far more people suffering from psychological problems than psychologists, psychiatrists, and other well-trained mental health workers available to deal with them. Primary care physicians treat mental health problems, yet they often have little knowledge of basic psychology. Their time constraints and busy schedules often do not allow them to deal with psychological issues, even if they acquire enough knowledge to help their patients.

Some internists and family physicians feel that psychological problems should be dealt with by other professionals. The idea is not incorrect, but in reality, more often than not, there is no referral to a specialist. Many primary care physicians (PCPs) do not take care of their patients' emotional dysfunctions or family problems.

Many insurance companies often place restrictions on mental health coverage, making referrals to competent psychotherapists difficult, if not impossible. One of the reasons may be the number of patients who are in need of psychological counseling. Since so many people suffer from behavioral dysfunctions, mental and emotive pathology, too many people qualify for referrals to psychotherapists. Very few health insurance companies would like to carry that kind of burden.

Two thousand years ago, Hippocrates stated that obese people die younger than slim people do. Obesity was not considered a disease until 1985. There are so many obese individuals that the recognition of obesity as a disease implied costs that no health insurance was happy to cover. It took 20 centuries to prove Hippocrates right! The cost of obesity, in terms of health dollars spent on obesity-related conditions, is staggering.

Electronic Health Records (EHR): Psychotherapists and other health professionals will be required to use electronic medical records. This requirement just went into full effect. The US Government has already instructed the medical profession to use EHR. Eventually, perhaps in a couple of years, all medical personnel in the United States will be obliged to comply with this regulation. Those who fail to do it will not be reimbursed. Many doctors who are practicing with the new EHR system do not like it. They prefer old-fashioned medical records, where professionals write a report or dictate it to a transcription company. Whether they like it or not, they will have to work with EHR.

The Privacy Issue: Electronic health records are kept in computers. Employees have access to these records. What will happen to the extreme privacy that psychological, marital, sexual problems and other intimate confessions require? The wrong people on almost any government or insurance company computer screen could read these details. To me, medical records should always be private, but there is a difference between recording gout, kidney failure, or peptic ulcer disease and soft erections that result from marital unhappiness.

I believe that *psychologists will need to deal more closely with physicians* to understand the medical conditions and their association with all kinds of emotive-behavioral dysfunctions. You rarely see a psychologist in the area of the emergency room. People with an acute heart attack have serious preoccupations and concerns that would benefit from appropriate counseling.

Psychologists are also badly needed in schools, communities, corporations, organizations, and businesses.

I will give you an example regarding the usefulness of psychology and the dire consequences that occur when it is not applied the way it should. George W. Bush got involved with the Gulf War, invaded Iraq, and dropped bombs at will. The United States did not study sociologically and psychologically the social-religious anatomy of that country and the possible adverse consequences for Iraq, as well as for the United States, before getting involved in a war with a culture about which they were ignorant.

Psychologists are needed not only to treat people, but also to prevent them from getting into trouble and provide counseling for their dysfunctions. They are also needed to educate people and the medical profession.

Dr. Paul: Ed, as usual, you have articulated a number of remarkably important issues, which affect not only the role of psychologists, social workers, and psychiatrists, but really have a larger impact on the future of mental health in this country and in other countries where similar problems exist.

As you know, I have been involved in the medical education of physicians for close to 35 years. While I now primarily teach and supervise psychiatry residents, I also have taught medical students during their medical training.

Physicians typically go through a six-month rotation in psychiatry and have small group instruction in psychiatric and mental health issues. They do leave medical school with knowledge of psychiatric principles. You mentioned time constraints as one possible reason for a lack of involvement in identifying and managing mental health issues. Another possible reason, for some, may be that mental health and psychiatric issues are simply seen as a confounder to their medical treatment and may not be a real area of interest to that particular physician.

Many physicians are keenly aware of the need for referrals to specialists within the mental health field. A handful of local physicians make up the bulk of my referrals. Once again, I think we need to be cautious and not paint with too broad a brush. Some physicians are sensitive to mental health issues and some less so.

One additional real reason many physicians do not take the time to counsel their patients is that the remuneration rate for psychotherapy is very low compared to what physicians could earn in the same time frame. Not only that, when your waiting room is packed full of people, it is genuinely difficult to take the time needed to get into psychosocial issues. Many of these issues cannot be simply opened by the doctor and not properly closed because the doctor must then send the patient out the door in order to see their next waiting patient. Opening up important and painful issues without the time to adequately deal with these issues can be damaging. Most physicians know this and simply pass on dealing with such psychological issues, even if they are obvious.

Dr. Chapunoff: It is true that the remuneration for psychotherapists is unfair and painfully low when compared to the compensation enjoyed by other medical specialists. Patients with mental disorders take time and patience. Many tests done by cardiologists, gastroenterologists, and other subspecialties don't take that much time or patience and are better compensated.

Dr. Paul: Psychiatrists are among the lowest paid physicians, and psychologists make less than psychiatrists do. To some extent, this is based on the arcane way remuneration is determined. There is this construct called the usual and customary fee (UCR) used to determine rates. I do believe that there are some lawsuits currently ongoing to try to make public how these numbers are cooked up because they appear to have little relationship to reality.

There is also an attempt to balance the importance of work, as it relates to payment. Surgeons, for example, can make 50 to 100 times more than psychotherapists can for working the same amount of time. I obviously have a rather strong bias here, as I started my professional life working for two years in research surgery and believe that, while some surgeries are remarkably technical and draining, what psychotherapists do is, at times, just as difficult.

Dr. Chapunoff: ...or more difficult! If we are going to judge what situation is more preoccupying and stressful, say removing an appendix or resecting half of the stomach versus dealing with a severely depressed patient with suicidal thoughts, I do not hesitate to tell you that the harder work is done by the psychotherapist. Years ago, I spent long hours in operating rooms, assisting surgeons performing major operations. Many times, the surgeon cracked a joke while doing his job, and on a number of occasions, I saw surgeons singing while working in the operating room. I can't imagine a psychotherapist singing *La Traviata*, while interviewing an emotionally disturbed person.

Dr. Paul: Ed, the suicide rate among all physicians is highest for psychiatrists and a few other medical specialties. This is a clear commentary on how stressful this work can be.

A few years ago, when the utilization of mental health services began to rise, due to some reduction in the stigma of going to a therapist, as well as greater public awareness of the benefit of psychotherapy, our government, in conjunction with insurance companies, developed a plan to contain costs by managing care, especially care for mental health. Insurance companies say they need to utilize these restrictive procedures in order to contain costs, as well as reduce abuse by therapists, who may see insurance companies as annuities and who provide services without regard to outcome or cost.

Speaking only for myself, I am a therapist who is acutely aware of the cost of providing treatment. I work diligently to make sure that no one is in my office for one session more than is necessary. As I have said previously, I tell people that my job is to *get rid of me,* as soon as possible. I have been working with patients for 45 years, have my doctorate degree, am board certified, have over 100 scientific publications, and am the book review editor of a professional journal, which means that I read many of the new books being published, so that I am very up to date. It is rather annoying to me when someone with far less training tells me that I must firstly, beg (ask permission) to treat somebody, have it restricted or cut off prematurely, or tell me how to do my job.

Mental health is the unfortunate stepchild within health care. These attempts at reducing health care expenditures do not bode well for the future of mental health in this country. All anyone needs to do is watch the six o'clock news to understand that easier access to and more mental health services are needed, not less.

Ed, in your series of questions, you suggest that far more integration of medical and psychological services would be beneficial. You also suggest that psychologists need to understand more about the human body and be more collaborative with physicians regarding treatment. I could not agree with you more and believe that I do practice what you preach.

I agree with you that psychologists must be almost as well trained as physicians in physiology and biology. One of the lectures I give to the behavioral medicine students at the medical school emphasizes the need for psychologists to be well-versed, not only in psychotropic medication, but in the general medications used to treat conditions such as hypertension and endocrine dysfunctions.

I was once referred an individual for what was suspected to be an intermittent catatonic psychotic reaction. A careful history, including a medical history and current medication usage, revealed that he was seeing a number of different physicians, two of whom had prescribed him, without checking what the other had prescribed, an antihypertensive. His so-called catatonia was, in fact, him suffering from hypotensive episodes!

You mention obesity as a prime example of a disease that has both biopsychosocial and medical elements, requiring both medical and mental health interventions. You are correct that the cost of obesity is staggering. Almost one out of every 10 dollars spent on health care goes to some disease or condition related to obesity. The cost is estimated at about 150 billion dollars!

The total estimated cost of health care dollars attributable to smoking is about 100 billion dollars. For smoking alone, the loss in productivity to the country is also estimated at another 100 billion dollars.

The cost of problem drinking on health care dollars has been estimated to be equal to the cost of smoking and obesity combined and is a staggering 250 billion dollars! Three conditions that all have psychosocial and emotional components; add up to about a half a trillion of our health care dollars. If the government is really serious about reducing health care costs I, personally, do not believe they will achieve their goal by cutting funding, where it may be needed most. We need more psychological interventions, not less. We need more trained mental health professionals, not less. Given the economic mess that our country is in right now, I must admit to some degree of pessimism regarding how things will unfold over the next number of years.

Ed, you brought up the most important issue of confidentiality. Your concerns over confidentiality and the inexorable drift towards electronic record keeping are right on target and very well stated. I do not need to repeat your concerns but simply say that I share them. In many instances, the lack of confidentiality you mention is already upon us. I occasionally treat people who are involved in work-related accidents and who are covered by workers compensation. I also treat people who have been in car accidents and are covered by the personal injury protection plan (PIP) of their car insurance. It is harder and harder for individuals who have work-related injuries or who have been injured in a car accident to find a psychologist or psychiatrist to treat them because of the onerous management that has been placed on providing these services. I must include with my bill, photocopies of my treatment notes, in order to gain payment from the insurance companies. I cannot treat without providing a written narrative and a treatment plan, in order to gain permission to provide treatment, and then I am told how many sessions it must be completed in! I warn my patients that there will be absolutely no confidentiality and their insurance company is entitled to detailed information about the treatment they receive, as well as what they reveal to me in treatment. This is a sad state of affairs. I keep on saying to myself that I will no longer become involved in such cases; however, when people call me, and they lament that they are simply unable to find a provider, I relent. I do plan to retire within the near future, and honestly, I do not know where I can refer these people; it is that bad.

I mentioned earlier that there has been a slight reduction in the stigma associated with seeking mental health services. While it has been slightly reduced, it is still very much there, especially for professionals. For example, if physicians report that they are having mental health issues, they are often treated punitively and harshly by their local licensing boards. I have had instances where I have helped people overcome conditions, such as obsessive-compulsive disorder when they were teenagers, and because of the diagnosis given then, they were later rejected from employment by some government agencies. I wrote very clear letters stating that they had done good work in therapy, and they no longer suffered from the problem at any level that would cause problems at work. They posed zero security risk yet they were still rejected. I have one patient with the diagnosis of OCD who was denied life insurance because of his psychiatric condition. These kinds of circumstances still make people hesitant to call a therapist. Many parents are quite concerned about my having to place diagnoses on their children when I treat them. I share their concern. For the most part, the limitations imposed by mental health issues can be reduced; however, the limitations of bureaucratic meddling and stigmatization have not been.

Ed, regarding your idea that psychologists are badly needed in schools, communities, corporations, and businesses, I once again can only heartily agree with you. I am not only a clinical psychologist, but I am also a certified school psychologist. In one of our previous conversations, I mentioned how while working as the leader of a school special services program, I tried to reorganize the culture of the school by changing the report card to be more supportive of all the students in the school, not just those who were the brightest and best achievers. Sadly, the culture reverted to business as usual shortly after my departure.

There are graduate programs providing coursework in business psychology and community psychology. Clearly, there is a shortage of trained professionals who can make an impact in these important areas, and there is a lack of perceived need in many of these areas, leading to little utilization of expertise that might be available. In too many schools, the school psychologists are so caught up in simply assessing the many children with potential learning disabilities that there is little time left over to do mental health intervention. Schools are often focused on maintaining zero tolerance policies, rather than using the kind of social and emotional learning programs that have been recently developed that have been shown to be effective in reducing bullying and improving morale, as well as the mental health of students.

You also hit on an entirely crucial component regarding mental health - prevention. In our discussion on marriage, you proposed a questionnaire meant to stave off problems at the start. It is a fabulous idea, and as is often the case with primary prevention, remarkably underutilized. There is more and more effort being placed on prevention within training programs, especially community psychology training programs. We can only hope there are enough individuals interested in this area and enough funding available to train properly interested people. An ounce of prevention is worth a pound of cure; however, most insurance companies will not pay for preventive services, apparently preferring that you have a disease and then they will pay. If I do an evaluation and find that the problem does not reach the level of severity to require a diagnosis, and if I do not give one, there will be no payment from insurance.

Up to this point, my conversation has been somewhat pessimistic. I would like to take some time looking at what is going on positively. There are quite a number of very dedicated researchers and clinicians devoting themselves to improving the craft of psychotherapy.

Researchers continue to work on identifying and developing procedures that will have greater efficacy and ease of delivery. Unfortunately, there is a disconnect between what we now know works and what is being typically delivered in many local community mental health centers. I have only infrequently mentioned social workers in our conversations. Social workers tend to be the individuals providing the bulk of mental health treatment in this country. Fortunately, schools of social work are becoming more focused on providing training in empirically supported treatments. While significant progress has been made in developing effective, empirically supported procedures for many psychiatric and social-emotional conditions, empirical support does not mean that these procedures work for everybody. In some of my professional writing, I noted what I called the *70 percent conundrum*. Our validated procedures work for 70 percent of the individuals we treat. Of the 70 percent who benefit from the treatment, 70 percent still have some residual symptoms. So while good progress has been made, more work remains to be done. Fortunately, we are no longer limited to one type of validated procedure. Well-trained therapists can begin with behavioral interventions and add cognitive interventions where necessary. For those procedures that prove to be less than efficacious, therapists can switch to what is now receiving more and more interest and study - a focus on acceptance and commitment as a form of treatment.

As science progresses, there are incremental improvements in the effectiveness of our medications, with decreases in problematic side effects. There are increases in our awareness of the neurobiology of many disorders, which may in the foreseeable future, translate itself into better procedures, better medications and better understanding of the complicated issues we face.

Psychiatric hospitals are often called *puzzle factories*, given the complexity of the presentations and problems that people bring to mental health workers. Little by little, some of these puzzles are being solved.

It will be interesting to see what the emerging status of psychiatry, psychology, and social work will be, as the future unfolds.

As long as mental health is on the bottom of the totem pole, I am fearful that the social ills of our country and the cost of remediable medical disorders that have psychosocial components will proceed unchecked.

I can only hope that this conversation, coupled with the others that we have had, may make a small but positive difference in this most important, critical area.

Ed, I must admit to have thoroughly enjoyed our conversations. In some of our discussions, I mentioned that a challenge faced by many people happens when their heart and their head are not on the same page. There are many, many times when what people really wish and what they know is best, are not the same. I offered my definition of maturity as being able to choose what is best, over what is desired.

When love, the most devastating of *heart* diseases, is added to the mix, *head* is often the loser in the contest. In our conversations, I think heart and head have gotten along just fine and have produced the best of both worlds, which occurs when what we would like and what we believe is best, happen to be the same. It has been a pleasure having these conversations with you and trying to answer your many poignant and probing questions.

Dr. Chapunoff: Howard, in the course of our lives, we go through experiences of different kinds. Some of them are good, while others are not. Our conversations about the mysteries of the mind have been, without exaggeration, one of the most wonderful and fruitful events I have experienced since I was born! Your intellect, the depth of your knowledge, and your analytical acumen were clearly exposed during our chats. I learned a lot, and I am sure the readers of this book will be grateful for the information and wisdom you provided.

If it were up to me, I would like to continue having conversations with you about additional subjects, but everything has an end.

I consider your willingness to share your thoughts and knowledge with me one of the greatest privileges I have ever had.